Introduction

I couldn't figure it out. I had a great consulting business, financial security, a super family, a good relationship – but it wasn't enough. I wasn't happy and I had to know The Answer. Plus I couldn't seem to stay healthy and I wanted to know why. I consulted a globe, strapped on a backpack, donned a pair of orange socks and left on a Nomadic Goddess journey. I found the most amazing, bizarre, but most incredibly simple answer to The Big M – The Meaning Of Life. It looked nothing like what I thought it would.

"Orange Socks is a winner! It is honest, fun, inspiring and guaranteed to help you pull up your socks and step into a life of adventure and connectedness. I loved it! Valerie, thankyou for magically weaving your own true story to inspire us all to know wisdom, peace, and courage."

Judy Armstrong —singer, songwriter,
recording artist, guest speaker,
workshop facilitator

"Wonderful, wonderful, wonderful. It's just what the gods ordered, was your book."

John Shelley — District Sales Manager
Bantam Books/Doubleday Canada

"What a thrilling experience to trek with Valerie Simonson while donning my Orange Socks. Many of us seek "the answer" and Valerie has shown a way to achieve the inner peace we baby boomers desire, now that our other basic needs have been met. Orange socks has been read by some of my contemporaries who are now anxious to meet this brave, spirited and spiritual lady."

Don Thonger — President, Derby Explorations Ltd.

"I don't know you, Valerie – yet I feel ever so close to you. When I read a "healthy" book they only talk about one way of healing one's self, one way of finding your way to come "home". Your book, Valerie, is different. It is ORANGE! Right at the start you create an appetite...there is so much truth! It is informative – colorful – majestic – witty – humorous – uplifting, and yet down to earth. This is how your book touches me, my senses, and my soul."

Judy Johnson, waitress

"What a fantastic book. Once I started reading it, I could not put it down. I started it one evening and the next day I traveled to Regina, so I put your book in my briefcase and every minute I had to spare was taken up reading. On the plane, at the airport – and once I got home, I just continued reading until I finished it."

Sarah Nykiforuk — Human Resources Supervisor,
Public Works Canada

Orange Socks

How A Yuppie Goes Yogi

Valerie Simonson

Canadian Cataloguing in Publication Data

Simonson, Valerie, 1955
  Orange socks

ISBN 0-9681438-0-6

1. Simonson, Valerie, 1955---Journeys. 2. Spiritual biography. I. Title
BL73.S55A3 1997   291.4092   C96-910847-8

Cover Design: Michelle Phelips
Page Layout & Design: Sage Creek Books
Cover photograph: Carolyn Sandstrom
Editing: Leslie Johnson

This book was printed and bound in Canada by
Friesens Corporation for Eternal Giving Inc.

Eternal Giving Inc.
P.O. Box 61108
Kensington Postal Outlet
Calgary, Alberta
Canada
T2N 4S6

For
My Baba

Contents

"Whatever you can do, or dream you can, begin it. Boldness has genius, power and magic in it."

— Goethe

Until one is committed there is hesitancy,
The chance to draw back, always ineffectiveness.

Concerning all acts of initiative and creation,
there is one elementary truth,
the ignorance of which kills countless ideas
and splendid plans.

That the moment one definitely commits oneself,
then the Divine Hand of Providence moves too.

All sorts of things occur to help one that would
otherwise never have occurred.

A whole stream of events issues from the decision,
raising in one's favor all manner of unforeseen
incidents and meetings and material assistance,
which no one could have dreamt would have
come their way.

"The soul, because of a certain kind of amnesia, has forgotten its true identity and also the Soul World from where it has come. That memory is now being re-awakened. Now, know thy self and have fresh memories of the self, the Supreme and of the Sweet Home."

— God

A Word Of Thanks

I, myself, did not create this book. God played a big part in its creation, as did many other dear, sweet souls. A big hug and thanks to Tim Kitting, for lending me his studio apartment, his bicycle, his Porsche and his color computer. One might ask why one would *need* all these things to write a book, and one would answer, "One is not always writing!" My daily forays to the soft, white sands of Asilomar, and climbing the rugged, rocky outcroppings around Pacific Grove, California, helped to bring clarity and restore hope to this struggling, first time writer. And thanks to Leslie Johnson, who undertook the most valuable, yet most incognito effort of all – the task of editing. What would I have done without you? As a guide, you taught me how to find my way through the challenging maze of story creation. You brought out the best in me, and had a way of firmly showing me what was essenceful and what was extra – and you did it in such a way, that I never lost my confidence or became disheartened. Your love and encouragement were tremendous, and the force of your gentleness was a wonder.

To Troy Lenard, who taught me the meaning of the color orange, a big ORANGE SALUTE! Your zeal and enthusiasm and carefree nature helped me remember my own lost treasures. To June Cobb and Susan Letourneau, thankyou for your care and understanding in pointing the way to my well-being. And what would I have done without my girlfriends; my sweet, loving, incredibly talented and intuitive goddesses? To Marlene, Patrice, Kathryn, Lisa, Colleen, Gerda, Patricia, Diana, and my sister Laura – I thank you from the deepest part of my soul. Together, you taught me the real meaning of the song, "That's What Friends Are For." You are truly angels. And so are you, brother Darrel – aren't all big brothers? You and Mary and Bill Ambrose kept insisting this message had to get out to people. I read somewhere that a book is a letter to the world. Thankyou, everyone, for helping me write this letter. And to brother Robert and sister Liz – much love. *Thankyou* for introducing me to Baba.

And thankyou to you, Mom and Dad, for your love and unwavering faith in me. I never knew how proud you were of me – until you told me. I'm still smiling. It was the greatest gift in the whole world.

Valerie Simonson   January 1997

Preface

Once upon an eternity, there was a little Nomadic Goddess who had broken her wings. She knew she had lost something of great value, but didn't know where to look for it; she only knew she had to find it. She left the shores of Canada, and flew off into the big unknown world to discover the answer. After searching many foreign lands – she arrived at the Paradise called Bali. It was there she found what she was looking for. It was a brilliant, glowing, ever so tiny, magical diamond. At first she didn't see it because it had been covered up by lifetimes of disuse. But she was determined to find her treasure, so she dug and dug and when she uncovered it, it was SO beautiful and SO enchanting, its power radiated upwards and outwards and filled her with a love and a light and a peace like she'd never known. She was happier than she could ever remember in her entire life. In her heart, she knew she had finally come home.

The little Nomadic Goddess spent day after day in her idyllic paradise learning as much as she could about the essence of her beautiful diamond, but soon it came time for her to return to the land of her birth. She didn't want to go, but she knew she had to.

When she landed on its quiet, familiar shores, she was still clutching her new-found treasure close to her breast. She vowed to never let go of it again. That diamond meant more to her than all the gold and jewels in the whole wide world, because there – shining back at her – was her soul.

xi

ONE

*But I'll Just Die
If You Stick Me
In The Accounting Department*

It was never really my plan to backpack around the world. Quite the contrary. My dream was to become a world-class volleyball player. I played every sport high school had to offer, but my real love was volleyball. I positively ate, slept, and breathed volleyball.

When it came time to graduate from high school, I thought, "How can I keep playing volleyball *and* earn good money when I have to go out and get a *real* job?"

I went to talk to the school career counselor. I hadn't even sat down before she suggested I go in for lab technology or nursing.

I walked out.

There was no way I was going to pay money to learn how to inflict pain in people by drawing blood out of their bodies and then embarrass them by asking them to go into the bathroom and void into a cup the size of a thimble. "No way. Uh uh," I grumbled, as I walked past the sports trophy case outside the gymnasium door. I glanced in at the gold *Athlete of Year* statue with my name engraved across its base and frowned and thought, "Besides – I'm an athlete, and every athlete knows

1

technical institutes don't have decent volleyball teams. University is where the best coaches are, and if I want to become a top-class volleyball player, I'll need to find the right one. And if I'm going to do any post-secondary training, I want to do something women haven't done for a career – something important – something that gives me a feeling of accomplishment and pays a top salary."

"But what could that be?" I asked myself, still frowning – as I entered the women's locker room to get ready for volleyball practice.

The answer came two days later when I was talking with my cousin. She worked at a large financial institution, and when I told her of my quest, she told me her boss – the vice-president – was a chartered accountant, or what she called a CA. I didn't exactly know what that was, but when she told me everyone looked up to him and that he made lots of money, my face lit up like a pinball machine. I could hear bells ringing in $50,000 a year in my bank account. I made an appointment to interview him immediately.

"What better way to find out how to make money?" I thought. "Besides – I've always wondered how the world of business works. I'm sure this guy can give me some excellent insight."

The next day I knocked on his office door, and when he called to me to enter, I suddenly felt nervous.

"What's going on?" I asked myself.

I recalled the first time I showed up at the high school senior volleyball team tryouts. I was what they called a Freshie – a Grade Nine student – and I saw myself standing self-consciously in the middle of the gymnasium floor facing the challenging stares of the senior team members as they sized me up.

"But you're interviewing him!" I reminded myself. "Relax!"

"Oh, yeah," I laughed. "Right!"

I turned the knob. As I opened the door, the man rose from his high-backed leather chair, came out from behind his enormous, shining, oak desk – and walked towards me. He extended his hand, and with a big, booming voice – graciously welcomed me to his office. I was so impressed by his powerful presence, I was momentarily speechless. I quickly recovered and said hello, shook his hand and thanked him for taking time out to see me.

When I told him of my mission, he looked me straight in the eye and told me few women ever became CAs. I thought to myself, "Hogwash. How perfectly ridiculous. I think it's high time we changed all that, don't you? I'm up for the challenge!" Thirty minutes later I emerged from his office with my sights set on becoming a Commerce graduate.

As I look back, those were pretty big words for what was really a scared little girl.

I arrived for my first day of university as nervous as a rookie on a team of four-year veterans.

I looked around at the flurry of activity going on all around me and thought, "All this excitement for a cup of coffee and a doughnut? What are they, addicted or something?"

I had just stepped into the Buffeteria – the university coffee shop – and everyone was looking stressed right out of their brains. Judging from their age, and the proliferation of lines on their foreheads, I guessed they had been in the institution for at least three years.

"An institution is certainly the right name for a place like this!" I said. "This place looks like Loony Tunesville!"

I looked around for a free table. It was a tough assignment – the place was jammed with bodies and books and packs of playing cards and crib boards. I set down my pile of newly-acquired textbooks and cleared away a couple of Jacks and a King of Hearts and laughed and thought, "Maybe Commerce won't be so hard after all!"

I remembered how my friends had warned me to take Physical Education if I was planning to play volleyball and go to school at the same time. They said it would be a lot easier on me. I looked at them with a look of utter disgust and retorted, "No way. No power or money in that."

I somehow got through my first day of classes, then walked over to the Physical Education building to report to the volleyball coach to get my new training schedule. He had written to me my last day at high school and asked me to consider coming out to play for his university team. He had seen me play in the Provincial High School Championships and said he was very impressed with my level of skills – although I still needed a lot of work on my defensive and setting skills.

3

We practiced diligently for three hours each day. He even had us come out on weekends. He wanted us to be the best in the country. I knew I had found the right coach. Commerce turned out to be something I did in between volleyball practices. I barely had time to do my homework assignments – let alone write my term papers or study for exams. Most weekends we went on the road – traveling across Canada competing against some of the best university teams in the land. I was in heaven. I had become one of the top hitters on the team, and after countless hours of grueling drills designed to eliminate my weaknesses, I was overjoyed to see my overall playing ability improve dramatically.

By the end of my first year, I was invited to try out for the Canadian National Team, and a few months later, I was asked to consider trying out for the Canadian Olympic team. The 1976 Montreal Summer Olympics were still three years away, but they wanted to start recruiting and training as soon as possible.

Canada's new Korean coach warned me it would be tough training if I decided to go ahead. He said to expect demanding schedules and lots of sacrifices. I didn't care. It was my dream come true, and I was going to give it my all. I was not about to pass up a chance at the Olympics.

"What more could a girl want?" I asked myself.

The answer came about a week later as I stared down at the 42 on my accounting exam.

"Some chartered accountant I'm going to make," I thought, frowning. "I can't even tell the difference between debits and credits!"

The professor called me into his office and demanded to know what the problem was. Before I could answer, he suggested that I think about what was more important to my life – my "extracurricular activities," as he called them, or my Commerce degree.

I walked out. I was livid. "Extracurricular activities!" I exclaimed. "I'm not exactly playing intramural sports, here! This is top international competition!"

"What does he know?" I said, shifting my sports bag to my other shoulder, and stomping angrily past the accounting tutorial hall. "He's not an athlete! Besides – if he'd quit being so stubborn and let me write the weekly accounting quizzes I keep

4

missing when I'm on the road, I would pass his stupid old course. He's not playing fair ball!"

I decided to major in Computer Science instead. Computer Science and Accounting sounded kind of the same to me. They both had numbers in them, and I had gotten good marks in my high school math. Besides, a high school friend told me that his brother was a systems analyst – whatever that was – and he made around $55,000 a year. It was all I needed to hear.

I barely squeaked through the computer class with a 51. Canada's national team had decided to host the Pacific Rim Volleyball Conference in Vancouver, and I ended up taking extended time off from school to train and compete.

I loved volleyball more than anything else in the world, but now it was standing between me and my Commerce degree.

"What am I going to do?" I thought. "How am I going to make time for both?"

It turned out I didn't have to. I injured my back playing in the finals of the National Conference University Championships and after extensive physiotherapy, the doctor recommended I consider giving up volleyball for at least a year – maybe longer. As a middle hitter, he said it was much too hard on my back muscles – all the twisting and contortionist moves had finally taken their toll on my body. He told me if I didn't take the time off, I could do irreparable damage.

I was devastated. I had no idea I had been that hard on my body.

"No volleyball?" I whimpered. "But volleyball is my life."

I sulked for weeks, but then I decided that if volleyball was out of the picture, and a career in accounting or computers was highly unlikely, I had better switch to Marketing.

I was determined to make the most of my university training. It was all I had left.

"Besides," I told myself. "Marketing is more conceptual. Maybe that's what I need – something less numbers-oriented."

It worked. My marks soared and I began having visions of becoming a $70,000 a year high-flying advertising executive.

I ended up graduating a little later than most of my classmates. I had to take summer session classes to make up for my low marks in Accounting and Computer Science. Leaving my friendly little city of Saskatoon in search of fame and fortune, I hit the big city lights of Calgary just in time to be turned down for an account executive position with a good-sized national advertising agency.

"WHAT?" I screamed at my apartment wall, as I reread the rejection letter. "NO SECOND INTERVIEW? BUT I'M A COMMERCE GRADUATE! THE PROFESSORS TOLD US WE WERE VALUABLE! WHAT DO THEY MEAN THEY DON'T WANT ME?"

I threw myself down on my bed and cried for hours. "There's no future for me!" I wailed. "First my volleyball career – and now this! Oh God, what's to become of me?"

It took me a few days to recover from my disappointment, but then I decided it was time to apply to the oil companies. It was quite the concession for me. I hated the idea of working in such an incredibly boring industry. Oil rigs and geophysics did nothing for me – especially compared to the glitz and glamour the advertising industry had promised. Besides – everybody and his dog was working for the oil business. I wanted to do something different – something totally unique.

I begrudgingly dropped off my resume at a few of the bigger companies, and secretly hoped no one would hire me. I got a response almost immediately. They wanted me to come in for an interview the very next day.

All the major U.S. oil companies were building Canadian head offices in Calgary and they needed large numbers of new graduates to staff them. The price of oil was skyrocketing. It was no secret Western Canada was rich in oil resources. Money was pouring in from all over. It was 1978 and construction was going on everywhere. I could not walk half a block without being bowled over by a cement truck, or being forced to cross the street in search of a sidewalk – any sidewalk. I realized my chances of finding one were next to nil. Men armed with hard hats and jack hammers were in the process of ripping them all up to turn them into construction sites. Everywhere I looked, building cranes were silhouetted against the horizon. It was destruction and creation on a grand scale.

I dodged every obstruction imaginable, and eventually reached my destination. Walking up the fancy inter-locking brick sidewalk leading towards the glowing, gold-towered office complex, I suddenly came to an abrupt halt. High above me, the noon-day sun was pouring down its brilliance upon the newest home of one of Calgary's largest and most prominent multi-national oil companies. I was momentarily blinded by the sun's intense light as it reflected off of the enormous expanse of sparkling, gold-flecked glass. I shielded my eyes and smiled. But then I let out a heavy sigh. "Whoa," I said tersely to myself. "Don't let anything stop you now. Just keep right on walking. You need the money, and it looks like they've got plenty of it. Besides – once you're in, you can always look around for something that suits your interests. Who knows? Maybe they've got a marketing department!"

I began to smile again. I entered the shining marble foyer and pushed the elevator button. Waiting to ascend to the 35th floor, I smoothed down my navy blue pin-striped skirt and reached up and straightened the shoulder pads under my matching navy blue suit jacket. I had read in a *Dress for Success* book that it was the best color to wear if I wanted to climb the corporate ladder.

I was still mentally polishing the glass on my degree certificate and sporting my obligatory Commerce chip on my shoulder when I arrived at the door. It read: Employee Relations – Please Walk In.

I did as the instructions on the door said, and came face to face with a hard-nosed, tight-faced woman sporting a rather severe, short-cropped, Vidal Sassoon hair style. One of her eyes was completely covered by a large downward-slanting block of hair, and I thought, "The poor thing's half blind!"

"That is the strangest haircut I've ever seen," I thought, staring and cocking my head to one side, trying to decide which eye to look into.

She gave me a penetrating look– as if she had read my thoughts – and I suddenly felt extremely uncomfortable. I squared my shoulders to match hers, flicked my long blonde hair out my eyes, stretched myself to my full height of six feet – and confidently introduced myself.

She said she had been expecting me, and directed me to follow her. Turning quickly on her heel, she led me down a wide, dimly-lit hallway, lavishly decorated with very expensive-looking bronze sculptures and beautiful large paintings.

When we got to the end of the hallway, she ushered me into a small boardroom and curtly asked me to sit down. She walked around to the other side of the table, put on some stylish-looking French-made half-glasses, then took out my resume and started to look it over.

While she was studying my credentials, I busied myself admiring the beautifully-crafted rosewood furniture, then stared out the floor-to-ceiling windows marveling at the magnificent view of Alberta's own, snow-capped Rocky Mountains, far off in the distance.

"Well," she said – looking up at me through her glasses and hair. "It seems you are of little use to us, Miss Simonson. You have no work experience. You only have a Commerce degree."

"Only a Commerce degree?" I repeated incredulously to myself. *"Only a Commerce degree?"*

I felt the chip on my shoulder slowly begin to slide off.

"You'll need some on-the-job training," she said – looking stolidly at my blank expression. "We'll start you in the Accounting department; it's where we start all our Commerce graduates. Please introduce yourself to the department manager on the 15th floor, and I'll join you later to give you your induction papers."

With that, she rose and motioned for me to step through the door.

I watched the chip bounce off the parquet wood floor, roll under an immaculately ornamental side-table, then come to its final resting place beside a beautifully-polished, rose-colored lacquer waste paper basket.

A siren went off in the region of my brain usually reserved for extreme emergencies. I did not move. I was not about to make any motion that would put me any closer to the Accounting department than I already was.

I walked stiffly out into the elevator lobby muttering vehemently to myself, "I *hate* accounting. I absolutely *despise* it." I punched the elevator button and waited – fuming. I looked up at the floor indicator and silently wished it would get stuck – forever.

After a week on the job, I discovered their form of accounting wasn't at all like university textbook accounting. I had somehow managed to get myself assigned to processing employee expense accounts in the Accounts Payable department. They only dealt in debits. "Oh yeah," I rejoiced. "There *is* a God, after all!" It turned out to be too easy. I was bored in no time. Days passed, then weeks dragged by, and I sat brooding in my little partitioned cubicle with its fake walls – listening to my co-worker whisper sweet nothings to her boyfriend and dial her mother for the twentieth time to tell her to get off her back. My mind finally exploded in a rage. "This is horrible!" I thought. "Even solitary cell-mates are afforded the dignity of having some walls! And I'm sick of playing relationship psychologist to my co-worker. I didn't exactly graduate in Commerce to rot away in this dumb old accounting department, consistently having to stuff down my envy every time I process an employee's expense report and find out they've gone traveling on yet another exotic trip. Geez! I thought I would get to travel on company business when I got out of Commerce, but no. Here I sit – waiting."

"So tell me," I called out to no one in particular, "what on earth am I doing here?"

My co-worker handed me the new company directory.

"What's this?" I asked.

"Read it," she said. "Maybe it'll give you some new ideas."

I opened it up to a page marked, Corporate Planning.

"Hm," I said, running my hand affectionately over the page. "There it is, all right – gleaming up at me like a jewel in a sea of shells. Corporate Planning. It sounds incredibly prestigious – plus – they handle the money."

I reached for a glazed jelly doughnut, downed a can of Coke, stamped *Paid* on top of the *Dollars Owing* column of an expense report, then leaned back in my chair to contemplate what to do.

I reached for another jelly doughnut. This time, I reverently held it up to the fluorescent lamp and delighted in watching the light reflect off its delicious, sugary-coated exterior. I smiled. It reminded me of a brilliant splash of tiny, sparkling diamonds.

"Oh oh," I thought, suddenly dropping the doughnut. "If you don't find something soon to make you happy, you are going to turn *into* one of those!"

9

I picked up the doughnut as if it were some toxic piece of waste, took careful aim, and viciously slam-dunked it in the waste basket.

"Phew!" I exclaimed. "That was close! Time to go on the offensive."

I pictured all my faculties rallying into a huddle, and thought about how much determination it had taken me to play volleyball and to get through university at the same time. I knew if I set my mind to it, and if I really believed in myself, I could get into Corporate Planning. Training for the Canadian National Team, the coach had told us to visualize game scenarios and play them out in our mind as if they had already happened.

"Why not use those same skills here?" I asked myself, cracking open another can of Coke. "It's a competition, right? Well – you want to win don't you?"

If I learned nothing else from being a rookie in sports, it was to keep on trying. It was the only way to make the first string.

Employee Relations said they were too busy with performance evaluations to see me right away, so I spent the next few days visualizing my game plan.

The week ended and I still hadn't heard from them. That weekend I was plagued by nightmares of jelly doughnuts gleefully jamming themselves into my open mouth and then – horror of horrors – helplessly watching my body swell to mammoth proportions, and observing jelly doughnut dimples beginning to occupy the spot where my elbows used to be.

I decided not to wait. I went straight down to the Employee Relations department Monday morning and demanded their attention. I wasn't going to be put off any longer.

One of the officers freed herself up and told me she would phone the manager of the Corporate Planning department to see if there were any openings. I thanked her for her help and went back upstairs.

The next day she phoned and said I was in luck. They had an opening for a computer analyst – was I interested?

I gulped hard and said, "Sure."

Three days later I found myself sitting in front of a brand new Univac computer trying to figure out how to log on to the company's Ten Year Financial Plan.

"Amazing – simply amazing," I thought, flipping through my new operating manual. "Not only am I the first woman to be hired as a computer analyst in this department, but the manager hired me without knowing I barely passed Computer Science! Talk about a miracle! I guess that's what they mean when they say, "Fake it till you make it."

I typed in my new password and studied the strange, foreign-looking symbols that appeared on the computer screen. "Hm," I thought, frowning. "This is not going to be easy." It was not exactly my dream job, but it paid excellent money, and I had a real live office with real live walls. And even though I did not have a clue about what I was doing, I spent long hours teaching myself and before I knew it, I had become fairly proficient at consolidating the company's financial plans – all 14 departments' worth.

"Not much different from volleyball," I thought, smiling smugly. "I never thought I'd be playing top caliber ball that first day in Grade 8 when I went to set a volleyball and it hit me square in the face. Yet I went on to become an accomplished volleyball player."

The more time I spent dealing with corporate scenarios in the nine figure realm, the more preoccupied I became with money. I even started looking for new ways to make what I began calling, Serious Money. It was a handy little term I picked up from my new stockbroker. I liked the sound of it. It meant Big Money.

My greed for money grew quite slowly. It was incredibly insidious and sneaky, because before I knew it – I began putting in long hours playing Overtime At The Office, instead of playing Overtime At The Gymnasium with my new Club volleyball team. The doctor had given me the go-ahead to play again, but now I could not quite seem to find the time.

I began wondering why, and I suddenly felt alarmed. I realized a lot more had changed than just my attitude towards my sports. I was also spending a lot more time at upscale cocktail parties, and actively seeking the company of MBAs (Master of Business Administration) from the University of Western Ontario – Canada's equivalent of the Harvard Ivy League. I was even trying to talk myself into learning how to play *Trivial Pursuit*, the latest board game created for the new, fast-growing category of aspiring young executives. They were young, they were ambitious, and they were upwardly mobile – and people were calling them Yuppies.

"But you're not a Yuppie, Valerie!" I exclaimed, looking down at the *Izod* alligator logo staring up at me from the front of my expensive brushed- cotton designer T-shirt. "You're an athlete, Valerie! Athletes don't play board games! That's for intellectuals. Athletes play sports!"

"Right," I thought. "So where did I go off base?"

My answer came a few weeks later when Patrice walked into my life – or rather – ducked into my life.

TWO

Boil, Boil, Toil and Trouble

Patrice and I met when she was ducking out of the 21st floor elevator. I stopped dead in my tracks. I had never seen anything like it. Here was this woman trying to unfold herself from the elevator, and it was not a small elevator. Come to think of it, it was an unusually tall one. But then – so was she.

I looked up at her and my eyes lit up. All I could think of was, "Volleyball! Got to get her to join our team. She'll be a sure-fire ringer!"

I closed my lower jaw – which was hanging somewhere down below my belly button – pulled myself together and said rather nonchalantly, "Why – you must be Patrice."

"Why yes," she said, smiling down at me and looking very surprised. "How did you know?"

"Your boss, Bill, phoned me last week," I said. "He wanted to tell me he'd hired a new writer for the company newsmagazine, and took great pleasure in teasing me about having to relinquish my position as the company's tallest woman! So when I spotted you, I figured you must be the competition!"

I looked towards the top of her head and said, "I must admit that when he first told me about you, I thought to myself, "Well I'm six feet – how much taller can she be? One, maybe two inches?" "I'm six foot five," she replied, her large brown eyes shining brightly back at me. "Oh?" I said, laughing. "Is that all?" She smiled.

I decided to ask her to join me in my office for a little chit chat. She said she would be delighted. After talking for a bit, I discovered we had very few things in common – large shoe sizes and specialty clothing stores for tall women. Other than that, we were really very different. She was a Classics and Theology major and I was a Commerce graduate. She did not play any sports and blamed her inability in sports on her lack of coordination. She told me about how she had been plagued with physical pain because her body had grown so quickly, but I hardly heard a word she said. I was too preoccupied and aghast, thinking, "Poor thing! Imagine. A life without volleyball!"

We got together a few more times after that, and she told me about her love of writing and how she believed in the nether world of gods and goddesses and fairies and tree devas – which she said were some sort of invisible plant kingdom deities. I looked at her and smiled mischievously, then made a face and teased, "Not exactly a corporate planner's first thought when she wakes up in the morning, now is it? Balance sheets? Yes. Fairies dancing on blades of grass? Not likely."

She giggled.

I laughed and decided to change the subject. I started talking about making money and climbing the corporate ladder, and her eyes glazed over.

"Well then," I said, holding her gaze. "How about religion?"

I found out Patrice was a Catholic. I did not really know what that was, exactly, but I did know it had lots of rules and rituals and a Pope and something called Confession. I grew up as a Lutheran and I had a complex about hell and eternal damnation. Patrice told me Catholicism was pretty much the same. She said they both had two things in common; that we were all sinners and we had to be saved.

14

As I thought about it some more, I reflected on how I resented being called a sinner. I hated growing up feeling guilty. Most of the time I never even knew what I was supposed to feel guilty about. The pastor was never all that clear on the subject, so in my as-yet-unformed juvenile imagination, I assumed he meant I should feel guilty about everything. That way, I could not go wrong. Or was it I could not go right? As you can see, I was a pretty confused puppy. My motto soon became: I exist, therefore I am bad.

"Valerie," I thought to myself, laughing weakly, "that's not funny."

I thought back to my early twenties and remembered how I had tossed out religion and turned my sights on the world of business. It gave me something I could really sink my teeth into – something good and logical and rational. They never once talked about blind faith in the oil industry. They relied on statistics and science. They only dealt in reality. The other thing I liked about business was I could see immediate rewards for my efforts. It was called money. With religion, the process of rewards took much longer. You had to live your entire life, then die – and then you had to wait to find out if you entered the Kingdom of Heaven or – God forbid – entertain a less desirable alternative.

Even though Patrice and I had different ways of viewing the world, I still felt drawn to her. She had something none of my other friends had– at least, not that I knew of. She had a deep belief in a higher power – one she often referred to as God. She talked about him as if he was her closest friend – like it was perfectly natural to have him along with her everywhere she went. I watched her eyes light up as she talked about her experiences with him, and I could see he was very real to her. I felt a small pang of envy, and it surprised me. I thought I was beyond all that. I suddenly realized my own religious upbringing had left me longing for something – I just did not know what. I also liked the way she had a grasp on her own inner guidance system – or what she called her intuition. It was something I knew almost nothing about. I was not even sure if I believed I had it. But I was still very interested to know more about it. I figured she would be a good teacher.

We spent many days drinking tea in my office, talking about life philosophies, and I began to feel a heightened sense of comraderie – even though we still seemed to be so incredibly opposite in so many other aspects of our lives. But somehow, as I look back, it never quite stopped us from becoming roommates – a fact which still confounds me to this day.

Wanting desperately to cut our living expenses, we agreed to share a basement suite together. I had only been with her a few weeks, when I began wondering if it was such a good idea. I never knew Patrice was so completely enraptured by the realm of psychic and paranormal activity. It was not at all unusual to catch her indulging in what I began calling, Heebee Jeebee Stuff. I made light of it most of the time, but if I was really honest with myself, I found it quite frightening.

When she wasn't doing something heebee jeebee, like relating encounters with demonic forces and visitations from departed souls, she was singing. And when she wasn't singing, she was in the kitchen humming away, concocting some sort of strange substance she called, Food.

She was virtually a full vegetarian – something else I did not know.

"You should ask more questions before you get into things, Valerie," I said to myself.

"Too late," I thought. "She had a stereo."

I loved music.

I also loved eating. Quite often we would go grocery shopping together. I always lost her on my weekly pilgrimage through the butcher's section. She would be in the produce department while I was poking and prodding the delectable selection of chicken thighs and side pork and debating the relative merits of a filet mignon versus a T-bone steak. Oh how I loved meat. I was mesmerized by how the butcher hacked off my order from a large, blue-tinged carcass. I silently congratulated him on his aim. After I was finished, I headed off into the cookies and potato chip department and rendezvoused with Patrice at the checkout counter.

As I watched her ever-so lovingly place her mostly-green grocery treasures on the revolving countertop, I thought about how bland and disinteresting it all looked. I decided to label her choices, "The No Meat, No Additives, No Preservatives,

No Artificial Colorings, No Sugar, No Salt, NO FLAVOR Diet."

Quite often I would sit across from her at the dinner table and slice neatly into my T-bone steak and eye her plate and play my favorite food game. I called it, "Identify One Of The Things On Patrice's Plate."

I lost every time.

I loved observing her parade of UFOs – *Unidentifiable Food Orders*– passing by the dinner table. I would often sit back and listen to her philosophical musings about cosmic consciousness and unreal reality, and watch my mind jump up and down and yell out, "SHE IS, SHE IS FROM ANOTHER PLANET!"

One day she caught me completely off guard when she started relating an incredibly arresting story about a vision she'd had – something she called a past life recall. We were sitting in the living room listening to music from Crosby Stills and Nash and she started talking about witches.

"I was practicing herbalism and other forms of natural healing," she began. "It was during medieval times in the forests of England, and I found myself being dragged from my dwelling and charged with heresy for doing what they called Devil's Work. They put me on trial and burned me at the stake for witchcraft. Even now – when I recall that vision – it's as if I can still see the flames licking at the hem of my gown. I can feel the agony of my flesh burning and I can smell the acrid scent of my body as it melted into the fire."

My stomach lurched and I asked her if she could be just a little less graphic.

She smiled back and continued her story, choosing to totally ignore the twisted look of disgust that had somehow taken over the entire square footage of my face.

When she finished, she looked over at me and said, "Valerie, I have since learned that if I want to discover my past lives, I must be especially careful not to go back with my emotions – lest I come upon yet another tortuous scene!"

"But Patrice," I said, grimacing, "why would you want to go back? Besides – as far as I know – nobody has really proven whether or not such things as past lives really exist. Science certainly hasn't come up with anything to support it. Besides –

17

my early religious training only talked about having this one life. They were pretty definitive about it. They said, "You live, you die, and then depending on the kind of life you lived – you go to Heaven or Hell."

She smiled back and danced merrily off to the kitchen to make some Crystal Dragon herbal tea.

"It all sounds pretty straightforward to me!" I called out after her.

She did not respond.

I cracked open another beer and switched on the television to the Wimbledon Tennis Championships – then reached across the coffee table to grab my bag of Dad's chocolate chip cookies.

I playfully started calling Patrice, The Whacko Wicca of the West. I chose wicca, because Patrice had told me it meant witch, and witch originally meant "wise woman," or, "one who was knowledgeable in the healing arts and herbal remedies." It seemed in the Middle Ages, men were increasingly taking up the profession of becoming physicians and it conflicted with many of the natural healing methods the herbalists were pre-scribing at the time. What better way to dispose of the compe-tition than to have the church declare the herbalists heretics and have them burned at the stake?

Whenever Patrice was in her heebee jeebee mode, she would sit silently and impassively in her room and call up entities from the nether regions of the cosmos. She called it her, Tel-epathic Chit Chat. One of her most frequent visitors was her father. He had died tragically ten years earlier, and she missed him terribly. She said she loved to "bounce things off of him."

"Now that's a trick!" I exclaimed. "If he's a ghost, don't things usually just bounce right through him?"

She did not answer. She was too engrossed in making her phone call.

One night when she was out, I was getting into bed and I suddenly felt I was not alone. I looked around, but could not see anything out of the ordinary. I chided myself for being so silly and thought, "You've been living with Patrice for much too long, Valerie. Now you're starting to imagine things!"

I switched off the light and decided to forget the whole thing and just go to sleep. That turned out to be wishful thinking. The absence of light simply fueled my imagination.

A few hours later, with the covers pulled up tightly over my head, I eventually fell into a fitful sleep. The night became a living hell – filled with nightmares of grotesque disembodied entities carrying messages to me from the beyond. I was glad to see the morning sunlight come streaming into my room. "Thank God it's over!" I exclaimed, hoisting myself up heavily from my bed.

As my feet hit the hardwood floor, I was startled by a loud knock at the door. Before I could say, "Come in," Patrice came bounding into the room, jumped gleefully onto my bed and excitedly announced she had fallen in love with a local folk singer named Jared.

She told me all about how they had met and how they had stayed up all night getting to know each other, and how they had shared the same dreams and aspirations in life, and how if things worked out, she would probably be moving out.

"Wow," I said, laughing. "All this on a first date?"

She smiled. I could see her mind was made up. Besides – I knew she never did anything without checking in with her intuition, and it was right 100 percent of the time.

I smiled and gave her a giant hug, then wished her the best and went off to shower for work.

As I waited for the water to heat up, I thought about her pending departure, and realized that even though I found her heebee jeebee escapades a little unsettling, I would miss her calming personality. It slowed me down a lot, and I found myself going out less – out to discos, out to parties – out of my mind. My mind was continuously racing wildly out of control with thoughts of work and responsibilities, and trying to devise ways to fit in my demanding social and sports activities. I was the kind of person who said yes to everything. I guess you could say it was my obsessive pattern to achieve, achieve, achieve. Plus – I did not want to miss anything.

One day I was at the print shop overseeing the publication of the company's Annual Report to Shareholders. It was part of my newest job promotion. We were facing what seemed to be an impossible deadline, and all of a sudden I felt my head exploding. I told my co-worker I wasn't feeling well and I needed to go to the bathroom. I quickly made a beeline for the toilet, relieved my turbulent, bursting bowels, almost blacked out twice, managed to weave my way towards a black leather bench next to the toilets, and flopped down. Suddenly, I found I could not breathe. I gasped for air and swallowed hard two or three times, but no air was coming in. I panicked. Then, as if watching myself playing the starring role in a scene from, *The Exorcist*, my body began convulsing out of control – bouncing me mercilessly up and down on the bench. I was scared to death. My mind started screaming, "OH MY GOD! WHAT'S HAPPENING TO ME? AM I GOING TO DIE – RIGHT HERE IN THIS TOILET?"

My co-worker came in just as I was about to bounce right off the bench. She turned as white as a sheet and ran out to get help.

The next morning I went to see my doctor. She assured me it was no big deal. She called it a minor stress attack brought on by overwork and bad eating habits, and told me to take a couple of days off work.

I lay in bed for the next few days, and was alarmed to notice how I could not quite seem to unclench my fists – or my teeth. The few times that I turned on the television to watch the soap operas, the fighting scenes made me even more tense.

"Uh oh," I thought. "I'm in big trouble. Here I've been worried about performing at work, when now it's my body that won't work! How am I going to climb the corporate ladder without my body?"

I began recounting the events leading up to my stress attack and I realized I had always been blessed with a good, strong, healthy body – a body with boundless energy; a body that played all kinds of sports and stayed up late and got up early; a body that was always there for me; a body that supported me whenever I rushed myself off my feet trying to balance simultaneous love affairs with flying all over the countryside doing back-to-back business trips.

"Gee," I thought, smiling sardonically. "I managed to do all that, plus find time to devour a bag of marshmallow chocolate-layered cookies, two packs of Twinkies and an O'Henry chocolate bar – not to mention two Orange Crush pop – all in the time it would take a person to change planes!"

"Yep," I thought, shaking my head and smirking, "And that was all between-meal snacks!"

I sat bolt up-right in my bed and exclaimed, "God, Valerie! If you need all this food, what are you trying to fill up? What is it that's making you feel so *empty*?" I turned on the television and switched to the sports channel. "I'll think about it later," I told myself.

I discovered it was not an easy question to answer; at least – not on my own. Luckily, reinforcements came romping into my life a few weeks later in the form of a five-foot-nine blonde bundle of energy called Marlene.

THREE

The Truth Hurts – A Lot

Marlene and I met the first night I went to practice with my new Club volleyball team. I had just made a good, strong spike, and was bending down to pick up the runaway ball, when a blur of a red jersey tackled me and pinned me to the gymnasium floor.

I looked up into the face of a glowing, tanned, blonde young woman. I quickly gathered up my senses and exclaimed, "Just *what* do you think you're doing? Who *are* you, anyway?"

She didn't answer. She simply smiled at me, snatched my volleyball, and ran over to the next court.

I couldn't believe my eyes. No one had ever stolen my volleyball.

"Just who does she think she is?" I retorted. "What audacity!"

I went back to the spiking line-up to wait my turn, and covertly looked over towards the other court to take another look at my assailant.

She caught me looking at her and smiled back. I detected a challenging twinkle in her eye.

I poked one of my teammates in the ribs and pointed toward the woman and said, "Who *is* that? And why did she tackle me and steal my ball?"

She laughed and said, "Oh. That's just Marlene! Her practical jokes are her trademark. She loves to tease. She calls herself, The Big Kid."

"I can believe that!" I exclaimed, rubbing my sore elbow. "But she's a bit of a ruffian!"

The next week we were in the middle of the final game of the match, and I was being substituted in to replace what I judged to be the most perfectly-coiffed, hair-in-curls, girlie type of a teammate. I stepped to the sideline to wait for the referee's signal, and all of a sudden I heard a voice yell out, "OH, HEY! LET'S JUST EXCHANGE ONE BARBIE DOLL FOR ANOTHER, SHALL WE?"

I looked over. It was her again.

My blood began to boil. "Just *who* is she calling a Barbie doll?" I blurted out.

The referee blew his whistle and waved me onto the court. There was no time to retaliate. I vowed to deal with her later. I ran to the net, took up my position – then quickly looked back and glared at her.

She smiled and laughed – then stood up on the bench – held my gaze, and started doing a pantomime of polishing her nails while trying to set a volleyball.

I could not believe my eyes. I scowled back and thought, "She's got some nerve! I'll get her! Just wait!"

I pictured her sardonic smile on the face of my next set and pounded the volleyball with such a fury, I pictured it leaving a smoldering hole in the gymnasium floor.

The referee blew the whistle. The game was over. We had won the match.

I walked over to Marlene and demanded an apology. She simply smiled sweetly and said, "The truth hurts, doesn't it?"

I was stunned. I could not believe someone could be so rude. I asked why she was being so mean, and she answered, "Because I know who you are. You're not a Barbie doll. You just appear to be one."

"Oh yeah?" I replied. "Just what does that mean?"

She didn't answer. She just smiled. I was flabbergasted.

"There's no reasoning with people like her," I mumbled, and turned to walk away. I bent down and picked up my nail clippers and nail file and threw them viciously into my makeup bag and stomped off to the locker room.

I really had no idea what she was talking about. I happened to like the way I looked. I thought I looked pretty normal – just like all the other professional women I worked with. Besides – I hated being teased. My father teased me a lot when I was growing up. I guess I still had to develop a sense of humor when it came to anything involving my precious little ego. A few days passed, but I could not stop replaying the scene in my head. She had caught me totally off guard, and I was still peeved. Nobody had ever had the nerve to challenge me like that.

I could feel a deep furrow beginning to form on my fore-head, and a funny feeling suddenly came over me and I thought, "You know, if she's got that much courage to confront me, maybe she has something I really need to hear. I've been wondering what's been going on with me, lately – maybe she's the one to help me figure it out."

I decided there was only one way to find out. I invited her out for a drink.

We got together after the next volleyball practice, and I found out she was game for just about anything. Name a sport, and she had played it. She was full of life and wonder and joy. I slowly began to let down my guard, and discovered she was only 20 years old, yet she had an amazing wealth of experience in so many fascinating aspects of life – aspects I had never even touched on. I suddenly realized my life had been entirely made up of sports and school and business.

A few weeks passed, and we became quite close. I was surprised at how fast it all happened. Then – when volleyball season ended, we took up playing tennis together, teaming up to compete in several Women's Doubles competitions around the city.

I loved spending time with her. She made me laugh, and she made me notice the natural beauty around me. She also taught me how to stop taking myself so seriously. She said I could still work in the corporate world and have fun.

"Really?" I thought, scratching my head. "That never once occurred to me!"

I began looking more closely at myself. I soon realized I had been acting like a stuck-up, grown-up, uptight businesswoman, and Marlene's regular doses of playfulness started to loosen me up.

We spent many quiet moments together – walking her dog and talking about life and love and sharing our ambitions and ideals. I discovered that underneath her playful exterior lay a surprisingly deep thinker – a woman fascinated with the mysteries of life and magic – kind of like Patrice. She was also a gifted writer – and composed some of the most eloquent, profoundly moving poetry I had ever read. She said it was because she was a Pisces. I didn't care what she was – I found her refreshing and fascinating and joyful. Something inside me told me to stick with her; that this was only the beginning.

When volleyball season started again, I was surprised to see how much I was opening up to her.

At first I could not figure out why, but then it came to me.

I had never had a best friend.

"Imagine that," I thought. "I wonder why?"

It was not like I had not had any friends – I had had plenty. But I had never let any one of them get too close to me. I had always held them at a distance. They must have sensed my detachment, because they always kept our friendship on a superficial level. They never pushed me, and I appreciated it. But with Marlene, I felt compelled to talk to her. I couldn't help myself. She was like a magnet.

What I loved most, was watching her intuitive powers at work. They continually amazed me. One day, she turned them on me, and blew me right out of the water – or should I say – right off the tennis court.

We had just played a game of doubles and she came over for a cold drink. We were sitting at the kitchen table and she peered at me from over her glass of Seven-Up and said, "Tell me, Valerie. Who's hiding in there behind that Miss Perfectly Together Blonde Barbie Doll role? You may have fooled everyone else, but you haven't fooled me. Just what is it you're covering up under those blonde curls and blue eye shadow, hmmmmmmm?"

With that, she sat back confidently in her chair, raised her eyebrow and looked me directly in the eye.

I didn't answer. I really had no idea what she was talking about.

26

She folded her arms resolutely across her chest and challenged me again.

"Come on now, Valerie," she said. "You know I'm onto something. Admit it. I'm here to help. I promise I won't hurt you."

I still said nothing. I was stumped. Not only had I lived a life apart from everyone else, but I had also lived a life apart from myself. I honestly didn't know where to begin.

"I've been watching you for months," she said, smiling compassionately, her warm blue eyes shining brightly. "And I've been waiting for just the right time. So tell me, Valerie – won't you at least *try* to get in touch with what's going on inside of you?"

I suddenly felt like a balloon that had been deflated. I had been holding myself so very tightly together – and for so long – I had no idea my body was so tense. "I've been doing this for the better part of a lifetime!" I said to myself, feeling stunned. "And the joke of it is, I had no idea! Look! It even translates into the way I hold myself!"

I let go and sank down in my chair, and stared dejectedly at the floor.

Marlene leaned forward, picked up my hand and simply said, "Valerie, I think it's time."

I suddenly burst into tears and cried convulsively for a full ten minutes. Marlene picked up her chair and came around to my side of the table and sat down and started gently cradling me in her arms.

"It's okay," she whispered gently. "It's really okay, my sweet friend. You can trust me with your secrets. There's obviously something you have to get off your chest."

I sat protectively wrapped in her arms, feeling her love and compassion, and I realized this was a side of Marlene I had never seen. She had always been so outwardly tough; it took me a minute to adjust. When I did, I looked up and smiled. I reached over to the cupboard and grabbed a Kleenex tissue. I got it just in time, before another torrent of tears flooded in, and I thought, "What's going on? I haven't cried like this for years! I can't believe how incredibly sad I feel. Actually, it's even more than that – I feel an overwhelming sense of grief!"

I looked up at Marlene through my wet, swollen eyes and sobbed convulsively and choked out, "What on earth do you suppose is causing me so much emotional pain?"

I didn't give her a chance to reply. A giant dam suddenly burst open in my mind, and a torrential flood of unbelievably painful childhood memories rushed out – incredibly ugly, demeaning memories which had left me feeling deeply tainted and defeated. An endless parade of negative comments from my parents and teachers and mean comments from my playmates and classmates had left me deeply wounded. They had left me feeling inferior and negative and incredibly ugly. "Not good enough," flashed across the screen of my mind more than once. "You don't accomplish enough," was another. "You're not worthy of anything," was another recurring theme – usually when it came to lovers.

Marlene was right. I had, indeed, spent the better part of my life masking my insecurities behind my role as a self-confident, self-assured businesswoman – not to mention my secret hiding spot behind my starring role as an accomplished athlete.

As I contemplated it some more, I realized it was not so much that I lacked self-confidence. That was not it at all. I must have had a fair dose of it to have been so successful in the corporate and sports arena. What I did lack, though, was self-esteem. But most of all, I lacked the grand daddy of them all – self-love.

Self-love was a biggie for me. I had always steered clear of it because my dad was not exactly the most positive guy in the world. He always taunted me – constantly saying things like, "You never seem to be able to do things right. What's *wrong* with you – don't you know how to *think*? You're always putting *Val* first – you're so self-centred. Just once, can't you think of *other* people first?"

I began believing it was a bad thing to think about myself – so I went the extreme opposite and started denying my own self-importance and self-worth and ended up feeling inferior and inadequate instead.

Something else I had blocked out was the times I had been molested by a neighbor when I was a little girl. I used to ride my bicycle down the alley past this man's house and he would give me money if I kissed him and spent time talking to him. He was extremely lonely. It hardly involved anything at all, and it seemed so innocent at the time – but I realized that by doing this, I had sacrificed a lot of my self-respect.

I also remembered being chased and touched in personal, inappropriate ways by my evil, lecherous uncle when I was a young teenager.

"No wonder I don't trust anyone!" I said to myself, wiping back my tears.

I also realized how much I disliked the way I looked. Growing up, I had always allowed others to make me believe there was something wrong with me. I was tall and gangly and the boys at school used to tease me about being so skinny – then they would point at my chest and say I was flat as a blackboard. It didn't help that my dad also teased me about my slow development. He would grin and say I did not need a bathing suit top to lay in the sun, "Since there was nothing to show anyway!" I was devastated. At such an impressionable young age of 13, it wounded me deeper than he knew – deeper than I knew. I knew he loved me, but I thought he sure had a strange way of showing it.

I looked at Marlene and burst out, "You know – until this very moment, I never knew how much I really hated myself!"

Marlene looked back at me and smiled. I suddenly realized what I had done. For the first time in my life – I had actually let someone in.

I suddenly felt embarrassed. I quickly looked down at my hands and reached for another tissue, and blew my nose again.

A curtain of silence fell between us.

Marlene was the first to speak.

"Valerie," she said softly, "I knew that. I could tell by the way you always put yourself down. You always make jokes about the way you look, and you've never showered with the team after a game. I knew something was up. You also call yourself 'dummy Val' a lot. Did you know that?"

"I do?" I replied. "I obviously do it sub-consciously."

"It's okay," she replied, smiling brightly. "Because I know you're not!"

"Thanks," I replied, laughing weakly. "You're truly a friend! And you know what else I've realized? I've been burying myself in my job and sports to escape taking a deeper look at who I really am. I've been so busy trying to prove to myself – and to everybody else – just how strong and talented and capable I am. Yet the irony of it is – all along I never really believed it. It also explains why I've always felt so empty – even though I've managed to reach all the goals I've set for myself. I've even had some of the most special, loving relationships any woman could ask for – but every time my partners got too close, I would freeze up. I refused to talk to them, so they'd eventually leave – feeling as exasperated and frustrated as I did."

"It's okay Valerie," Marlene replied, smiling softly. "I know. I've been trapped in a lot of negative stuff myself. Why do you think I recognized it in you?"

I looked in her eyes and burst into tears all over again – but this time my tears were tears of joy. I was so grateful to have found such a treasure. Marlene was truly a godsend.

After the crying episode Marlene pushed me to go even deeper into my childhood traumas. She spent hours digging and cajoling me to come out from behind my roles. She showed me how I had been living my life as if I had been detached– like I had been living in the third person. I knew she was right. I even wrote letters to my friends using words like 'she' instead of 'I'. I also realized I had lived as a stranger to myself. I didn't know who I was, so how could I possibly love myself?

For months Marlene challenged me to remove my masks – to show her and the world, who I really was. But because I was not entirely sure which part was the real me, and which was the role, I found it tough separating the two. Later on, I found out why. I read a warning in a book which read: "To all full-time mask wearers; be careful how long you wear your masks, because when you go to throw them away you might just throw away your face."

FOUR

How To Save Your Own Life

My early attempts at mask removal were extremely painful. I never quite got around to clearing up my emotional issues until about four years after meeting Marlene, so when it finally came time to remove my masks, I almost ripped off my face. I can honestly say it felt nothing like removing a facial mask at the local beauty salon. It hurt. It hurt a lot.

Even though Marlene helped me become more aware of what was causing me to feel empty and separate, I found it easier to allow the glamorous world of career-building and status-seeking to keep pulling me outside of myself. That way I didn't have time to look too closely inside. I ended up accumulating an ever bigger stock of problems – along with a few more broken love affairs.

The suppressed anger and resentment eventually took its toll and sent me spinning into a downward spiral of pain and depression and debilitating lethargy. It knocked the stuffing right out of me.

It was time I faced the music. I was more desperate than I had ever been in my entire life. I was an emotional and physical cripple.

First I had to stop my incredible back pain, so I went to a chiropractor and came away smiling sardonically at the sight of two sayings posted on his bulletin board. One said: "If you wear out your body, where will you live?" The other said: "Self-discipline is not nearly as limiting of one's personal freedom as disease is."

"Touché, I thought. "The truth hurts. I hear ya loud and clear, Mister. Roger. Transmission received. Over and out."

After a few more trips to the chiropractor, I could not seem to get any lasting postitive results, so I went to see a highly recommended holistic medical doctor. As I was reading through his credentials, I realized he happened to be a psychoanalyst as well.

"Oh good," I thought. "A two for one special. Just what I need."

When I first walked into his office, I was thoroughly convinced no one was more determined than I was to get to the bottom of my physical and emotional illnesses. I followed the nurse's directions and sat down to wait my turn. I picked up a pamphlet on stress-related diseases and thought about what an extremist and a high-achiever I was, and said to myself, "Why not apply your talents to something *really* important – like saving your own *life*?"

It was no exaggeration. By the time I had arrived on his doorstep, I had entertained thoughts of suicide more than once.

As I sat thinking about all of the ways I had come up with to kill myself, the receptionist called my name and asked me to go and sit in the treatment room. I sat down on the cold metal chair and waited – sweating. For months my perspiration had been out of control. I had no idea what was causing it, but I did know it was ruining all my favorite, expensive business suits.

A few moments later the doctor entered and politely introduced himself. He asked me what the problem was. I described my symptoms and he looked me over and said I had what he suspected was probably one of the most extreme cases of hypoglycemia he had ever seen. I was not surprised. I had developed short term memory loss, a myriad of debilitating high and low mood swings, and I could not fall asleep. I was living on sleeping pills and valium, and having trouble with slurred speech. I described one occasion when I sounded drunk while making a design presentation to the Board of Directors. My boss quickly ushered me out and told me he would handle it. I left feeling totally humiliated. I described how I fainted in the stairwell, somehow revived myself, then crawled down the stairs, and tried desperately to recall where my office was. Then – when I finally located it, I inched my way along the walls, holding onto them for support, then eventually staggered into my office and collapsed into my chair.

"You're a nutritional desert, Valerie," he said, looking pointedly at me from over his bifocals. "Your mega-stressed, fast-paced lifestyle and junkfood junkie binges have been robbing your body of all of its vital nutrients. It can't function. I suspect what you've got is what we call, The Yo Yo Syndrome. Your moods and energy go up and down just like a yo-yo, and with hypoglycemia in as extreme a case as yours, it's the kind of imbalance that won't kill you, but I bet sometimes it makes you wish you were dead. Am I right?"

"Bingo," I replied, mustering a weak smile.

He started me on a healing program immediately, then recommended I book in for weekly psychotherapy sessions. He felt he could help me get to the bottom of the emotional causes of my illness.

Week after week he taught me more and more about what was happening inside of me. I could see it would be a long road back. I followed his diet and vitamin and mineral program to the letter, but after several weeks, I was still struggling horribly with the symptoms.

I felt as if a big black cloud was obstinately hovering over me, somewhere in the vicinity of my forehead – casting dark perceptions inside my mind – causing feelings of hopelessness and self-destruction. Whenever I would catch a glimpse of myself in the mirror, I would see a shell of a body – a gaunt, drawn-out face staring back at me through lifeless, colorless eyes. It was a horrendous existence.

Many nights I lay in my bed shaking my fist at God and yelling, "IT'S ALL YOUR FAULT! YOU'VE GIVEN ME MORE THAN I CAN HANDLE! I'M *DYING* DOWN HERE!" I was convinced it had to be one of his tests of faith, something like they had taught me in Sunday School.

Not only was I angry with God, but I was extremely angry with myself. "HOW COULD YOU HAVE ALLOWED THIS TO HAPPEN?" I yelled at myself. "YOU'RE TOO SICK TO WORK, AND YOU'RE EVEN TOO SICK TO EAT!" Food – any food – seemed to make me feel even more ill. "When will it all end?" I cried, looking desperately up at the ceiling where I supposed God would reside. I was hoping for a response – any response.

I guess I thought the answer lay outside of myself.

FIVE

If You're So Psychic, Why Don't You Know My Cat's Name?

Five months passed and I dedicated myself to staying on the new program, but my recovery was very slow. I wanted faster results, so I decided it was time to move on. The same friend who had recommended the holistic doctor was seeing much faster improvement with a herbalist named June, so I felt it was time for me to take the next step.

Leaving the realm of professional medicine to seek alternative therapy was a major decision for me. I had always been scared to death to look too far afield. Naturopaths and herbalists were being called quacks, and a lot of the newspaper reports served to reinforce my negative beliefs.

But I was desperate for more answers. I decided to close my eyes and take the plunge.

When I opened them I could not believe my eyes. Miracles were happening all around me.

After one month my mental fog cleared and my energy started coming back. It was a dream come true. I phoned June to give her the glowing report and she was thrilled – but she also cautioned me. She said I should be aware that my complete healing would take a bit longer, and explained how herbs worked much slower than drugs because they go to the root of the problem – rather than simply masking the cause like drugs do. She said it would take a while for my biochemical balance to be totally restored, and asked me to be patient. After I hung up I did not feel one bit disheartened. I was willing to do whatever it took to get well. She was right, though. Every day I had a lot of ups and downs, but none of them stayed as long as they used to. I simply willed myself to stay positive and waited for my body to respond.

I spent long hours in the kitchen experimenting with all kinds of foreign substances like bulgur and Quinoa and before long, through trial and error, and sheer iron-willed determination, I taught myself how to cook the whole, unrefined natural foods I used to watch Patrice prepare – the food I used to call, UFOs – Unidentified Food Objects. I swallowed my pride and my newly-purchased granola – and demonstrated more humility than I had ever shown in my life. I wanted desperately to get well.

A year passed and I was able to get back to full-time work, then one year later I started my own small communications and public relations consulting business. I still wasn't feeling 100 percent well, so I had to be sure I worked only a quarter of the time – to give my body a chance to heal. Food continued to sabotage me for no apparent reason, and I was never quite sure when another attack would happen – but I knew the attacks were almost entirely connected to the levels of stress in my life.

It was time to look for more answers. I continued to see June every two months or so and kept up the special diet she had recommended, but I also enrolled myself in some natural healing courses. I was determined to learn more about how I had destroyed my body. At the same time other things began to interest me. For one, I became more and more curious about psychic phenomena. Two women I was consulting with in the oil business, were taking weekly meditation classes and told me about how they were able to contact disembodied spiritual beings for information on different aspects of their lives. I decided it was time to have a psychic reading done.

"Living with Patrice had to have rubbed off on me somehow," I reasoned. "After all, what have I got to lose? I've tried everything else. I know I'm still blocking out something – otherwise I would be well by now." When I read the pamphlet for what one gentleman promoted as a Life Reading, I felt a wave of trepidation. I really had no idea what it would be like. I did not want to make a fool out of myself if it turned out to be some kind of a hoax. I was not even convinced that such a thing as psychic abilities really existed, but something inside of me – something I could only describe as a little inner voice – kept saying to me, "Why not? I mean – *look* at yourself. You're a mess."

I picked up the telephone and dialed his number. As I listened to the telephone ring I was tempted to hang up. People had continually warned me to watch out for charlatans. Suddenly, my little voice jumped in and exclaimed, "Look Lady! Let's be fair! If you were really honest with yourself, you've been curious about this stuff for years! And you've been covertly asking around for at least *five* years for a recommendation on a reputable psychic! Now, here's a guy who's been highly recommended by two of your friends – how *sure* do you want to *be*?"

A saying suddenly sprang into my mind and I thought, "Choose to live or die, Valerie, but for God's sake – don't poison yourself with indecision."

"Well, that's that I guess!" I said, smiling to myself.

I waited for someone to pick up the phone. I could hear my little voice cheering me on, calling out, "Now or never, Valerie. Just do it!"

A soft-spoken gentleman answered the phone. His voice was warm and clear and exuded an air of purity. He introduced himself as Troy.

"Wow, what a voice!" I exclaimed. "So smooth, so melodious." I felt absolutely captivated. He sounded so gentle and sensitive.

I booked an appointment.

I arrived still feeling somewhat skeptical and felt obliged to ask him if he knew the name of my cat. I figured if he was a true psychic, he would know these things. He just smiled.

He was a handsome man, about two inches shorter than me, but then it occurred to me, wasn't everyone? I was taller than virtually every kid in my class when I was growing up.

I surveyed him a little while longer and guessed him to be about 35. His blonde hair was mixed with streaks of gray and his bright blue eyes seemed to sparkle and dance. While we were standing in the waiting room he explained what a psychic reading was about, but I didn't hear all of his description. My mind was preoccupied wondering why he hadn't answered the question about my cat.

He lead me into a large, very white room – sparsely decorated with a poster depicting what I imagined to be a symbolic representation of some heebee jeebee metaphysical principle. In other words – I had no idea what it meant. Off in the corner, a white table and two chairs were pushed up against a stark white wall, and on the table sat a small tape recorder.

He asked me to sit down, and turned on the tape recorder. He went around to the other side of the table, sat down, smiled beatifically at me, closed his eyes, and started making a strange sound – kind of like a monotone hum with plenty of volume. I thought it seemed a bit odd, but was willing to give it a minute. Next, huge beads of sweat began forming on his forehead and his face and arms took on a reddish hue. Perspiration began pouring down his face as if someone had just turned on a water faucet full blast.

I began to wonder if I had made the wrong choice. I mean, what was happening to this guy? He was obviously on fire, yet the room temperature was a little on the cool side. His yellow shirt was soaked clean through in a matter of minutes.

It was the weirdest, most bizarre scene I had ever seen. He made Patrice's psychic episodes look like a walk in the park. I started to feel alarmed. I thought about leaving, but I could not get up. I was riveted to my seat.

Minutes passed. Then, while still debating what to do, he began to speak.

"There is a consciousness here that is of the first ray, or fire principle," he said. "It represents red. It represents orange. It is the fire nature in the consciousness of elements and comes in like a flame, a fire – a sword at times. It represents the consciousness that is transformative, cataclytic. It brings change. It is power, it is will, it is directorship. It has come to tell you that you are the sword bearer and it is time to take up the sword of courage to cut through your limitations. Orange is the color of courage and of fire."

As he spoke, his voice seemed to grow in intensity and volume. It was as if he was trying to convey something of extreme importance.

He suddenly stopped speaking and sat perfectly still. He seemed to quit breathing entirely. It was all very eerie.

"Well," I thought, reminding myself to keep breathing. "This is just too weird. I sure got my money's worth, though. Time to go. I'm *outta* here. Say bye bye!"

As I got up to leave Troy cocked his head to one side and pressed his eyelids tightly, yet gently together, and looked for all the world as if he was trying to adjust his antennae. It seemed to me as if he was attempting to tune into some other frequency and scenes from *My Favorite Martian* flashed onto the screen of my mind. It was my favorite television program when I was a kid. I didn't move. I just stood there – mesmerized.

I decided to shelve my reservations. Such bizarre behavior deserved an audience.

"Besides," I thought. "Once in a lifetime, hey Valerie? Why not stay around and see how it all turns out?"

I sat back down in my seat.

I watched him for a few more moments but nothing else seemed to be happening. My mind wandered off and I started reviewing my list of questions. He had asked me to write them down when we talked on the phone, and told me he would try to answer them if we had time.

While I was busy taking mental inventory, he sat bolt upright in his chair and exploded with the word, "SHIVA!" The sound blasted out of his mouth like a rocket.

I was shocked. After a few seconds, I composed myself. I looked frantically around the room – half expecting to see some firelord named *Shiva* standing behind me – his sword raised menacingly above his head, looking wild-eyed, muscles tensed and ready to attack.

No such entity appeared. I gratefully relaxed and breathed a long sigh of relief.

"Just what *is* he talking about?" I thought to myself. I figured if he was truly a psychic, he could read my mind and answer the question.

Meanwhile, he sat in front of me, sweating uncontrollably – eyes closed and cheeks all aglow – looking like an unsuspecting tourist who had found his way into a cannibal's steaming kettle.

Suddenly – he spoke. *"Shiva* means to call and communicate to a greater sound of your totality, of a greater group of which you are a part. For you are not alone and there are many who function in this consciousness. You are of that group that represents the fire principle that comes into the pattern of our planet, especially radiating from the sun. You are a portion of that energy that brings transformation through the fire principle. So the *Shiva* consciousness is within you. You are of that devic nature."

I started to giggle. He sounded just like my cosmic friend, Patrice.

"You are of the nature of form – of colors," he related, "in terms of radiation that comes from you aurically. It might not be understood by you at this time, but it is there to bring transformation."

I listened and thought, "Mister. You've got to be *kidding* if you think that is the only thing I don't understand. I've actually understood very little of what you just delivered through that fiery little oratory of yours. Devic; fire principle; aurically. What are these words? Don't you speak *English*?"

I ranted on in my head, but decided to concede. I could not really communicate my complaints, because his eyes were still closed. He was obviously consumed by some otherworldly source.

I thought about how at the start of the session, he had told me that by allowing what he called, The Source, to use him as a channel, he acted like an information pipeline. The businesswoman in me saw him playing the role of a middleman. He was providing a way for my soul – or my intuition as he called it – to give me answers to my long-held questions.

"Oh yeah, sure!" I thought, sarcastically. "I get to use the information provided I can decipher it!"

Troy galloped on with his firelord's bugle call to action, and left me in the dust of my own thoughts.

He spoke of gods and goddesses and the sun principle spreading knowledge, and a whole bunch of other weird and unfamiliar themes. But then he started talking about Amazons and I snapped to attention.

I thought, *"Finally* a familiar word in this firelord monologue of his!"

All of my life I had a lot of tall, strong female friends – including my sister. We would all stand around surveying each other and joke about the possibility of having shared Amazonian past lives.

"Well," I thought. "There's an answer to another one of life's mysteries!"

"But *is* it?" I thought. "I'm not even convinced reincarnation actually exists!"

It seemed pure conjecture – in the same realm as fantasy. Besides, I saw myself as much too practical and pragmatic for that kind of nonsense. I was a businesswoman and an athlete. We only dealt in concrete things.

Troy launched into a dissertation on what he called, Truth. I quickly came out from my silent meanderings to pay attention to what he was saying. I had agreed to pay him $95.00 for the reading; I was not about to waste my money.

"Do not stop from being who you are," he said, "in terms of the level of truth that has to sometimes take the sword of courage that is within you – for the warrior of the Amazon has also been part of your past and you've had to be the warrior principle with the shield and the sword. But she is also holding the scale that symbolizes balance, and you must recognize just where there is an imbalance and take away that which is diseased. You are to do this through truth, power and application."

My heart jumped when he said the word, "imbalance," and I said to myself, "Now that's something that hits home. Didn't June say my hypoglycemia was a result of a biochemical imbalance, and didn't she also say it was related to long-held thoughts of anger and resentment? And didn't she also tell me my constant barrage of throat infections were caused by my core beliefs of being powerless and not speaking up for myself?"

As I thought about it some more, I recognized Troy's words to, "take up the sword of courage" as advice to stop procrastinating. I had to go through my fears and cut through my emotional blocks, because that was what was keeping me struggling in my search for happiness and fulfillment.

41

As I thought about it, Troy went on. He said, "So it is very important for you to now accept that role in life, to speak up and be heard – especially in the capacity to again speak – to orate."

I froze. An explosive charge went off in my head and the shattering sound reverberated throughout my entire being. A chill tingled up and down my spine and my knees began to shake and I thought, "Whooping cranes."

I flashed back to when I was nine years old and I was standing and choking at the front of my Grade Four classroom. My cheeks were beet red and I was nervously shuffling my feet. My classmates were taunting me, and I was trying with all of my might to focus through a growing haze of tears on my cue cards. They were lying soaking in the palm of my hand. I was delivering a speech on the threatened extinction of whooping cranes.

"I hate public speaking," I said vehemently to myself. "One of my biggest fears is getting up in front of a large group of people and making a speech. No way. Uh uh."

"You will be talking to small groups at first," he continued, "then – eventually – to multitudes."

"Multitudes?" I thought, laughing. "Not on your life!"

"I also see you writing," he said.

"Not according to the marks my Grade Five teacher gave me in grammar," I thought, scowling.

Troy suddenly opened his eyes and started giggling in a high pitched squeaking sound – which soon graduated to a full-fledged belly laugh. Then he sat back in his chair and mopped the sweat from his brow, and exclaimed, "Phew! It sure is a hot energy coming through!"

"I'll say," I replied, nervously. "I'm sweating just *watching* you."

"All this fire of energies is beautiful!" he cried out, "but has not yet been *accepted* by you. I'm burning up! Just look at me," he said, pulling his sweat-drenched shirt away from his skin. "The sweat, you know, comes pouring! Whoo! This has never happened to me before! We must have tapped into some powerful energy!"

I said nothing. I simply sat and smiled indulgently at him. If he believed I had something to do with this fiery stuff, it was his prerogative. As for me – I didn't buy it. No matter how spectacular a show he put on, my ingrained skepticism overrode it all. I didn't trust him. As far as I was concerned, he still had to prove himself.

"Besides," I thought, "how can this amazing firepower possibly have anything to do with me?"

Troy closed his eyes again and started describing my limited view of power.

"How uncanny," I thought. "How did he know I was thinking about that?"

I laughed at myself and thought, "Gee, Valerie. Did it ever occur to you that maybe he *is* psychic?"

"Your power still has not been accepted," he began. "For a part of you denies the role of being *as* powerful, *as* strong and *as* capable as any other individual because you have a limited perspective of power as you look at others and see them in what would be called earth power or power of position in life that may be corporate in nature."

"Whack," I thought. "If a word possessed a sound, "corporate" would sound like "whack."

Wasn't I, after all, the consummate corporate ladder-climber and power seeker? Yes indeed, he was right on the money. And – speaking of money – wasn't that exactly how I defined and gauged power? I focused on money the most. I had even sacrificed my free time to get more of it.

"And that wasn't all you sacrificed," my little voice piped up. "You also offered up a living sacrifice to the Altar Of The Money Gods. Your body."

I frowned and watched Troy continue on his merry way elaborating on the Shiva fire theme and talking about strange things like brahmins, yogis, fire initiations and Loki the troublemaker– some Norse god he said represented change.

I began contemplating the cost of adding asbestos suits to my wardrobe, and dreamily longed for the good old days when fortune tellers sent their clients on their way with the promise of, "You will meet a tall dark stranger," dancing in their imaginations.

The reading ended and Troy and I discussed some of my questions, and then he suggested I take his Sound, Color and Vibration course to learn about the qualities and sounds of color.

"It will help you gain some insight into how to use color to open up new avenues of awareness and change in your life," he said. "I think it's obvious from all the things we've talked about, that it would definitely benefit you."

He said he had taught the course to June, my herbalist. My reservations suddenly began to dissipate. I trusted June's judgment. I decided to give him the benefit of the doubt, and promised to sign up.

We finished the reading, and he gave me some excellent advice about my father – plus clarifying a whole bunch of other issues I had been struggling with. As for his entertaining account of Shiva the feisty firelord, I figured I would have to wrestle with that one a bit longer. I remembered a Taoist saying and thought, "Valerie – let your mind rest in not knowing."

When I stepped out onto the sidewalk, I realized that by saying yes to Troy's offer of a course in color vibrations, I had snagged myself a first class replacement for Patrice.

"Yes," I thought, smiling. "Wind him up and watch this guy go! No need for batteries, folks. This one is *soul*-powered!"

I reflected on Patrice, and thought about how she was definitely the strangest friend I had ever attracted. We were so incredibly opposite – or so I thought. Yet here it was seven years later – and *things* were beginning to happen to me. Strange, unexpected, woo woo things.

"The changes were really quite imperceptible," I thought, suddenly feeling alarmed. "If they'd happened all at once, I would have noticed them."

"I mean – here I am, promising a pyschic reader I've only *just met*, how I would be *happy* to enroll in his Woo Woo Heebee Jeebee Color Vibrations class after having just stayed up half the night with my nose buried in a book called, *Healing Herbs of North America!* And as if *that* doesn't just about take the cake – which, by the way, I am not allowed to eat because of my sugar intolerance – my standard bacon and eggs breakfast has been mysteriously and magically transformed into five-grain granola with raisins and real fruit. Real fruit! I *never* ate fruit – unless, of course, it was dehydrated fruit in a box of Fruit Loops – my favorite sugar-coated breakfast cereal. Fruit always tasted awful by itself – especially after my ritualistic evening of cigarettes, beer and a bag of Dad's chocolate chip cookies."

I reached up and felt my hair, and realized it was growing much longer than it had been in years. Plus – somewhere along the line, I had virtually stopped wearing makeup. I thought about how I had caught myself humming along to meditation tapes like, *You Are The Ocean* – which was Patrice's favorite tape, and I thought, "Oh my God! What's *happening* to me?" I began to panic. I contemplated getting Patrice on the telephone and *calmly* saying to her, "YOU WICCA! WHAT KIND OF A SPELL HAVE YOU CAST ON ME? WHAT MYSTICAL, MAGICAL INCANTATION HAVE YOU GOT HIDDEN AWAY IN YOUR WHACKO WICCA KIT THAT'S TURNED ME INTO A CRUNCHY GRANOLA COSMIC COSMONAUT LIKE YOURSELF?"

I walked up the front walkway to the house, opened the door, walked briskly into the kitchen and made a beeline for the telephone. But then a major revelation hit me and I put the telephone back in its cradle.

"It wasn't her at all," I said, leaning weakly against the kitchen cupboard. "It was me! I did it all by myself." First my body refused to work, then my friendship with Marlene uncovered lots of deep, hidden issues, and my time with Troy had now answered even more key questions. Quite simply, all the events taken together made me stop and pay attention to myself – my true self, that is – and forced me to embark on this journey of self-discovery. Instead of covering up with masks like I had always done, I was now peeling them away – one by one. What's more – it felt good.

"I would rather know, than not know," I thought, smiling confidently. "At least that way, I can do something about it."

A chill suddenly ran up my spine. I felt instantly empowered. For the first time in my life, I felt invincible – like I could do anything I set my mind to. I knew I had closed the door on my old life – forever.

SIX

Orange Socks
Take The Lead

Troy's SCV class – that was
what I soon found out was the class lingo for Sound, Color
and Vibration – turned out to be absolutely fascinating. I had
no idea colors had so many profound meanings.
Troy explained how each of the seven colors in our spectrum possessed a wide range of characteristics: some positive
and some negative. Then he drew a chart on the blackboard
and wrote down the names of each of the colors; across from
each name he listed their qualities.
"If you look at the positive and negative qualities of colors
they represent harmonious and resistant qualities. For instance
– on the positive side red represents leadership, freedom, initiative, determination and power. On the negative side, it sig-
nifies anger, rebellion, impatience and force. Once you know
these attributes and begin recognizing the qualities at work in
your life, you can start using the colors to enhance and understand your daily experiences."
"Let's begin with the color red," he said, pointing towards
the blackboard. "It's the first ray of the color spectrum. Now
go down the list of positive and negative qualities and intuitively

pick out which of the two qualities you feel are most dominant in you. Once you've finished doing that for both categories, try identifying which of the characteristics you want to build into your life and which ones you want to change."

"Next, simply wear that color and begin building a day-to-day awareness of the qualities red represents. It'll help draw attention to those issues in your life and you'll begin looking at them more closely. After a little while you'll begin noticing some changes happening – particularly if you start taking action on some of your issues. Wearing the colors gives us a valuable tool; it helps us recognize when we are facing up to a problem, and when we are running away from it."

I listened intently. He seemed to have a good point. I also realized I was having a whole lot more fun than I expected – especially when he showed us how to make the sounds of the colors. I never knew colors had sounds – but according to Troy they did – and boy were they powerful– when I could make them that is. It was awkward for me because I never believed I had much of a singing voice. The weird noises coming from my mouth were nothing like the sounds Troy was demonstrating. But then I thought, "All of my classmates sound like screeching, ailing fire engines too!" They were making a high-pitched, red EEEEEEEEEEEE sound. We were novices, after all. None of us had any voice training. What we did have, though, was a good sense of humor.

Troy told us to use the sounds in the same way as wearing the colors; both techniques helped us build awareness of the colors' characteristics. When it came time to wrap up, he suggested we start by wearing red for the next week. He said we would move onto the other six colors in the weeks following.

I liked wearing red and yellow and blue and green, but as the fifth week approached I knew something big was about to happen. I could feel it. Working through the first four colors raised some interesting issues for me. But when orange took center stage, all my internal sirens started going off.

I hated orange. Out of all of the colors in the spectrum – next to purple – I positively loathed orange. Yet there was Troy standing at the front of the class saying I actually had to wear it.

"Yuch!" I said out loud when he was explaining the qualities of orange. He looked over at me and smiled. He knew this was going to be my big test.

I sat making faces at him and screwed up my face every time he said orange. I suddenly felt filled with uncertainty and fear, and had an overwhelming urge to fly out of the room. I did not want to play his game anymore. Just the thought of putting orange on my body made my skin crawl. I wanted to gag. Then – as he elaborated about the color of orange even more – I exclaimed even louder, "Double yuch!"

He ignored me, and started listing the details of orange on the blackboard. Then he looked over at me and grinned. He held my gaze and said directly to me, "*ORANGE* represents courage, illumination, assertiveness, confidence and change. On the negative side, are the qualities of sluggishness, stubbornness, aggressiveness, inferiority, and procrastination. As you can see, it's a very strong color, but that's because all the qualities of red are also in orange. It is, after all, a mix of red and yellow. Pretty powerful stuff, hey class? No wonder fire has so much power! Where do you think the term 'firepower' comes from?"

He winked at me. He knew he got me – what with *Shiva the Firelord* still fresh in my memory.

"Very funny, Mister," I thought, glowering at his back.

"Boy, did I hit the jackpot, or what? These are all the qualities I've successfully avoided most of my life. Yet here they are, bold and sassy – and not to mention stubborn! But then that's their nature – according to old Smarty Pants Troy. And here they are, staring me straight in the eye and yelling, "Hey Lady! You can run but you can't hide!"

I imagined myself making a last ditch attempt to escape and pictured myself darting for the door, but those little qualities never left my side. They ran neck-in-neck with me chiding, "Hey Valerie! What you resist, persists!"

"Bingo," I replied. "Okay you guys. You've caught me red-handed – or maybe I should say, *orange*-handed. I must say, I have never met a more *aggressive* color in my life! Okay, so you figure it's time I faced the music, hey guys? Then bring on the orchestra fellas! Let's see, now – I need a B flat. Maestro – if you please!"

I walked back into the room and sat down to wait my turn. I was going to make the sound of the color orange. While I waited, I brooded. But then a solution flashed onto the screen of my mind and I felt elated. "Why, I'll wear orange socks!" I thought. "Yes. That's it! Of course! A person doesn't always notice socks, right?"

Wrong.

The orange socks were with me from the very moment I put them on. Peripheral vision being what it is, it took in a panorama view of everything going on around me – including what was going on with my size 11 feet. And I couldn't miss the fact that they were wearing orange socks. I saw them every step of the way. As a matter of fact – they were all I could see. Maybe it was because they happened to be fluorescent orange socks. They were on sale. I certainly wasn't going to pay full price for a color I hated!

That week I refused to wear the socks anywhere else but around the house. God knows my corporate persona would never let me risk my reputation by wearing them in public. But for the limited time I wore them, I couldn't help but notice how there was something about those little orange babies which positively compelled me to move forward – whether I wanted to or not. I chose the 'or not,' but to no avail. I couldn't resist their power. They were so noticeable and so bright, they demanded – no commanded – that I walk forward.

And so I walked.

One year later I found myself enrolled in an intensive, confrontational, experiential, push-all-your-buttons self-development course called *Personal Best*, and a friendship with a bizarre new artist friend followed quickly on its heels. But the orange socks were what made it all possible. They were, after all, the first step, and what they say about taking the first step I found out to be true: "The first step puts you half way there."

Shortly after pulling on the socks, I went to see Susan – a counselor trained in the power of visualization and the changes I made in a few short weeks were nothing short of miraculous. She helped me to finally answer the nagging question, "Why do I keep the people I love at a distance?"

She stunned me with her incredible insight. She told me that at a tender, highly impressionable young age, I learned to connect love with hurt – with my dad especially. She was sure in his heart of hearts he felt he was showing me attention and love the only way he knew how – by teasing me and unconsciously putting me down. But I took his criticisms to heart and learned to hold him and everyone else I loved at a distance. "With so many hurtful experiences in my memory," she said, "how could I not have grown up equating love with distrust?

I knew Susan was right. I carried this fear throughout all of my relationships – no matter how many times my partners complimented me or told me they loved me. The fear of not being attractive enough, plus the nagging feelings of being unworthy, had left me a distrustful, emotional wasteland.

I knew I needed to confront my father. I had to banish the ghost of his negativity once and for all. I also knew the feelings of powerlessness I felt whenever I was in his company were keeping me weak. I felt like a young, helpless child. No wonder I blew in any direction a strong wind might take me. I had no sense of my true self.

I decided to fly home.

I was at home for a full three days, but never quite got my dad alone until we were actually walking to the truck to drive me back to the airport. I couldn't believe my eyes – my opportunity was slowly slipping away. I quickly thought to myself, "I am not leaving until I talk to him. We'll just have to do it in the truck."

As my dad pulled the truck out of the garage, a raging blizzard quickly enveloped us, and my spirits abruptly sunk even lower as I pictured us having to shovel ourselves out of a snow drift just to reach the plane on time.

I pulled my jacket around me and sat bundled up in the passenger seat and began to shiver uncontrollably. I knew it was not the cold. I was scared.

"How will he react?" I kept asking myself over and over. "Maybe I should just forget about it. It's a silly idea – past is past. I can't change what's happened so why say anything?" Then my little voice piped up and said, "True – but unless you assert your power *now* with your father – you'll remain an unhappy wounded child *forever*."

I could not bear the thought. The radio was blasting out some inane Country and Western *You Done Me Wrong* song and

I found myself lunging towards it, switching it off and suddenly blurting out, "You know, Dad – all those mean things you teased me about as a child; about my slowly-developing body and how I often seemed self-centered and how I was just out to take care of myself, well I've felt unworthy all my life and it's affected every relationship I've ever been in. I *resent* how your negativity and ugly comments have affected my life and because of *you*, I've never had one *normal* relationship with a man. I hate it. I *absolutely* hate it. Your negative comments have affected me *un*believably. I don't trust *anyone*. Why? Because I think they'll hurt me just like you did. Sometimes I don't even know if I trust *myself*."

He was so caught off guard by my uncharacteristic boldness, he simply turned and looked at me. I could see he was stunned. He recovered quickly and vehemently denied ever having done such a thing – then demanded to know where I had gotten such a silly idea.

I continued on – relentlessly. I was not about to stop. I knew all too well how quickly I could give in to his anger and his unquestionable authority. He had gone pretty much unchallenged in the family the whole time I was growing up. His word was law. There was never any room for questions. If I ever unwittingly ventured to ask him about anything – he would explode. I learned to just keep quiet – to swallow my words. But I paid a high price for my silence. All my pent-up anger and resentment created the horror of my hypoglycemia.

I had been waiting for an opportunity to challenge him for years, and he was going to listen whether he liked it or not. I had him cornered. There was no escaping me.

I quickly visualized my orange socks and charged ahead – describing in detail the damage caused by what he called, 'his harmless comments', and watched his expression slowly begin to change. For the first time in my life, I could see he was finally beginning to believe me. Now it was my turn to look shocked, because here he was – finally lowering his shield of self-righteousness and beginning to see things from my point of view. Then he really blew me away. He apologized. He said he had no idea he had wounded me so deeply – or for so long.

We pulled up to the airport loading zone and got out of the truck and solemnly walked to the airport ticket counter. While we waited for the ticket agent to check my bags I could see my dad was visibly shaken. He was standing off to the side looking down at the linoleum and self-consciously shuffling his feet. He suddenly looked very very old. I did not know what to say, so I said nothing. After what seemed an interminable stretch of time, I turned and walked through the security gate and boarded the plane. Sitting on the airplane I looked out the window at the flakes of snow swirling around outside and began to cry. The realizations about all of my broken relationships and the ugly self-hatred I had endured all these years was too much for me.

"At least the deed is done," I said to myself, wiping away my tears and silently thanking my orange socks. I knew I could never have faced my dad without them.

After that day, I busied myself taking courses in visualization and reading books and listening to tapes on forgiveness. Slowly I began to forgive him. My health and energy improved dramatically, and when I asked June about it, she explained that so much of my energy had been channeled into thoughts of hatred and resentment, it made me sick. Now, it was being used in a positive way – for living my life, rather than just enduring it. She also told me that hypoglycemia's main emotional cause was a feeling that life is a burden, characterized by thoughts of, "What's the use?"

"How true," I said, grinning to myself. "Growing up, every time I wanted to speak up for myself, I'd swallow my words and think, "What's the use? He'll just make me out to be wrong, just like he always does. But now that I've confronted him, I've actually taken back my power, and now he can't hurt me anymore."

"You're right!" she said. "Congratulations, Valerie. You've made a major leap forward. I'm very proud of you."

I thanked her, and hung up the phone. I walked onto the deck of my house and looked out over the dark office towers standing like silent sentinels – a sharp contrast to the bright blue sky above – and began to review my 12 years in the oil industry.

"This new-found energy and growing sense of balance is absolutely wonderful," I thought, feeling a sense of lightness and brightness as I felt the warmth of the sunlight dance on my face.

I stood for a few moments, eyes closed, basking in my happy, carefree thoughts, when all of a sudden a dark thought came barging into my mind and I began to frown.

"Geez," I thought. "*Where* do those thoughts *come* from? I'm peacefully minding my own business, feeling happy, and whammo – there they are. I know I need to look at how the stress of my work keeps me from feeling consistently balanced. And I know that somehow, I need to change all that – but how?"

Right then my orange socks danced onto the screen of my mind and gleefully blurted out, "Change? Did we hear you say, *change*? Why – that's our specialty, dontchaknow? What do ya say? Gonna let us have a go at it?"

I smiled at them and replied, "Why not? What have I got to lose?"

SEVEN

Sacred Retirement
Savings Fund
Bites The Dust

The orange socks danced into my life, and something inside of me changed. Even some things outside of me changed. For one, I began looking at my oil clients in a whole new light; my main client in particular. It was my principal source of revenue and my most loyal and regular account. Oil prices were dropping dramatically, and my other clients were cutting back their public relations budgets. I was one of the casualties. But my main client never abandoned me – they were always there for me. Even though they gave me steady work, I began to tire of the same stressful routine – and so did my body. I loved the money. It was more than I had ever thought I would make. But still – what to do?

The more I thought about changing my career, the more I resented it. I always believed my Commerce degree would give me a lifetime career in the world of business, yet here I was – seriously considering leaving the corporate world entirely.

One day a relatively new acquaintance said something to me which absolutely knocked my socks off. And no – they were not orange. They were in the wash that day.

Her name was Natalia. She was Troy's wife. I met her at the

Esoteric Centre when I was taking his color class. We spoke very briefly then, but one day when I called seeking Troy's advice, she answered the telephone. We got on the topic of my growing boredom working in the oil industry, and she said something so outrageously insightful, it left me dazed – for days.

"Valerie," she said, "rather than considering your main client as someone holding you up, have you ever considered it may be holding you back?"

I gathered up my socks – composed myself and weakly replied, "Well no – not until now."

I suddenly began to cry. I apologized for being so emotional, and quickly hung up.

For weeks I was plagued with indecision. Then the weeks turned to months. My every thought and action seemed to be dominated by confusion and fear of change. Feelings of restlessness and peacelessness continually assaulted me. They seemed to last for an eternity.

I suddenly thought, "What exactly do my career and oil clients have to do with eternity?"

I laughed as the answer came flying back at me like a boomerang.

My little voice popped up and said, "Don't concern yourself with that right now. You'll get to it. Eternity's like that. It happens – eventually."

I took its advice and started contemplating the concept of security instead.

Security was something near and dear to my heart. I remembered Troy bringing it up in his color class. He asked us, "Is security real or an illusion?"

I thought about it some more, and realized it never existed even in my parent's day – even though they would have had me believe otherwise. "Security is a figment of your imagination," I said to myself – "an illusion; something you've bought into. So Valerie – why have you been hanging on to an illusion?"

I began thinking about my relatively sizable retirement fund, and laughed and exclaimed, "But you're only 34 years old! Why, that's absolutely ludicrous! Why on earth are you so concerned about something so far in the future? People retire at 65. Sixty five! Why – that's 31 years from now!"

I was astounded. I realized I had bought into all the retirement savings ads the financial institutions and mutual funds salesmen had been getting fat on. I bought it lock, stock and barrel. I did not want to find myself destitute and eating catfood like some of the unfortunate little old ladies I had read about in the newspapers.

"The brainwashing worked," I thought, grinning sardonically. "It made me believe the only way I could avoid such a gruesome, inevitable fate, was to diligently sock away my money into a registered retirement savings fund and now it is positively bulging with bucks – and for what?"

"But if I could save that much money in five years," I thought, smirking, "and I still have 30 more years to work, and I already have my house virtually paid for and I own my car – what more could I possibly need for retirement?"

"Not much," my little voice answered.

"Well," I said, laughing, "that *hardly* warrants saving thousands more dollars and stressing out my mind and body to carry on a demanding business that I don't even find challenging any more!"

Not only had the retirement scare been working overtime on my consciousness, but I also realized how easily I had let myself become enticed by the promise of acquiring all of the goodies in life. I had let the goodies seduce me into believing I would be a lot happier if I had them. Yet when I got them, I never found lasting happiness. I simply wanted more.

A deep sense of melancholy grabbed me as the full weight of my realizations sunk in. I had always believed a good career and striving for personal achievements and finding a satisfying, stimulating relationship was what life was all about. And they were – to a point. But now I was beginning to look at them from a, "Been there, done that" perspective. I even started noticing that almost without exception, every one of my experiences had a recurring theme. I had just never seen it before. I had been totally caught up in all the sensory experiences and perceptions. Now – when I had stepped back – I could see the themes were actually alternating – giving me the illusion of something new each time – when in fact they were really just more of the same thing.

"But I still want more out of life," I thought, frowning. "But if more isn't money, or a new career success, or a new relationship, what is it?"

EIGHT

Color Me Uptight

If I learned nothing else from Troy, he taught me if I wanted something badly enough, and if I was willing to open myself up to the possibility of it happening, something he called The Universe would give it to me. At the time I had no idea what The Universe was, but he said it with such conviction I could only believe that it was true.

Well, as it turned out, The Universe was right on cue, because as soon I decided I wanted to do something different with my life, The Universe delivered the goods. Her name was Lisa.

Lisa was an artist. A bizarre shock 'em, rock'em, revolutionary artist. In short, she was a rebel. If everyone else was doing one thing, she was doing something else. From her perspective, art college didn't allow for a student's individuality of expression – so she quit.

I always thought artists were kind of an unconventional lot – maybe even a touch eccentric. Notice I did not say touched. Lisa was by no means a flake. Quite the contrary, I thought she was positively brilliant – but I did not realize how much so until I got to know her a little better. She also had this child-like, devil-may-care attitude and her bizarre methods of clothing her body made her stand out in a crowd – and me along with her.

The more time I spent with her in public, the more I realized just how preoccupied I was with worrying about what other people thought about me – or more precisely, what they thought of me based on the company I kept. I realized I was really quite the conventional, conservative Yuppie. I was super-conscious of following societal rules – whatever those were. I reflected on how I lived an ultra-restrictive life – just to be sure I didn't commit any societal no-nos. I didn't particularly like *being* a conservative, but I found myself surrounded by people just like me. I figured it was part of the herding instinct. How else could I account for all those pin-striped suits and Vidal Sassoon hair styles?

When I met Lisa, I had just enrolled in my second Personal Best self-development course. The facilitators spent a great deal of time helping us to oust what they called, The Approval-Seeking Mechanisms. I loved how the facilitators categorized people like me. They were so sensitive and sweet. They called us Approval Sucks.

I realized I still had a fair distance to go. My friendship with Lisa proved it, because whenever I felt particularly exposed under the watchful eye of The Public, I willed myself to remember the saying: "What you think of me is none of my business." I thought it might help put my concerns in perspective. It didn't, because then I immediately thought, "Nice, concise little ditty of information but try applying it to *real* life." I usually found myself saying it with clenched teeth and sweaty palms – then I would go back to worrying about what other people were thinking of me. Lisa's friendship tested me on all fronts.

Lisa talked of art projects and political rallies, and how she was a vocal women's rights activist, a Jewish rights activist (she was Catholic by birth), an animal rights activist, a butterflies' rights activist, and a 'have you hugged a tree today' activist. I could not think of one cause that escaped her attention. She personified all that was disturbing and unacceptable. I mean, she was doing things people just did not do – and getting away with it. What's more, most of the time people did not even seem to notice. I liked that. Not only did I like it, I wanted to learn how to do it.

"She's perfect," I thought, "the perfect teacher for me. What better person to teach a straight-laced, uptight, pantyhosed, high-heeled corporate consultant and societal rule-follower like myself to loosen up. Yes – if anyone can do it she can."

Right then my orange socks bounced onto the screen of my mind and rallied around me in an unprecedented show of support. They were absolutely ecstatic – positively bursting at the seams. I realized they were just as anxious as I was, to break free of the shackles of mediocrity and conservatism. "*She's* the one to help you do it, alright!" they exclaimed.

I was so mesmerized by their impassioned soliloquy, I failed to notice the gigantic multi-colored neon sign flashing above Lisa's head. It was yelling out, "THIS IS IT. CHANGE YOUR LIFE FOREVER. COLORING LESSONS. ENROLL NOW."

One night Lisa arrived at my door with a large shopping bag. The bag read: Games Galore. She handed it to me and walked into the kitchen. I looked inside and found a Peel and Paint set. I laughed and thought, "It's just a child's game."

I followed her into the kitchen and put the bag on the kitchen table and went back to cutting vegetables. Lisa was an avid reader of the Tin Tin comic book series, so I assumed the paint set was just another one of her bizarre eccentric interests.

Little did I suspect the paint set was Lesson Number One For Corporate Syndrome Sufferers. It was her way of easing me out of my sheltered existence in the world of corporate communications and launching me into a world filled with creativity, imagination and possibility thinking. The paint set was also a prerequisite for what she later called, The All-important Aid To Understanding The Meaning Of Life – Coloring Books.

Lisa noticed my blasé reaction and said, "Valerie, the paint set is a gift for you. I thought you might be interested in taking a new approach to your life. Didn't you tell me one time about how you used to draw when you were little, and how much you missed it? Well – why not try this?"

I let out a peal of laughter and kept right on slicing my mushrooms.

"Who does she think I am?" I thought. "A child? That's not *art*; that's playing. I don't *play*."

61

My reaction didn't deter her one bit. "I'm serious Valerie," she said. "You may enjoy it. I know my Tin Tin comic books weren't up your alley, but just give this painting thing a chance. How will you know until you try? Where's your spirit of adventure, hm?"

"Lisa," I said, turning around and looking her squarely in the eye. "I'm *not* interested in wasting my time playing with children's toys. I have more important things to do."

"Do me a favor," she said, smiling sweetly. "Just try one. If you don't like it, I promise I'll leave you alone."

I could tell her mind was made up. I reluctantly conceded.

"Okay," I said, "but just one."

Two hours of painting and peeling later, I got up from the kitchen table and pasted my newly-created works of art on the microwave oven window – on display for all the world to see. From my victorious smug, one would swear I had just painted the Mona Lisa.

Lisa grinned. She knew. She knew from the jubilant shine in my eyes – that I was hooked.

"I certainly never expected you'd be ready for step *two* this soon!" she said, not even attempting to hide her amazement. She gathered up her paint set and gave me a big hug and said good-bye. She returned three days later for what she called, Graduation Day. She arrived at my front door loaded to her chin with supplies. She was carrying a veritable cornucopia of coloring books and pens and crayons. One book advertised Instant Color, Just Add Water. Another sported a Connect-the-Dot with an intricate collection of crosswords and mazes, with a cover that featured Christmas trees and Santa Claus and his adorable elves. Since it was September, I wondered where she had bought them.

"No matter," I thought, "color me excited." I sat down, and began to leaf through her pile of fascinating, ever-so delectable selection of coloring books and brightly-colored crayons. I must have looked like a prisoner set free to discover the world after 34 years in the slammer.

Lisa looked on in quiet amusement, and watched my eyes dance from book to book. When I looked up, I could see her eyes were sparkling as much as mine.

"She's obviously enjoying our happy little adventure as

much as I am," I thought, smiling.

"I love the way you teach," I said to her, feeling my face glowing as I flipped through the books. "Doing something completely *un*corporate makes me feel absolutely terrific! You obviously knew I needed this. Why – this is ultimate freedom, compared to the way I normally spend my time. The work world can be so restrictive. At least here, I get to create and play and cut loose. I love it."

She smiled and spread out more books. I wondered why she was being so quiet, but then I thought maybe she didn't want to interrupt my little exercise. I never once suspected our innocent little scene was anything more than just a straightforward coloring exercise.

I lost myself in the multitude of books for a full hour – sitting and merrily coloring away and carefully selecting the right crayons – then diligently concentrating on applying the colors just so.

"You're such a perfectionist," I thought, chuckling. After finishing a few pictures, I stopped and leaned back in my chair and surveyed my work. I liked what I saw. All the pictures were so colorful and pretty. But most of all, they were neat.

I looked over at Lisa and smiled.

Just as I was about to start a new picture, Lisa suddenly lunged forward, grabbed a crayon that did not even match the colors I was using, then boldly and swiftly and with not so much as a 'Pardon me, *Miss*, but would you *mind* if I just *trashed* your perfect little masterpiece?' she dove in and smeared the offensive color all over my drawing. Not only that, but she had the audacity to color *over* the lines and into the white areas outside my picture.

A siren went off in the vicinity of my brain and a flashing billboard started screaming at me, "YOU CAN'T DO THAT. THAT'S NOT ALLOWED. GO DIRECTLY TO JAIL."

When the noise and bright lights died down, I realized what it was. It was another limiting belief.

"There it goes again," I thought, fighting to regain my composure. "It's those darned limiting beliefs– loud and annoying, as usual."

I was cross. Actually, no – I was downright livid.

Lisa could see I was upset, but she just smiled. She handed

me the crayon and stepped aside and said, "Here – *you* do it." She may as well have slapped me across the face with a glove and challenged me to a duel.

The athlete in me rose to the challenge. I ripped the crayon out from her hand – looked her straight in the eye and said, "Okay, Miss Leeeeesa! It can't be *that* hard. After all, it's just a picture and an itsy bitsy crayon, right? How hard can it *be*?"

For all my bravado, I watched my hand approach the perimeter of the little girl's skirt and then stop. I inched my hand a little bit closer – but then stopped again. For some reason I could not seem to bring my hand to go over the line.

"I know," I said, pumping myself up and feeling a little more confident. "I'll try a *new* color! That'll do it. I'll even change my focus and color another part of the picture."

I deliberately reached over her, grabbed a nice bright, fuchsia crayon, flung her a defiant I'll Show You What For look, and confidently moved towards the bow in the little girl's hair.

I stopped again. I could not do it.

I changed crayons again and again, but every time I got close to the line I stopped.

"I *hate* this play session," I burst out. "Why, I'm not even having any *fun* any more."

Lisa jumped to my side, put her hand over mine, and sent my crayon skidding wildly through the outline of the little girl's bow.

I was horrified. As I watched my crayon go careening off the edge of the page and fall head-first on the carpet, I pictured it lying there whimpering in pain. I flinched.

It hurt. It actually hurt. I felt as if something had been torn apart inside of me. Another one of my limiting beliefs had been torn to smithereens.

I suddenly began laughing hysterically.

"That was positively ludicrous!" I exclaimed. "I can't believe this insane little coloring exercise has got me so upset! It's just a *picture* ! What's the big deal?"

"Obviously something is," Lisa replied, holding my gaze. "What do *you* think it is?"

Without a moment's hesitation I answered, "Society. That little girl's bow was just a stand-in for my beliefs around what's right and wrong according to my understanding of society and its status quo. I really *am* quite the conservative, stick-in-the-mud-rule-follower – aren't I?"

Lisa smiled and said nothing.

I suddenly felt absolutely euphoric. It was as if I had been cut free from all limitations. I picked up a crayon. Not even stopping to see what color it was, I galloped recklessly over each page, splashing bits and pieces of color all over the place. I even combined two or three colors for the little girl's hair bow, and laughed demonically, plotting new and aggressive ways to assault the page. I was on a creative rampage. I had been locked up for far too long. There was no stopping me now.

"HA HA. TAKE THAT SOCIETY, " I yelled, as I dove for another fistful of crayons and called out, "MORE AMMUNITION!" "Ah. What a rebel," I thought. "This feels positively fantastic! Victory at last!"

Never once had I suspected how my family and grade school teachers and beloved childhood friends had programmed me to become such a rule follower. Under their tutelage I was an easy mark. I followed merrily along – never questioning the status quo. And whenever I did, they always gave me a pretty good answer and that was that. Their programming was so subtle, so incognito – I bought it lock, stock and barrel.

A memory suddenly flashed across my mind and I pictured myself sitting at my mom and dad's big kitchen table. All of my coloring books were spread out before me, and I was humming away coloring in the pretty pictures. My tongue was sticking out. I looked pretty intense. Who knows, maybe my tongue helped me aim my crayons.

Anyway, there they were. My dear sweet Mom and my Auntie Norine and Auntie Gladys from the farm; all sitting next to me watching me color.

It was Sunday, and they were waiting for the chicken to cook. They sat sipping their coffee, smiling sweetly at me, and dutifully patting me on the back every time I colored within the lines. Then, when my performance started to flag, they quickly bribed me with promises of angel food cake and extra helpings of Neapolitan ice-cream for dessert. Oh, how I loved Neapolitan.

When I finished coloring, I raised my picture as high in the air as my short little arms would allow, and triumphantly shouted, "HEY LOOK AT ME! I DID IT RIGHT, DIDN'T I? HUH HUH? DIDN'T I?"

Doing it right meant I had produced a drawing that was perfect – perfectly *acceptable* that was.

I told Lisa and she laughed and teased me and exclaimed, "So, that's how you became such an avid, conscientious rule follower. It began at an early age; *The Age Of Coloring Books!*"

NINE

Retirement Is Not
A One Shot Deal

After the coloring book episode, Lisa and I became closer than ever. Every day, her carefree ways and daring attitude kept me on my toes. One time, when it looked like I was lapsing into my old ways, she winked at me and said, "Remember the crayons!"

I laughed and said, "How can I forget?"

I decided I had better enroll in next part of the *Personal Best* program – just to make sure I did not lose my momentum.

"I never want to lapse into complacency or conservatism again," I vowed silently to myself.

I signed up for the course, and worked harder than I did in the previous two. I was determined to learn everything I could. During the second month, we were asked to do some goal setting. I thought about what I wanted to do and thought, "I'll pay off my mortgage by the end of the year. That'll give me seven months. It'll be challenging, but I'm sure I can do it."

The facilitator came around and looked at our goals. When she came to mine, she surveyed my paper and smiled. She looked very amused.

"Valerie," she said, "remember how I said we should choose our goals based on living our dreams – finding something that would make us feel really exhilarated and alive – and powerful?"

"Paying down my mortgage would make me feel that way!" I said, looking at her hopefully.

She looked back at me with a blank expression.

"Okay," I said, shuffling my goal sheets. "It may not be the most *exciting* thing in the world, but I know I'll feel good when I achieve it!"

She kept staring at me.

"You're not buying it, are you?" I said.

"I'll be back," she said.

She moved on to the next individual.

"Geez," I thought. "She's right. What could be more boring?"

"You're *such* a Yuppie," I mumbled to myself, ripping up my goal sheet. "You're playing it safe and boring, just like you've always done. All you really know is how to make money. Why not break out and *live* a little – *risk* something."

I suddenly felt utterly defeated. It was as if my ego had deflated. I realized I had no idea what I wanted to do. I had never really given it any thought.

As I sat brooding, my loud, pugnacious orange socks danced onto the screen of my mind and yelled out, "HEY YUPPIE! WHAT ARE YOU? YELLOW?"

"Now hold on just a minute!" I retorted. "Just who are you calling *yellow*?"

"If the sock fits, wear it!" they replied.

"Why you belligerent little..." I replied, getting out my mental eraser. "I'll show *you* guys. I've had just about *enough* of you. Get ready to meet your *maker*. I'm going to wipe you out of my mind – forever!"

As I lifted my invisible weapon, my little voice interceded and said, "Hold on just a minute."

"Yeah, yeah," I said, lowering my arm. "I know what you're going to say. The socks are perfectly right. I just hate to admit it. It really is time to do something different. I mean, why would I have gone to all the trouble to get well, take Troy's crazy Ooga Booga spiritual classes and then battle with Lisa and her coloring classes, if I really wasn't going to *do* something with everything I've learned?"

"Like *change*, you mean?" my little voice said, smiling ever-so sweetly.

"Now you're talking!" my orange socks jumped in. "And don't you worry, Valerie. We'll be with you every step of the way. You can count on us. After all, you *created* us – remember? *You're* our maker, Valerie. Didn't Troy teach us orange not only stands for courage, but it also stands for *creativity*?"

"Yeah," I said, smiling. "I forgot!"

I felt distinctly lighter all of a sudden – as if I had had a monkey on my back, and it had magically vanished.

I picked up a clean piece of paper and wrote down a goal of traveling the world.

"Why not?" I asked myself. "I've been thinking about quitting my business and taking time out to discover the other aspects of what June and Troy call my "spiritual nature." Why not just do it sooner than I had planned?"

The next week we were asked to make up what the facilitator called a Treasure Map. We were directed to cut out some pictures from magazines that represented our dreams and aspirations and paste them on a large bristle board. In the center, we placed a visual image that represented who we were, then drew lines connecting our goals to ourselves. Next, we were told to place it somewhere in our house where we would have a chance to look at it as often as possible. The facilitator said it would help tap into the vast, limitless power of our minds, and help us manifest our dreams.

I loved it. It felt like magic in the making. It was great to be a kid again – armed with scissors and giant glue stick – diving headlong into an endless sea of magazines. It reminded me of my coloring book escapade with Lisa. I smiled and pulled out a photo of Thailand.

A few weeks passed, and I realized I had a problem. Even though my treasure map was half-covered with pictures of exotic travel destinations, I never really believed I could actually travel the world – especially alone. I was simply toying with the idea. It was something I liked to dream about.

"Besides," I thought. "It's just one of my many goals. My mortgage idea is still there – it's just number two on the list. Maybe I'll pay it off first, then save money for traveling."

The travel goal was the first to materialize.

I was petrified.

"Darn," I thought, scowling. "It must have been that Treasure Map. The facilitator said it would bypass our conscious mind and go to work on our imagination. But I never actually believed it would work! I would *never* have chosen such a heralding goal. *Now* what am I going to do?"

I could feel myself beginning to sweat.

I suddenly found myself catapulted into contemplating the totally unfamiliar and mysterious territory of what backpackers called, World Travel – exposing myself to what I called, Life Outside The Office. It was a mighty scary proposition. Out there, there were no hermetically-sealed windows to keep the outside world *outside*. There were also no security personnel to screen my visitors, and not one bit of protection from the elements. To me, the elements represented robbers, rapists and con artists – to name a few.

I don't know if other backpackers considered backpacking mysterious – but I certainly did. All I ever knew was corporate business travel. Call it intuition or just plain gut feeling, but somehow I knew five star hotels, valet parking, room service and concierge offerings were far from being options for an *Around the World on a Shoestring-type* backpacker.

My little incognito orange socks had quite an impact on my life. They were determined to introduce me to the *Big M –The Meaning Of Life*. But some of the vistas they promised to open up I suddenly wished would remain closed – for an eternity.

"There's that word eternity again," I said, frowning. "I've managed to go my entire life without really thinking about the word, and now it's hanging around making a darned nuisance of itself!"

"It's because of those orange socks," my little voice said. I scratched my head and retorted, "Yeah. Before *they* arrived on the scene, things like money and volleyball and tennis and lovers and consulting contracts and the consummate lunch engagement easily grabbed my attention. But *eternity*? Almost never."

I suddenly started eyeing my retirement fund as a travel fund. All kinds of fears started rolling in.

"What will you do when you return from your travels?" they said. "How will you pay your mortgage and living expenses?"

On and on they went for hours. "Blah blah blah blah blah." I was determined not to let them get the best of me. They had won out all my life. It was time I stood up to them. I decided to challenge them and called out, "Remember what they taught us in *Personal Best*? Remember when I actually went *mountain* climbing? I hate heights, yet I proved to myself I could do anything if I put my mind to it. Remember how petrified I was – frozen with fear and hanging off the side of that sheer cliff – clinging to the side of the rock-face by my fingers and toes? Even though I was thoroughly exhausted, I still managed to hoist myself up over the top of that last ledge! And didn't I stand up and ecstatically perform a victory dance – jumping up and down and crying out, "I DID IT! I DID IT!"

As I brought my thoughts back to my fears about quitting my business, I remembered something they had reiterated again and again in the *Personal Best III* course. It spurred me on to take new risks whenever I felt afraid. They said, "Today's stretch is tomorrow's boredom."

"Well," I thought, "I certainly stretched when I quit my bi-monthly paycheck and went out consulting, and then I stretched again when I confronted and forgave my Dad. Then I stretched again when I overcame my fear of falling off the mountain. Well – now I'm bored, so it must be time once again – time to stre..........tch!"

I pulled the doubts up onto the screen of my mind and shouted, "TAKE A HIKE, DOUBTS! I'M IN CHARGE NOW!"

The next weekend I shared my travel plans with two friends who had just returned from traveling. They were enthusiastic about my news, but when I told them I really did not want to rush into anything – at least not until I was good and ready, they looked at me and laughed. They said it was best I jump ship as soon as possible – before I had a chance to chicken out. They even offered to coach me on travel routes and teach me how to pack my backpack.

I could feel my resistance and fear begin to resurface and I swallowed hard. I willed myself to keep an open mind.

We sat and drank herbal tea long into the night, and as I listened to their fascinating tales of Thailand and Indonesia and New Zealand, I found myself completely in awe of their amazing courage and adventurous spirit. Their eyes positively shone. I saw a light in those two I had not seen in any other friend or business associate. They were alive. They had taken the challenge and gone out and lived their dreams. They had refused to let any fears of the unknown stop them.

"You know what guys?" I said, suddenly brightening. "I can use my *retirement* fund for just that – retirement! Who says I have to retire *once* in a lifetime?"

They both laughed. Raising their mugs, they proposed a toast.

"Why – it was probably *them*!" I exclaimed, holding my cup of tea high in the air. "You know – the little guys running around giving out the free advice! I'll bet it was also *them* who spread the belief that people only retired when they were *finished* working."

"Well," I said, beaming. "I'm by no means *finished* working. What I need, is a different experience of myself – plus an opportunity to think about a new career. An extended leave will also give me a chance to totally heal my body."

The clock suddenly struck 2:00 a.m. We looked up in amazement. They each gave me a big hug and wished me all the best, and told me to call them when it came closer to the time to leave.

After I bid them good-bye, I sat down in my wing-backed armchair, and suddenly began laughing hysterically. I thought about how I had discovered retirement was really not the one shot deal I had always thought it was. I now knew I could retire as often as I wanted.

I suddenly felt my body vibrating. I looked down and noticed goose pimples beginning to form on my arms. "This is the most *incredibly* freeing idea I've had in years!" I exclaimed. "Just *thinking* about it makes me feel charged! I haven't been *this* excited about anything for years. It *must* be the right thing to do."

A bunch of thoughts suddenly rushed onto the stage of my mind and started dancing excitedly around performing flying leaps all over the place. It didn't take me long to realize what all the kerfuffle was about.

They were celebrating!

TEN

Birth Of The Nomadic Goddess

The next day I found a letter from Patrice in my mailbox. She was reading a fascinating book on Greek and Roman mythology and was anxious to share some of its insights with me.

"Hm," I thought, feeling my eyes sparkle as I skimmed over the letter. "Sounds to me like she's talking about the mysteries of mythology, mysticism and mankind. Hey – kind of rolls off the tongue, now don't it? All the 'M' words and all."

Musing about the 'M's' coincidence, I reread her letter and realized she was talking only about womankind.

"Ah well," I thought. "No point in throwing out a perfectly good rhyming phrase. Let's just go with it, shall we?"

The book Patrice referred to was called, *Goddesses in Everywoman*. I went to the local New Age bookstore and bought it. As soon as I started reading it, I was completely engrossed. I could not put it down. It created the most magnificent tapestry of mythological knowledge and high adventure I had ever experienced. Not only that, but it felt incredibly real.

I got so excited I called up Lisa and another dear friend of mine, Colleen, and told them they absolutely had to read the book. We agreed to get together at my house the following weekend to share our discoveries.

We were amazed by how all our life experiences were reflected within the pages of the book. The goddesses' lives were actually our own lives – which meant we were living proof that goddesses had existed.

We were them.

As we skimmed one of the chapters on Artemis – the Huntress, we learned that she represented courage and determination. Lisa quickly looked up at me and said, "Isn't *that* what the orange socks represent? It's quite the tie-in, don't you think – what with your upcoming travel plans?"

I looked at her – stunned.

As I sat turning the idea around in my mind, Lisa and Colleen went on reviewing the various aspects of the seven main goddesses. Each goddess had her own unique set of characteristics; and each one was very much symbolic of the time we were living in. They were archetypes for our own behavior and attitudes.

What got me the most was how I had always thought gods and goddesses were some strange half-human, half-angel – even half-animal characters dreamt up by some weird and wonderful religions of the early Mediterranean civilization. But now I was learning it just was not so. They were actually the key to understanding life itself.

The more we studied the book, the more we loved it.

At first glance, the stories made perfect sense. But then we realized there was something important missing. The more we tried to pin it down the more frustrated we became, so instead of struggling, we opted to leave it alone. We knew it would show up when it was good and ready.

And true to form, it made itself known in a rather startling way. It ambushed us – or rather – it ambushed Lisa.

We were having a *Goddesses Go Ga Ga* movie night, and Lisa was touched by a divine vision. Actually, that is not quite true. She was not really touched because that would imply some form of gentleness. It seems the Great Goddess was positively fed up with our inept attempts as little goddesses-in-training, so she bonked Lisa on the head with a realization. When Lisa came to, she exclaimed, "Well girls! It's just so *darned* obvious!"

Colleen and I burst out laughing. It seemed an absurd remark – especially when we were quietly curled up watching an old Elvis Presley flick, stuffing our faces full of popcorn, and swooning over his romantic delivery of a touching love ballad.

It did not phase Lisa one little bit. She simply reached over us, grabbed the video remote control out of my hand, pushed the pause button, unfolded herself from her couch-potato position – and jumped up and exclaimed, "Ladies! The Great Goddess just whomped me on the head, and I've been awarded the missing piece to our puzzle. Do you remember when we first read the book and it appeared to cover all the bases? There was Athena the Warrior, Artemis the Huntress, Hestia the Hearthkeeper, Demeter the Nurturer and Mother, Persephone the Daughter, Hera the Wife and Aphrodite the Lover?"

"Yep," Colleen and I agreed.

"Everything was there alright," I said, "or so we thought."

"Right," Lisa replied. "Then along the way, something began to nudge at us, remember? Something didn't feel quite right. Well, Valerie, you know how we've been talking about your upcoming world tour? Well get this! Aren't we women of the 90s a whole new breed? I mean – look at *you*. Aren't you forsaking hearth and home, and lovers and children, and careers and upward mobility, and facials and aerobic classes – to hoist your backpack on your back and skip town while skipping to the tune of "I love to go awandering...?"

Colleen and I nodded.

"Well, then ladies," Lisa said. "It's time we added an *eighth* goddess to the realm, because standing before you, may I present to you, Valerie – The Nomadic Goddess. *You're* the missing piece, Valerie! Take a bow!"

My scalp suddenly sizzled with excitement. It always happened just before a life-altering event. This time the feeling was even stronger than ever. I knew something big was up. I could feel it clear down to my toes.

"Socks," I thought, laughing. I looked down at my feet. "It was those darned orange socks. Socks are on the feet, right? Well what would socks most love to do? Why, go for a walk, of course! Nomads, walking – and didn't I read a saying somewhere that said, "He or she who does not travel, does not know the value of man?" I sat quietly contemplating the thought, and began to realize it was a very deep point. Maybe that was what I longed for; to know the value of myself and others. One thing was certain; I was hungry for something.

After Lisa and Colleen left, I took out my journal and looked up some notes I had made on nomads a few years earlier. As I read, I began to shiver. One of them said: "There is nothing better than a change of air in this malady of melancholia, than to wander up and down – to be a nomad."

"Hm," I thought. "Isn't it interesting that I happen to be suffering from boredom and disinterest in my work? And isn't it also interesting that I was named after a German war-time march called, *The Happy Wanderer?*"

I smiled and continued reading. My goose bumps began to multiply.

"In Islam," the next quote read, "and especially among the Sufi orders – the action or rhythm of walking was used as a technique for dissolving the attachments of the world and allowing people to lose themselves in God."

I took a deep breath.

"*Big* enough for you?" my little voice piped up, smiling teasingly. "You've been struggling with this stuff for years – both with this thing about God and your propensity for gathering what you call, material goodies. Well – here's your chance, *Miss Nomadic Goddess!* What do you say? Are you *up* for it?"

"God help me," I whispered quietly under my breath. "*Whoever* you are."

I turned out the lights, and walked quietly upstairs.

ELEVEN

How Not To Pack
A Backpack

Oh how I loved my two fellow nomadic goddesses. They were, after all, nomadic goddesses in their own right. They were simply Nomadic Goddesses In Waiting – waiting to take their first solo journey. After we birthed the concept, we shared a closeness far different than before. It was as if some invisible force had gone to work and a powerful bonding had taken place. After that fateful night, we were inseparable.

Lisa and Colleen were the dearest, most daring women I had ever met. I loved the bizarre adventures we created. One of my favorite games was one Colleen dreamt up. She called it, Dares and Double Dares. We designed real life tests to see just how far we would be willing to go in our unquenchable quest for the spirit of high adventure. Because we had all gone through similar self-development courses, we were game for just about anything. If any one of us ever hesitated to take the dare, the other two would remind her it was time to str......e....tch.

We played together for two solid months, but because we were so busy playing, we did not notice how fast the time was flying by. All of a sudden, there were only three weeks left before I was to hop a plane to fly off to the nether world of the unknown.

One night I took out my new backpack, set it down on the floor of my bedroom, and surveyed it proudly.

"This is definitely not your run-of-the-mill backpack," I thought, running my fingers lovingly along its edges. "Why – this little baby's equipped with a chic, detachable day pack ingeniously designed to be used as a backpack or converted to a classy-looking briefcase; plus it has a top-loading feature for ease of organization and a beautiful leather luggage tag for my business card. Yesiree – a true Yuppie backpack if ever I saw one!"

I decided to try my hand at packing it. I thought it would be wise to do a test-drive – just to be sure I could fit everything in.

At first, I could not for all the world, figure out how to get all my stuff into such an itsy bitsy teeny weeny bit of what people so magnanimously called, *luggage*.

"I mean, really!" I exclaimed. "How's a girl to know what she wants to wear for the whole next year? Talk about a dilemma."

I decided to start down my checklist.

"Gold Cross pen. Check. Esprit walking shorts. Check. Tortoise shell leather belt and stunning brass buckle. Check. Fashionable combed-cotton jet black t-shirt with shoulder pads. Check. Leather-bound monogrammed travel journal. Check. Wrinkle-free black and gold skirt for an evening at the Sydney Opera House. Check."

I started rolling and cajoling all my belongings into the pack and suddenly found myself cursing and screaming at the pack. I discovered that soft-sided luggage (i.e.: a backpack) did not allow a person to force it shut by sitting and bouncing on it.

I decided to call Lisa. After all, what were nomadic goddesses for, if not someone you called to help you pack?

I was trying to stuff a third bikini and a sixth pair of shorts in when I heard the doorbell ring.

Lisa let herself in and came upstairs.

"Is there something I can *help* you with, *Miss*?" she asked.

I burst into tears.

It turned out Lisa had an excellent way of helping me decide what to take. She held my selections up one by one and made me defend my choices – kind of a like a Lisa The Crown

Prosecutor versus Valerie – The Defense Attorney. I did not have a hope. We were unevenly matched from the start. Lisa had nothing to lose. *She* didn't have to travel the world *without* any of the articles. She showed no mercy. My seven pairs of *Jockey* panties for each day of the week never saw the light of day; only four were allowed. As Lisa so wisely pointed out, "My dear Valerie – you can always *wash* them." I could see I still had a lot to learn about backpacking.

As it came time to leave, I began feeling more and more uneasy. Curiously enough, I began to burst into tears everywhere I went.

One day I was at June's – the herbalist. I was asking her for information on a first-aid herbal remedy package to take on my travels and she was in the middle of explaining how to use comfrey ointment for scrapes and sprains when I began to cry. She looked at me and said, "It's okay, Valerie. You've had an emotional time of it these past few weeks. Go easy on yourself. Everything will be okay."

On hearing this I cried even more. I cried right through her explanation on parasite control and did not stop until she covered off the dangers of malaria attack. I quickly jumped up and said I had to go, then climbed into my car and drove away. I pictured myself dying in some grimy little hospital in Bangkok and burst into tears all over again. The tears blurred my vision as I drove, and the vivid scenes in my mind wreaked havoc with my concentration. I had no idea how I got home, but when I walked into the house I locked myself in the bedroom and vowed that I would never come out.

The more I thought about it, the more I did not want to go. Then something hit me and my heart and mind began to race and I thought, "But you *have* to go. You gave up your business, rented out your house, found a home for your cat. Valerie, you've made all the preparations! You've even prepaid your health insurance for the next year. You *can't* stay. Besides – you *told* everyone you're going. How would it look?"

That was all I could take. I lay back on my bed and really wailed.

I sealed myself away for the entire day and relentlessly tortured myself with increasingly darker scenarios of ugly encounters in what I called Life Out There – fueling the stories with material from some of my worst nightmares. Each new scenario took on unprecedented dimensions of blood and gore and unspeakable atrocities. Everything seemed big and dark and horribly evil.

Suddenly, the phone rang. I let it ring. I was in no mood to talk to anyone. I just wanted to stay in my room and cry and fret and feel sorry for myself. Eleven rings later I began to wonder who could possibly be so darned insistent. Couldn't they just leave me alone so I could die of fear – peacefully?

The phone kept on ringing. I figured, "Someone must know I'm in here."

I decided to pick it up.

It was Colleen. When she heard the trembling in my voice she became extremely concerned and asked what was wrong. I told her my story. She listened intently. When I was finished, she said ever-so quietly and ever-so gently, "You know Valerie, you don't have to go if you don't want to. You'll still be a Nomadic Goddess in *my* eyes! And don't go thinking you won't be in other's eyes too. We all know you've already gone further than anyone else in making your dream a reality. If now isn't the time, it'll come when you're ready. Don't even think that it won't because it will. But right now you decide what's best for *you*. Forget about everything and *everyone* else."

We talked some more and I hung up feeling somewhat relieved. I realized I did have a choice – just like she said.

A few days later I went walking arm-in-arm with her through a nearby park and breathed a huge sigh of relief and exclaimed, "Boy! You know this trip of mine couldn't possibly be any worse than what I've just put myself through in that one day of mental anguish. All I can say is – thank God it's over."

"Actually," I thought to myself, "I'm *glad* I tortured myself with all those doubts and indecisions because now I feel like I'm through the worst part of the ordeal. Oddly enough, I even feel more empowered. I guess that's why it had to happen – I had to teach myself to be a warrior. My biggest limitation has always been a fear of the unknown."

From that day onward, whenever I found myself wavering or needing to strengthen my resolve, I simply remembered what Troy had said to me about the color orange and taking up my sword of courage and imagined myself confidently wielding a hefty, gleaming sword high above my head – reveling in my feeling of power and savoring my victory.

I knew I needed to leave home to find the answers to whatever it was that was going on inside of me. I wanted some special insight; some indication as to my life's purpose; some understanding about what intuition was – anything that would give me an understanding about the 'why' of life. Until I had locked myself away in my bedroom that fateful day, I really had no idea how much I craved the answer. Out there, everything would be unfamiliar. There would be no directions or guidelines; no sign posts reading, This Way To Your True Self and The Meaning Of Life. Yes indeed. I would have to find my intuition. How *else* would I find my way around?

I also had to contend with battling the remnants of my hypoglycemia. I was still plagued by it from time to time – especially when I was under stress or eating the wrong foods. But I was up for the challenge. My self-development courses had taught me that whatever I needed would come to me exactly when I needed it.

"If I can give up my business and dispel my fears about spending my savings," I said, "and I don't have a clue as to what I'm going to do for work when I return home, I can *certainly* tackle the challenge of using my intuition to travel the world alone."

Three weeks later we were all at the airport and I found myself crying again. Only this time it was because I was saying good-bye to my two dearest friends in the whole wide world. Suddenly the world looked even wider than before– especially since I had looked closely at a globe the night before. I realized I was heading off to the bottom of the world and putting thousands of kilometers between myself and my loved ones. It was a really scary thought.

As we walked around the airport arm in arm, I began joking about leaving the shores of the homeland. As I heard myself speak, it occurred to me it must be some sort of nomadic goddess lingo. Normally I would have just said "left home."

I felt puzzled and thought, "Could it be that some sort of transformation is beginning to take shape deep beneath the surface of my character – striking at the very core of my being? Could it be that I will be changed forever – doomed to leave

Canada and wandering the world aimlessly and endlessly – a lost soul? A nomad?"
My heart suddenly leapt into my throat and I felt panic rise to the surface. I quickly grabbed hold of myself and said, "You only have enough money for nine months – one year tops."
"Phew!" I thought, heaving a huge sigh of relief. "Saved by a realization. Thank God for budgets!"
The airline called my flight. I gathered up my belongings and waved a tear-filled farewell and trudged down the corridor towards the departure gate blowing my nose – wishing for all the world that I could take along my fellow goddesses. It was sad, this leaving. I decided it would be best to turn my attention to my backpack and surprised myself with the sound of my own laughter.
Wiping back my tears, I began laughing even more as I reflected on why I had chosen a red backpack.
"*Orange* was not an option," I said to myself, grimacing. "Just because I wore orange socks at one time doesn't mean I warmed *up* to the color. I didn't. I doubt I ever will."
"Yes," I marveled, "red was definitely the right choice. Red for Canada, red for willpower and red for freedom. Gee. What every nomadic goddess needs – a backpack with a hidden, incredibly profound meaning."
"Guess what?" my little voice piped up. "Red is *in* orange."
"Oh yeah," I said, chuckling. "I guess you're right. Come to think of it, I remember Troy mentioning something about all of the qualities of red being in orange – that and yellow."
"Hm," I said, smiling. "I guess I didn't escape the influence of orange *after* all. Well on that note, I think it's time we created something extra special for this little nomadic goddess journey of ours – what do you say?"
My little voice smiled.
"How about some helpful hints to help us along the way? What do you think of: Guidelines to Nomadic Goddessing? Point number one – Never lose your sense of humor?"
My little voice giggled.
We had a winner and we knew it.

TWELVE

Nomadic Goddess
Gets Adopted

The lights of Vancouver disappeared into the distance and the black void of the Pacific Ocean slowly crept in to take their place. A pang of fear stabbed at the pit of my stomach as I felt the darkness engulf me. I sank down in my seat and silently bid farewell to my country. I had a feeling it would be some time before I saw it again. I had promised myself I was not coming home until I had found what I was looking for.

It had been three hours since I had left my friends and I was already missing them. But I knew I had to leave. There was nothing else in the world that mattered more to me than going on this journey.

When I arrived in Fiji I struggled along like any other novice backpacking world traveler. First I panicked thinking the airport bus was leaving without me, then when I realized I still had not cashed any travelers cheques to come up with the $1.00 fare, I shouted to the busdriver, "HOLD ON JUST ONE MINUTE! DO NOT LEAVE WITHOUT ME!" and sprinted madly towards a Canadian-looking traveler (now I ask you, how can one really *tell* such things?) and unabashedly begged him for bus fare. Then, after a suitable amount of groveling, I captured my $1.00 prize and raced back to the bus. Wheezing for air and pulling my sticky sweat-stained T-shirt away from my skin, I climbed on board and silently thanked my lucky stars for my good fortune. I gratefully sank into a seat near the front of the bus, and kept my eyes on the road. I wanted to be sure the bus driver dropped me off at the right spot in Suva. It was my first stop and I was not taking any chances.

When we arrived in town, I jumped off and reached for my backpack, but as I was trying to put it on, I realized I had no idea how to adjust what I soon began calling, "My newly-acquired appendage." I began to curse.

First I got the straps totally twisted, then I managed to rip my watch from my wrist and send it skidding face-down (of course) across the pavement. Then, as sweat began pouring from my brow, I felt my cotton trousers beginning to stick to my legs.

"The humidity here is incredible!" I exclaimed – looking down at my fluorescent pink shirt, which was now changing color right before my very eyes.

"Sweat has a way of doing that," I thought, smirking.

Next, my beautiful thick fashionable leather belt – the one I had packed along against my better judgement – suddenly began sticking to my trousers, which in turn began sticking to my skin.

"Geez!" I exclaimed.

"Remain calm, Valerie," I cautioned myself. "Your temper is rising because you only snatched a few hours sleep on the plane. It's just the fatigue talking."

I decided to try adjusting the straps of my backpack again. When I thought I had done the job, I managed to cover only a few blocks before I discovered my heavy-duty waist strap was now resting on a newly-chaffed portion of my now relatively-raw hip bone.

"Aaaaargh," I growled. I looked up at the scorching, tropical sun, howled mercilessly at the gods, and vowed to put more meat on my bones. I was frustrated and I was hot – but I was determined to find the place the guidebook billed as, The South Seas Hotel – something they called, "The best backpacker alternative to cheaper hotels in Suva."

"Lonely Planet," I read out loud, as I held up the cover of the guidebook. Trudging heavily along the city's main thorough-fare, I said, "What a horrible name for a travel guide. It doesn't *exactly* encourage people to strike out on their own, now *does* it? If anything, it might scare people into staying home!"

As I passed by a store window, I took a good close look at my disheveled appearance and suddenly realized why backpackers looked so bedraggled and tired whenever I saw them trekking laboriously through the downtown of Calgary. They too had chosen to follow *The Call of the Wild* and take up the challenge to see the world. I glanced at the backpack pro-truding from my back muscles, laughed and decided to change it to *The Call of the Turtle.*

After a 24-hour flight and a four and a half kilometer hike – which seemed uphill all the way – I made my way up the last steep incline of steps leading to the hotel, gasped a "Thank you," to the smiling young woman who handed me a room key – then opened the door to my dormitory room. I quickly wriggled free from my now-soaked backpack and collapsed on the sagging mattress that the hotel so liberally called a bed.

I lay motionless for a moment, breathing heavily. I reached up and pulled my wet t-shirt away from my skin for what seemed the umpteenth time, and looked up at the rickety old fans wobbling precariously high above me. I prayed for a cool breeze to get me through the night.

Once I had caught my breath, I stripped down, jumped into the shower and leapt quickly back into bed.

I stretched out and turned on my side, then silently and sleepily took time out to congratulate myself for passing my first test as a nomadic goddess.

I had hunted down my first bed.

I spent my first week relaxing on Fiji's white-sand beaches. They were the easiest tourist attraction to find, and it didn't take much energy. I had no idea how exhausted I was. In the past few weeks I had deserted my job, my family, my friends, my house, my cat – not to mention my *life*. Gathered all to-gether, they had silently taken their toll.

I lay on the beach reflecting on my life, and pictured my cat Athena, unapologetically basking in the heat of the sun's rays streaming in through my kitchen window. I thought about how there would be snow on the ground back home and gratefully stretched out and soaked up the warm, tropical sun.

"This is great," I thought. "I'm free of all of my responsibilities. No telephones, no deadlines, no clients. All I have to do is find myself a bed and a meal and arrange my own transport. It's a dream come true."

I smiled to myself for what seemed the first time since I boarded the plane.

My first adventure was to try out Fiji's antiquated public bus system. The locals were friendly and curious and even though they stared at me a lot, I got kind of used to it. One time, a Fijian woman sitting next to me asked me to come to her home and visit her family. I graciously declined, but it got me thinking about spending Christmas in Fiji instead of New Zealand. I had prearranged to stay with my sister's friend in Auckland, but then I heard my little voice teasing me and saying, "What kind of an intrepid nomadic goddess *are* you? Where's your sense of adventure? Go look for a family here, silly. Can't you see it's right under your nose?"

I knew it was right. I had left Canada hungering for an adventure and here was my opportunity. I had heard a lot about an island called Benga from another traveler and he said that it was completely non-touristy and that the inhabitants openly welcomed foreign visitors. He had arranged his stay through a specialty travel agent in Suva.

I really did not want to go all the way back to Suva to make my arrangements, so I decided to go it on my own. I asked around and was told the best way to find a family was to go to Navua town and inquire at the local Saturday market. All the Benga families would be coming to the main island to get their Christmas supplies.

I looked at my calendar and realized Christmas was just two days away. I had been laying around at the beach for so long, I had lost track of time.

The next morning I hopped a bus in search of an adoption – mine.

The bus pulled into the little village of Navua and stopped in front the grocery store. I nervously jumped out. I could feel my heart pounding with anticipation; I really had no idea what to expect.

"What if no one *wants* me?" I said to myself. "What if I'm too late? Christmas means *so much* to me. It's the first one I'll be spending away from my family and I'll just *die* if I blow it. And what's worst, I've closed off all my options by *coming* here. I've cancelled my plane reservations to New Zealand. And for what? The chance – *the chance* – that I *might* find a Fijian family to take me home?"

I went on with my tirade for some time, but then I decided to stop berating myself. I could hear a calmer voice inside of me saying, "You believe in a higher power, right? In your metaphysics classes, you came to know it as the White Light. And when you were planning this trip, you said you'd never even consider traveling the world if you didn't actually believe you had *some* sort of guiding force to keep you safe. Once in a while you even called it God."

"Yeah," I said, feeling considerably brighter. "Besides – I'm a *Personal Best* graduate; and no self-respecting graduate would ever *consider* missing such an opportunity to stretch beyond their comfort zone!"

"Precisely!" my little voice exclaimed.

I walked towards the outdoor market. Everyone seemed to be staring at me more than usual. At first I could not figure out why, but then as I looked around I realized I was the only white person in sight. It was a market full of Fijiians.

I looked down at my giant Birkenstock sandals, my fluorescent pink shorts and bright yellow t-shirt and my long tanned legs with the sun-bleached orange hairs sticking out from inside them, and pictured my bright red backpack strapped to my body. I pulled a strand of long blonde hair free from beneath my shoulder strap and chuckled. I realized I must have looked like a space alien to them.

I adjusted my backpack's waist band in the place where it was fighting for space with my leather designer belt and vowed to never bring along such a ridiculous luxury again.

I steadfastly approached the entrance to the market. Two young girls were standing staring at me and pointing their fingers and giggling and whispering to each other behind cupped hands.

I figured they were as good a place to start as any. I went up and told them of my mission and they giggled even more. Then – they ran away.

I felt stupid. What's more, I knew I even *looked* stupid. My ego started to say a few choice words but I told it to shut up. The last thing I needed to hear was that it was a stupid idea to even try this. Besides – I had closed off all avenues of retreat. There was nowhere to go. I pictured my orange socks, summoned what little courage I had left and entered the marketplace to start looking for a friendly face that might help point me in the right direction.

No such face appeared.

I began to break into a cold sweat. Right then, the two young girls reappeared and started talking to two old toothless women behind a table piled high with vegetables. The two ladies listened intently, chewed thoughtfully on their gums, pulled at the whiskers protruding prominently from their chins, pointed their fingers at me, and began laughing uproariously. Once the initial entertainment factor had worn off, they went back to sorting their vegetables.

"This is humiliating," I thought, standing with my Lonely Planet guidebook dangling limply from my fingers.

I could feel my heart beginning to palpitate, and I remembered how I had skipped breakfast to catch the early bus. "Oh oh," I thought. "You didn't *eat*, and now the *stress* is getting to you!"

Just as I was beginning to feel faint, a little voice from behind me said, "You can come with me."

I turned around and found myself face to face with a tall, skinny waif of a thing – a young girl of about 16.

"Come with me," she said again – looking inquiringly into my eyes.

I couldn't believe my ears – or my eyes. Suddenly, the two giggling girls appeared again, and proudly announced that their friend Losana was willing to take me home to her family on the island of Benga.

I felt my knees go weak. I had had no idea how much stress I had put myself under. I willed my knees to hold me up and followed my new young host to an area in the far back of the market. We walked past a number of vegetable stands and I could feel the stall-owners looking me over. We approached a bright blue awning under which stood a tall thin man. He was not a young man; his face was weathered by long hours in the sun. But what struck me was his peaceful, calm presence and his amazingly brilliant blue eyes. She introduced him as her father, Sireli. He respectfully extended his hand and I shook it. "It's a pleasure to meet you," I said. He humbly bowed – then shyly turned away.

"He doesn't speak English," Losana explained.

They exchanged a few words – then she disappeared. He and I stood looking at each other, and about 20 minutes later she returned and directed me to go down to the dock. She said her uncle's boat was loaded and ready to take us to the island.

We went down to the boat launch and climbed on board a relatively small, low-slung boat. I was amazed to see how such a tiny boat was filled to overflowing with fellow villagers and Christmas supplies. I began to wonder if maybe it wasn't just a little *too* full to ensure a safe journey.

While I sat pondering the apparent complete absence of life-saving equipment, the boatman confidently turned the boat around and pointed us in the direction of the current.

We headed down river.

"How very different boating is here," I thought, "compared to going fishing with my dad. At least *he* had life jackets."

"Still," I thought to myself, "it feels great to finally be going somewhere – and for *Christmas* no less!"

I decided to lie back and turned my face to the sun and closed my eyes and relaxed. I had had a big day.

"Besides," I said, smiling to myself. "If my eyes are closed, I can't see what's going on!"

After about 10 minutes, a sudden buzz of activity made me open my eyes. Everyone was busy jockeying for position, trying to get underneath a big blue tarp that had somehow magically appeared from either side of the boat. At first I thought they were trying to protect themselves from the sun, so I shrugged it off and went back to basking in the sun – marveling at the passing sights on the nearby shore.

When we reached the river's mouth, the boatman turned the boat towards the open ocean and my head suddenly snapped backward. A huge wave had come out of nowhere and viciously slapped me in the face. After recovering from the initial shock, I realized an extremely important fact. I was seated in the least desirable position in the entire boat – the front.

"So *that's* why this was the only vacant spot when Losana and I climbed aboard," I thought, frowning. I wiped the salt water from my face and braced myself for the next wave.

As the huge waves rolled relentlessly towards our little boat, I looked back at the boatman. He was smiling confidently and puffing nonchalantly on a cigarette. Incredulous, I thought, "The size of these waves don't even faze him!"

"He must have done this a thousand times, Valerie," my little voice said. "Why don't you just relax and concentrate on shielding your eyes from the stinging salt water, and leave the driving to him?"

My attempts to keep the water out of my eyes proved fruitless. I tried closing my eyes, but then I felt nauseous. I didn't know which was worse – the nausea or the pain. Meanwhile, I looked over at Losana. She was also wiping the salt from her eyes – but instead of grimacing, she was smiling.

I smiled back at her and resolved to be just as tolerant.

After a two hour, hair-raising, shirt-soaking ride, we arrived safely on the shores of Benga.

We got out, and I could feel my legs were a little shaky; I was glad to plant my feet on solid ground. Losana and her father led me to a tiny little house next to a church and she explained this was their home.

It was a very humble house, looking odd with its rough plumbing protruding from its outside walls. I could also see a corrugated iron-walled outhouse off to the right. Next to it, stood a make-shift shower with homemade plumbing hanging heavily from its rippled sides.

I looked at Losana and her father and she signaled to me to go inside and proudly led me into the kitchen to introduce me to her mother, Arieta – a plump, sweet-looking woman with a toothless smile. She stopped long enough to welcome me – then went back to baking bread over an open fire.

I loved her instantly. She was cooking food.

I gawked at the cornucopia of food spread out over the kitchen floor, and felt my mouth begin to water. A gnawing ache began to emanate from the pit of my stomach, and I suddenly remembered I had not eaten. I began to feel faint again.

Before I could say anything, Losana took my hand and led me through to a spacious living room. I noticed there was something very different about the room. There was not one stick of furniture – save for a wooden cupboard filled with dishes. I looked around and saw how spotless it was, and then Losana signaled to me to follow her. She took me into the only other room in the house – the bedroom – and pointed at a queen-sized bed. She said it would be my room.

I stared at the bed and asked her where her parents would sleep and she pointed through the doorway to the straw mats covering the living room floor.

"You can't be serious!" I exclaimed. "*I'll* not kick your parents out of their own bed!"

She looked at me through her deep dark eyes and calmly assured me they liked sleeping on the mats.

"It's cooler," she said.

I was about to plead my case again, but a herd of children suddenly came tumbling in, and came to a halt directly in front of me. They stood ram-rod straight at attention, beaming up at me with their shining smiles and sparkling dark eyes. I had an overwhelming sense of being the wayward child – a newly-adopted member of the family.

I counted the children. I would be number nine.

The next day Losana took me across the way to a slightly larger house. She wanted me to meet her tukangu – her grandfather. He was the island chief.

"Hm," I thought, smiling broadly. "I certainly struck it big on *this* one. Here I am, the orphaned backpacker, and my new family turns out to be the Royal Family of Benga. What good fortune!"

We exchanged a few words and Losana translated for us. I detected a sadness in his eyes; he seemed rather distracted and distant. When I asked her about it, she explained how he had just lost his wife of 43 years. I looked over at him and smiled compassionately. "He is still very much grieving her death," she went on, "and sits day after day beside her grave – with a fire lit, sitting quietly – alone."

"But he *is* healing," she said, casting him a gentle, loving look. He looked back and managed a weak smile, then motioned towards some family photos on the wall. Losana went over and pointed at a picture of her grandmother, then showed me a picture of her grandfather standing proudly next to Prince

Charles – the next King of England. I looked over at her grand-father, and he began to smile. I looked back at Losana – a questioning look on my face – and she explained how the prince had visited Fiji in 1980. He had chosen to visit their island because it was the only island with a chief. She explained how – to this day – her grandfather's rule still extends to nine villages on the island.

"He has great power," she said proudly, "and everyone holds him in very high esteem."

We looked at a few more photos, then I reverently bid him a fond good-bye, and thanked him for his hospitality. We stepped out into the bright sunshine, and Losana pointed towards a distant hill, and said that when her grandfather died, he would be laid to rest on the top of the mountain – to symbolize his highest position.

I looked over in the direction of her gaze and smiled.

The next day the kids and I pasted together blue and pink Christmas streamers with flour and water and strung them all around the house. It was weird using such bright colors. At home I usually selected more subdued colors like red and dark green. Meanwhile, Arieta busied herself in the hot kitchen, making homemade breads and scones with a bunch of tin pots. I marveled at her magic. She didn't even have an oven. I never knew you could bake bread *without* one.

When the meal was ready, the children spread out a very long tablecloth over the floor– about two-thirds the length of the living room – and Arieta came in and covered it with her feast of delicacies.

They motioned for me to sit down. As I ate, I could sense them watching me. They were entertained by how large my appetite was – not to mention how enthusiastic I was. I smiled gamefully at them, poured my fourth ladle of lovo coconut gravy over the second fish they had just served – then slapped another knife-full of their mother's creamy homemade pineapple butter onto my third piece of freshly-baked, steaming hot bread, and looked to the heavens in appreciation.

They laughed.

I couldn't remember being happier in my life.

The next day I awoke at 4:00 am to the sound of Christmas carols wafting in on the lush, sweet-scented morning breeze through my open window. It was Christmas day.

I arose, smiled dreamily at my good fortune, and padded heavily into the living room – stepping carefully over the bodies of the children strewn sleepily over the mats on the floor. I was surprised to see Arieta and Sireli were missing, but then I remembered Losana telling me they would be singing in the morning choir. I went out on to the front steps and sat down and gazed out over the early morning mist and looked in the direction of the church. I could see the faint flicker of the kerosene lamps shining inside, and could hear the strong, sweet voices of the choir.

I closed my eyes and smiled.

It was pure magic.

That afternoon I was surprised to find out there was no gift giving. Instead, there was plenty of family, friends, music and lots and lots of singing.

"How absolutely precious," I thought. "These people don't suffer from the stress and exhaustion of the pre-Christmas flurry like we do – all in the name of gift-giving. But what we *do* share, is the same traditional Christmas carols. They're Christians– just like me. At least I think I am – at least until I come up with a better idea for a religion."

What endeared my new family to me the most, was sitting cross-legged in a circle in their darkened kitchen – looking at each other in the dim light of a kerosene lamp, and listening to them sing. Their voices had the most glorious, melodic resonance. I felt as if I was being joyfully serenaded by a group of angels; high, clear, and oh so sweet.

They wanted to make sure I did not feel left out, so they proudly presented me with their Christmas song sheets.

I gazed down at the unfamiliar-looking script – looked up at them and smiled – then shrugged my shoulders. They laughed.

I sang in English and they sang in Fijian; and it all came out sounding perfect.

On the last night before I was to go back to Navua town, I lay in bed and silently thanked God for the gifts I had received, and fell asleep marveling at the rewards of taking the risk of coming to Benga. My new family had taught me what it was like to have nothing – and yet to have everything.

THIRTEEN

Yuppie Goes Hitchhiking

I arrived in Auckland, New Zealand just in time to have the stuffing kicked out of me. And no – it was not the post-Christmas turkey stuffing. It was New Year's Eve and the place was shut tight. The entire city was closed – for the next seven days.

"Gee," I thought, looking up and down the empty rain-soaked streets. "These Kiwis sure do take the New Year's celebration seriously. Why – there's not a soul in sight – and *this* Nomadic Goddess is in no mood to celebrate."

I walked dejectedly back towards the hostel – mourning the week of closed storefronts and restaurants I had to look forward to. I also realized I would be spending New Year's Eve alone in New Zealand. There was no answer at my sister's friend's house.

I was cold and I was hungry, and I could not find a decent bit of food at the neighborhood corner store. I suddenly remembered seeing an advertisement on the outside of the hostel promoting an in-house cafeteria. I made a beeline back – only to find a new sign had gone up, announcing it too was closed for the holidays.

It was all I could take. I felt a flush of energy, and I could feel my back becoming inflamed. They were signs that my blood sugar had gotten dangerously low. Either I had to get some food soon, or I would probably faint.

"Great," I thought, "my spirits are as damp as the rain-soaked streets I'm standing on, and it's supposed to be a *Happy New Year*. I'm also about to fall face down on the pavement in celebration of this auspicious occasion, and I'm not the least bit excited about it. Welcome, *sweet* goddess – to 1990. This is *your* year!"

I felt totally ripped off. Not only could I not get any food, but I had also left the tropical heat and sunshine of Fiji to arrive in a cold, wet climate. I had no idea Kiwiland was so cold in January.

I began contemplating what to do and realized I was not only in the throws of having a low blood sugar attack, but my body was now beginning to demonstrate symptoms which looked suspiciously like what the Fijian's called, "Dengue Fever." My forehead felt like it was on fire and I felt dizzy and nauseous. I leaned up against the wall, took a deep breath, and recalled how so many travelers had been hospitalized and put on intravenous because of severe dehyradation and diarrhea.

"Wonderful," I thought. "First an empty city, then no food, now a deadly disease. How absolutely brilliant. What next?"

I felt totally alone.

"But you're alone for a reason!" my little voice exclaimed. "Don't you *see*, silly? It's perfectly accurate. Your being alone symbolizes the beginning of your new life – no ties, no responsibilities – just you on your own. It's what you've been asking for years – so take it. It's yours!"

"You're absolutely right," I said, smirking. "I almost forgot. Thanks for the reminder."

I went upstairs and laid back in my bed and watched the neon signs blinking their multi-colored brilliance outside my window, and contemplated what my New Year's resolution would be. "It's very simple," I thought. "The most important thing for me to start the new year with, is good health. I have to stop this Dengue Fever."

My herbalist had taught me how to use visualization to heal myself, so I closed my eyes and began imagining the bacteria as little infantrymen of Do-No-Gooders wearing black helmets – with my own little army battalion of white blood cells rushing out to "the front" with their cute little white helmets – mercilessly blasting the bad guys clear out of their trenches.

"Calvary to the rescue!" I shouted, as I watched waves of T-lymphocytes rush onto the screen of my mind. "What a great team of Do-Gooders!"

The next day I felt somewhat better. I got up and found some fresh fruit and sugar-free biscuits, then spent the rest of the day in bed envisioning numerous scenes of destruction and body reconstruction, while simultaneously wishing myself a Happy New Year.

By evening, I managed to oust the bad guys. I laid back in my bed and beamed.

"Wow!" I exclaimed. "This is absolutely amazing! Who would have thought?"

For years I had been experimenting with healing through thought, but I never really believed I could actually do it. I suddenly felt incredibly empowered.

"You really had no other recourse but *to* do it, Valerie," my little voice piped up. "You either healed yourself, or you suffered. It wasn't exactly like you had a herbalist or a doctor just around the corner!"

A saying danced onto the stage of my mind and held up an announcement board and shouted out as if it was the town crier, "THE ABSENCE OF ALTERNATIVES CLEARS THE MIND MARVELOUSLY!"

I laughed and saluted. I reached over and grabbed a glass of soda water and hailed my victory and reverently toasted my army of Do-Gooders. Another guideline quickly sprung to mind for what was fast-becoming my Nomadic Goddess Handbook.

"Point number two of being a Nomadic Goddess," it said. "*Never* surrender."

The next day I awoke to a crisp, fresh, sunny day. I pulled back the curtains to look out onto the sun-bathed streets below, and stretched and rejoiced in my newfound feeling of well-being. I decided it was my signal to go out and explore my new surroundings.

I started with a quaint little inner city district – about a twenty minute walk from the hostel. It was beautiful. I wandered around enjoying the elegance of its historical buildings, looking in the windows of all the expensive clothing shops, and thinking about how great it felt to be alive and healthy. I started to relax for what felt like the first time in days. I realized I was still adjusting to what I called, the civilized nature of New Zealand. It was a weird contrast to the third-world agricultural setting of Fiji.

At the end of the day I arrived home exhausted, then woke up early the next day and did more touring. A few more days passed, and one day I realized I was staying much longer than I had planned. I began to wonder why.

I was sitting on a carpet of exquisitely-sculpted emerald-green grass in the middle of one of the city's fabulous parks, and it hit me.

"You're stalling!" my little voice called out.

I looked at the harbor far off in the distance and tears began to well up in my eyes. I suddenly felt scared, and an overwhelming sense of fear tugged at my heart and throat. For a moment, I could not swallow.

"They're back!" I exclaimed. "It's those darned *doubts* again!"

I suddenly flew into a rage. I stood up and yelled at the top of my lungs, "WHAT NOW? WHAT DO YOU WANT FROM ME? I'VE LEFT MY HOME AND FAMILY AND I'VE TESTED MY METTLE IN FIJI – WHAT ELSE DO YOU WANT?"

Silence.

I began to cry. I realized that after my adventure on Benga I had become quite complacent. I had promised myself back in Canada, that I would be trying my hand at hitchhiking once I hit New Zealand, and now here I was, and I wanted to delay it as long as possible. The mere thought of it scared the living daylights out of me.

I dug a Kleenex out of my shorts pocket and dried my eyes and asked myself, "Didn't you promise yourself you would take up every possible challenge to live your journey to its fullest? Well, Valerie – you've given up everything that *counts* in life – you're certainly not going to back out *now* are you?"

I got up from my grass carpet and headed straight for the hostel. It was time to plan my route and draw up an itinerary. I knew if I did not get on with it, my imagination would grab hold of me. Hitchhiking was not only my number one fear, but it also went against a basic belief I had.

I thought I was too good for it.

"I'm a successful business woman, aren't I?" I kept telling myself. "I *certainly* don't have to beg some stranger for a ride, now *do* I?"

"Wrong," my little voice piped up, pushing aside my ego. "Get off your high horse, *Cowgirl*, and step out from under your covered wagon. Get out there and meet some people – experience the culture. There is no better way to do it, *dontchaknowit*? Hitch a ride with the locals and *learn* something, *Sweet*heart."

I knew not only was my little voice telling the truth, but it was also not done with me yet.

And true to form it came back – whooping and hollering out like some wild outlaw, "NOW GIT YOUR LITTLE BACK.........PACK OUT ON TO THAT HIGHWAY AND JUST DO IT! Remember what they taught you in Personal Best? Today's stretch is tomorrow's boredom. Now *git* along there, little Miss *Business*woman!"

I packed my bags and headed out.

It took every ounce of courage and blood sugar I could summon to go out there and stand on that highway. I called up my orange socks, and found them dancing to a Willie Nelson tune, doing the Texas Two-Step inside a pair of ostrich leather-covered cowboy boots.

"They've got good taste," I thought smugly to myself.

Just then, the same overwhelming fear grabbed me in the throat again, and I started gasping for air. Sweat began pouring down my sides, and thoughts of escape rushed onto the screen of my mind.

"New Zealand's a small country," they said. "There's only two good-sized islands and *one thousand* kilometers of territory to cover! Why not just sign up for one of those handy dandy – $99.00 – Do The Impossible – See New Zealand In A Day – tours?

My little nomadic goddess voice popped up and said, "*Not a chance, lady!* Remember the book title you saw the other day? *Feel the Fear and Do It Anyway*? Well – what are you waiting for?"

I wiped the sweat from my brow and took up my position on the side of the road – immaculately dressed in my new black

99

t-shirt functionally endowed with a brand new set of detachable velcro shoulder pads and sporting my newly-acquired Esprit walking shorts; complete with my lovely three-pound beltbuckle gleaming in the sun.

I looked down at my shining prized possession and smiled and said to myself, "Never know when a girl's gonna want to *impress* somebody."

The toughest decision of the day was deciding what to wear. A lot of backpackers warned me not to look too scruffy or people wouldn't pick me up, and others advised me not to look too affluent or people would not pick me up.

"Talk about decisions," I thought, feeling the hot New Zealand sun beating down on my jet-black t-shirt and shoulder pads. I began wondering why I had chosen black as the color to hitchhike with in the tropics, but then – I knew exactly why.

It was my ego. It knew blondes looked great in black.

No cars came into view, so I began reflecting on how it had only been three weeks since I had left home – yet it felt as if my life had become submerged in a sea of distant memories – a past life, really.

"Past lives don't necessarily refer to reincarnation," I thought philosophically to myself. "I can have any number of past lives in this one lifetime – considering the multitude of phases I've passed through in this one short year!""

I contemplated past lives some more, and began seeing the humorous side of it and asked myself, "Do you suppose standing on broiling asphalt in the tropical noon-day sun wearing a jet-black t-shirt and a black pair of shorts has anything to do with raising my level of consciousness into an etheric realm of existence?"

Before I could answer, my mind switched channels and I thought, "I never once suspected I would be standing on a highway in some foreign land with my arm extended – thumb pointed towards the heavens – trying desperately to charm someone I do not even know into allowing me to share their vehicle on the road of life."

"Actually – make that someone in a *speeding* moving vehicle," I thought, jumping clear of an onrushing truck, "passing *by* my body *and* my backpack at *breakneck* speed!"

"Passing by!" I cried out, as I watched the tail lights disappear over the horizon.

"How humiliating!" I exclaimed. "This is *some* introduction to life on the road!"

As car after car and truck after truck zipped by, I thought, "Yeah sure. Welcome to *friendly* New Zealand. *Geez* Valerie – didn't your well-traveled backpacker friends rave about New Zealand as being *the* place to hitchhike? "*So* friendly," they said, "*so* helpful – *so* easy!"

As the parade of cars continued to pass by I began to feel totally rejected, and doubts started flooding in unrelentlessly. I could hear myself lamenting, "Woe is me!" and thinking, "Hey, what's *wrong* with me? What is it? Aren't I good enough? Why won't they stop and give me a ride? What's the problem?"

I stood wallowing in self-pity for a few more moments, then decided it was time I either lifted my spirits, or flagged down a tourist bus to call out, "I SURRENDER!"

I was determined to go the distance, so I quickly reminded myself of Point Number One of Nomadic Goddessing; Never lose your sense of humor.

I detached myself from the whole scene and saw myself from up above – looking down at my cute little outfit and back pack. I laughed to myself and thought, "Do you suppose they maybe prefer Polo to Esprit? Maybe that's the problem – I'm wearing the wrong designer! Or maybe it's because my Canadian flag isn't visible enough – the one straddling *half* the surface of my already huge backpack. New Zealanders love Canadians, so that *must* be the reason! Or maybe they're not stopping because they don't like the way I'm holding out my thumb! Maybe I'm committing some offensive act. Maybe I'm making fun of some obscure rite of passage and casting impurity upon impurity on some innocuous and highly-revered 800-year-old sacred Maori custom. Maybe I'm being a real boor!"

I started experimenting with alternate thumb positions and shuffled my backpack around on the asphalt to make sure my humungous 12" X 8" Canadian flag was clearly visible, when another thought struck me.

"In the past," I thought, smirking, "I too have passed by hitchhikers. And what was I thinking at the time? Get a job bum and get your own car."

101

Synchronicity being the amazing thing that it is – a solid red brick struck me hard in the temple.

I came to, seconds later, to see what had hit me.

It was another realization.

"But why was it specifically a *red* brick?" I asked myself, absentmindedly rubbing my temple.

"Don't know, really," I thought. "Maybe realizations are like that; they just happen; instantly and inexplicably – in technicolor."

I picked up the offending brick and was surprised to see something written on it.

One word. Karma.

As the thought sunk into my consciousness, the brick started doing a loud annoying tap-dance inside of my head. I could see it grinning out at me and calling out, "HEY YUPPIE! WHAT GOES AROUND COMES AROUND!"

I laughed weakly, then raised my hands in mock surrender and replied, "Okay, okay. I get it!"

My little ego began muttering away, grumbling to itself and saying, "But I'm not a bum. I have a car. I have a successful business....."

Then another little voice popped up and said, "Yeah, but *they* don't know that."

"Humility," I thought. "What a concept. Welcome to the other side, Valerie."

I shuffled my feet, looked down at the asphalt and mumbled, "This is really horrible. They do have a point, though. I guess it *is* time I put my little ego to bed; time to tuck it in – say, "Nighty, night. Sweet dreams, little one. Time for beddy bye."

But like a naughty little child, my ego didn't really want to go to bed. Instead, it whined and whimpered and then yelled out, "BUT MOM. I'M NOT TIRED. I WANT TO STAY UP AND PLAY. I WANT TO WAIT UNTIL IT'S DARK. I WANT TO......"

"LIGHTS OUT!" I yelled back. "DO YOU HEAR ME, LITTLE MISS SMARTY PANTS? I'm saying it's time to *git* your little behind *into* bed and if you step one foot out of that bed, you'll be grounded for a *week*. *Got* it?"

As I watched it climb beneath the covers, and coyly look out at me, I diverted my gaze and turned my attention to watching more cars go whizzing by. A few moments passed, and a half-ton truck with a motorboat in tow pulled over and came to a halt a hundred or so feet in front of me. I could not believe my eyes. I stood in stunned silence for a moment, then snapped out of it when I realized this was my big chance. I hurriedly signaled the driver that I was coming, gathered up my belongings and clumsily ran towards the vehicle. The sheer weight and shape of my bulky backpack and day pack made it hard going.

A nice older gentleman greeted me, and I heard myself heave a huge sigh of relief.

"He looks nice and safe," I thought. "Thank God."

I said hello and he directed me to put my things in the back of the truck. I climbed into the passenger seat and we drove off.

As we passed through field upon field of incredibly green grass observing hundreds upon hundreds of lazing, grazing sheep, my host told me he was heading to Wellington – New Zealand's capital – and how he was on his way home from a fishing trip off the coast of the Coramandel Peninsula. He told me he was absolutely thrilled to be able to help out a lone backpacker, and I said he had no idea how thrilled I was!

He laughed.

He was a very sweet man and surprised me several times by stopping to show me the tourist sites – insisting I had to get the full experience of the North Island – otherwise I would head home to Canada "not knowing the beauty of New Zealand," he said.

We stopped at Huka Falls and picked up an ice-cream cone, then drove into Taupo and he dropped me off in the center of town. He waved good-bye and I thanked him for his kindness, then I walked up the road a little way and found an adorable little high school that had been turned into a hostel for the summer months.

At the door I was greeted by Barry and Joy – two fun-loving middle-aged Kiwis who had been running the place for the last 10 years. It turned out they positively adored Canadians; so much so, they had a list of Canadian friends the length of my arm – and flags of each Canadian province – including ones for the Yukon and the Northwest Territories, hanging from the ceiling.

"I live in Canada," I said, "and I've never seen the emblem for the Northwest Territories and the Yukon. You guys are incredible!"

They beamed back and offered to show me around.

I felt at home instantly, and soon forgot about the trials and tribulations of my hitchhiking adventure. I nestled myself into the bosom of their warm, southern hospitality, and followed them into the school gymnasium to set up my things.

I selected a mattress perfectly centered between the freeshot zone and the center line of the basketball court and thought, "It's good to be back on the court again."

I lay down on the mattress and stared up at the ceiling and smiled and reminisced about my glory days in the high school provincial finals.

I was still smiling broadly when a couple of young teenagers came bounding in. One blonde, and one brunette. The blonde girl was tall and thin and pretty, the dark one was stocky and olive-skinned and feisty-looking.

They both said hello, and I sat up and said hello back. Then they quickly ran to the corner of the gym, picked up their purses and make-up bags and ran out again.

"We're off on a hunting expedition," the dark one called out as they darted through the door. "We're in for *heaps* of fun. Tell you all about it later!"

We talked briefly the next day and they decided it would be brilliant to host a *Girls and Goddesses* pajama party. They said I really captured their imagination with my Nomadic Goddess theory and they wanted to learn more about how they too could become nomadic goddesses.

We chose the night before I was to leave to have the party – mainly because it was the night our chaperones, Barry and Joy, were going out for dinner. They were leaving me, "the eldest", as they put it – in charge of the hostel.

We got out our junk food and lay giggling on the mattresses spread out on the floor – wearing our sunglasses (it was midnight), and playing Beach Boys music and reveling in the joy of sharing that special brand of girl-talk only girls would know about – boy-talk.

My new aspiring young nomadic girlfriends were a riot. They told me tales about how they had run away from home on their bicycles and were "out on a tear up the middle of the island," and how they had just met their very first "groovy blonde bombshells" – two surfer boys from Venice Beach, Southern California, and how they were *in love*. They were positively bubbling over with excitement – dancing and singing to the Beach Boys song, *Surf City*, and saying they felt free for the very first time in their lives.

"No parents," they said, beaming back at me as Maria faked a double dip in Lorena's arms, then went straight away into a triple twirl.

"We didn't tell them we were leaving until we rode the 70 kilometres to end up here!" Lorena called out, stopping briefly to catch her breath. Then she and Maria performed a daring under-the-legs sliding finish, and collapsed on the floor exhausted. They reached for their refreshments and in between chomps on their Mars bars and noisy swigs from their Coca Cola bottles, Lorena – an animated Venezuelan with a penchant for Arnold Schwarzenager – explained how she and Maria – who was finishing up her elocution lessons to bury her New Zealand accent – were intent on initiating themselves into the realm of Nomadic Goddesshood.

"Yes," Maria piped up. "We want to be just like you! If we pass the test, does it mean my hair will turn as white blonde as yours and I'll be able to speak as eloquently as you?"

"You never know," I replied, winking.

We stayed up half the night exchanging nomadic goddess adventure stories, and after hearing some of their boldest moves, I assured them they were well on their way to becoming nomadic goddesses.

At 2:00 a.m. I called out, "Lights out!" and went off to the kitchen to begin planning my strategy for the next day's highway attack.

I climbed into bed about a half hour later, but found it difficult to fall off to sleep. I was contemplating what it would be like to step back onto the asphalt again.

"Will it be as tough as my first time?" I asked myself – laying there with my eyes open, staring up at the ceiling. "Well if I've done it once," I told myself, "I can do it again. The *real*

stretch was getting over my initial fear to do it the *first* time –
anything after that should be a piece of cake!"

Still – I had doubts.

The next morning I arose, packed up my things and walked
into the foyer and was surprised to have Barry offer me a ride
the two and a half kilometers to the highway.

"I almost never do such things," he said – almost apologeti-
cally. "I'm a firm believer in travelers finding their own way to
their destinations. But there's something about you that makes
me want to help you out, so come along!"

"Okay," I said, as I climbed enthusiastically into his brightly-
colored little Volkswagen bug. I looked at the color more closely
and burst out laughing. "How appropriate," I thought. "Orange!"

A few minutes later he dutifully deposited me on the outskirts of town and waved good-bye and called out to be sure to
visit again.

Much to my surprise, the first car that passed me, pulled over.

"Can you believe it?" I said, incredulously to myself. "I only
just stuck out my thumb!"

I gathered up my senses and my belongings, and ran towards the car – looking somewhat like a cross between a preg-
nant duck and a penguin.

"It's very hard maintaining any sense of decorum," I
thought, "when one is running with an 18 kilo backpack and a
10 kilo day pack and a bag of groceries – all strategically held
out in front of one's own body!"

My Angel of the Morning turned out to be a young nurse
from Wellington.

"I never ever pick up hitchhikers," she said nervously – watching me wide-eyed with wonderment as I hurriedly catapulted
my belongings into her back seat and climbed in next to her.

"I decided to take pity on you because you're a woman
traveling alone," she continued. "I was afraid if I didn't pick
you up, someone else would – and there's no telling *what* kind
of people they would be!"

"Hey, thanks," I replied, smiling. "I really appreciate your
concern."

We enjoyed a lovely six hour journey, talking about the holiday she had been on with her parents and how much she loved

growing up on a farm. She began to quiz me on how I had decided to go "on Walkabout," as she called it – equating it with the Aboriginal custom in her neighboring country of Australia, where they went naked into the desert on a Vision Quest – equipped with only a few tools and the power of their intuition. I agreed that it sounded similar – only mine was Yuppie style.

She laughed.

Before we knew it, we arrived in Wellington and she insisted on delivering me right to the door of my hostel – even though it was a long way from where she lived. I protested, but she raised her hand to silence me and said, "Just to be sure."

A few minutes later we pulled up to a huge old house and I thanked her and walked up the narrow brick pathway to the hostel. I was still smiling when I arrived at the reception desk, but my smile quickly disappeared when they informed me they were full.

"Rats," I thought, frowning and turning away – kicking madly at the air in front of me. I starting grumbling loudly and said, "This is *another* one of my fears about traveling; not being able to find a bed!"

Suddenly I felt thoroughly and unequivocally – exhausted.

I set my pack down and went to sit down on the bench at the end of the entranceway and began contemplating my plight in earnest. I must have looked like a dejected puppy turned away at the neighbor's door. "Make that a dejected, *hungry* puppy," I thought to myself, as I heard my stomach growl.

I sat for a few moments sporting a face as long as a basset hound, then thought, "I'd better resurrect myself from this immense show of self-pity – otherwise all is lost." I reached into my day pack and pulled out my travel journal and started flipping through until I got to a list of telephone numbers at the back. I got up, asked for change from the reception clerk, and dialed a gentleman by the name of John Stevenson. I really didn't know him very well, but he said to call him if I ever needed a place to stay in Wellington. He was my first ride on my first day of hitchhiking. I remembered him saying he was a Queen's Court judge when he wasn't playing fisherman, and I thought to myself, "What *better* person to call? Surely *he's* a safe prospect to stay with!"

I dialed his number and he remembered me right away. He said he was happy to hear from me and asked me to describe where I was, then said he would be there in ten minutes.

I sat back down on the bench and got out my new Swiss army knife and began cutting up a blushing ripe nectarine, smiling broadly and marveling at all the gifts coming my way. "Nice people and cars and beds," I thought.

I looked down at the juice oozing out over my fingers and running over my bare legs, and laughed and exclaimed, "And look at this! Even fresh fruit from Kiwi Orchard Country. Yessiree. Everything's coming along just when I need it most. Thank *God!*"

I finished my snack, got up from the wooden bench, and stepped out onto the front step.

Squinting into the sunlight, I could not believe my eyes. There before me lay the most beautiful, sparkling, cherry red BMW I had ever seen.

I caught my breath, reflected on the *"Welcome to Friendly New Zealand"* slogan on the bus passing behind him, and exclaimed, "Oh boy! I'll say – and how!"

I stood on the step savoring the moment. I watched John get out of his car and run around to the passenger side to open the door. He motioned for me to step inside and I smiled.

"Pure bliss," I remarked to myself, as I floated effortlessly down the stairway.

Wrapped in what seemed to be a pillowy soft cloud of etheric something-or-rather – like I had seen in the movies, I tossed my bags in the back seat, lowered my body into the car's deliciously fathomless, luxurious leather seats – sighed a deep sigh of satisfaction and turned to John. By now, he was grinning from ear to ear and I said, "You know, John – I can take this hitchhiking/hostel life any day of the week!"

He laughed, pointed towards the floor, and showed me how to adjust the seat to make more room for my legs.

"I have the same problem," he said, motioning towards his own, equally-long legs.

We pulled into the traffic and headed out of the downtown.

Moving along through the steady stream of vehicles, I sat back and watched and thought, "This really is what is meant when they say, "Go with the flow."

That evening John treated me to an exquisitely delicious meal at an upscale restaurant – a place way beyond my backpacker budget. I savored every mouthful. It beat the boiled pumpkin and brown rice and soy sauce I had been living on for the past few weeks. The next morning he drove me to catch a ferry to the South Island. I was off to Nelson to do some berry picking.

Three weeks later I arrived back in Wellington and telephoned him to tell him about my adventures hiking the Abel Tasman trail outside of Nelson – and how I had explored the sights around Queenstown and the Milford Sound, and how I had taken something called, a *Magic Bus* tour of the famous West Coast Trail with 40 other backpackers.

He was not surprised to hear how much I loved the pristine beauty of New Zealand, and said it was why he had chosen to live in New Zealand all of his life.

We also talked about how I was ready and raring to get back on the hitchhiking trail. People had recommended that I not hitchhike the South Island, since it had a smaller population and less traffic – plus it was the off season. John asked me where I was staying in Wellington, and I told him I would be spending the night with Lorena – my runaway teenage friend; The Nomadic Goddess of Taupo.

We said goodbye, and after walking down a few wrong streets, I found my way to her house via the commuter train. When I arrived, she let out a squeal of delight and leapt wildly into my arms. We spent a wonderful night reminiscing, and she told me of her plans to travel Europe when she finished highschool. She said I had inspired her to launch her very own nomadic goddess quest.

The next day, I laid out my plan of attack to begin hitchhiking again – this time to Auckland by way of the eastern seaboard through Napier – a city famous for its large selection of Art Deco building designs. The city had been virtually destroyed by an earthquake in the early 1930s and was rebuilt again in the style of the times.

I figured I could do the trip in a day. But after standing on the side of the road in the drizzling rain for an hour, I discovered that trying to get to Napier in a day was not such a good idea. I was such a novice. In my naiveté, I believed I could actually make it to the coastal city by sundown.

I must have endured one of the longest days of short rides any one hitchhiker could encounter. It was a veritable hitchhiker's nightmare. It took me six rides to cover what looked to be an incredibly short distance – at least as far as I could tell from looking at my map.

When I first started out, I noticed people were passing by me, pointing and laughing at my sign.

"What are they laughing at?" I asked myself.

"Don't worry about it," I told myself. "Eventually somebody will stop to let me in on their little joke."

As I thought about this, a couple of little old ladies pulled over and motioned for me to come to their window. They advised me there was no way I would ever get to Napier standing on the freeway.

"Oh – so *that's* the problem!" I exclaimed.

They laughed and asked me if I wanted to join them – saying they would be happy to take me a few miles up the road and put me on the main highway.

I thanked them, loaded my things in the car and climbed in. When we arrived at the highway intersection, I jumped out and said good-bye. Twenty minutes later, a car pulled over and the driver waved to me, signaling me to get in.

I ran to the window and looked in to see an elderly couple, and the husband asked if I would like them to take me to the next town – since that was as far as they were going. They both apologized profusely for not being able to take me further, but I told them that would be fine and climbed in.

They dropped me off a few minutes later at a roadside gas station and as I was standing on the highway holding up my cardboard sign, the gas station attendant walked up to me, pointed at my sign, and said, "Ain't no way you can get there before nightfall."

I looked closely at his face and he looked to be a bit of a sour sort.

"Maybe he has something against happy faces," I thought – since there was one smiling back at us from beside the words I had written in thick black felt pen that read, "NAPIER PLEASE."

I looked blankly back at him, moved a short distance away,

and acidly replied, "*That's* okay. I'm not from around here." Wandering down the road, I began chastising myself. I had been terribly rude. But I was hungry and hot, and I thought, "Who *wouldn't* be just a little irate hearing such disheartening news?" Then I realized what was really bothering me. I knew he was right. My ego simply prevented me from admitting it. "What a rookie you are," I said loudly to myself, trudging down the road. "I can't believe you didn't actually *research* this leg of the journey. What a *stupid* thing to do!"

Suddenly I stopped and said, "Listen to yourself. Your blood sugar must be really dropping quickly. It's the only time you're ever this vicious towards yourself."

A big semi-trailer truck with a large burly driver behind the wheel, suddenly pulled over. I debated whether or not to get in.

I decided to take the chance.

I looked up into the cab of the truck, said "Hi," to the driver and he introduced himself as Ron. He told me to climb on board.

He seemed to be a mild-mannered sort. He good-naturedly told me it was not company policy to pick up hitchhikers.

"But what the hell," he said, "it's late and you look tired, and I don't see why I shouldn't give you a break!"

"Thanks," I said, running around to the other side. I hoisted myself and my backpack up into the cab. It took all the strength I had to make it in. It had been a long day.

We drove on in relative silence.

He dropped me outside of the small Danish town of Dannevirke and said good-bye. He told me Napier was still another 90 kilometers up the road and said he would like to take me all the way, but he had an overnight load to pick up.

I thanked him and jumped out.

It seemed Dannevirke was the end of the line.

My back ached and I felt totally exhausted, yet I knew I had to find a way to get to Napier.

I looked around at the deserted sealed road– a gravel road pressed down and oiled which the Kiwis magnanimously called, *a highway* – and watched the sun begin to set.

I began to panic.

Next to having some crazy pick me up, my biggest hitch-hiking fear was being caught in the dark on a highway with no food in a foreign land. And now here I was – about to live out that nightmare.

"Oh God," I prayed. "*Please* say it isn't so. *Send help please!*" A half hour went by and I watched the sun dip below the horizon – turning the sky a deep fuschia and soft pink. Purple clouds began to reflect the sun's fading light off to the north – which was – by the way – exactly where I wanted to be – climbing into a nice warm bed and settling in for a good night's sleep. Normally I would have found the scenic sunset incredibly enchanting.

"But not today," I thought sadly to myself.

I suddenly felt a chill run up and down my spine and watched the dark envelope me and thought, "Better make that *tonight!*"

A big green tank of a car and a sea of dark faces went flashing past – and quickly squealed to a halt a few meters up the road.

"Uh oh," I thought, "*Gee* God. Remember when I put in that S.O.S. call? Well – I guess I should have been more *specific!*"

I watched the car back up towards me, and quickly ran down a list of ways to say as sweetly as possible, "GEE GUYS. Thank you VERY MUCH for stopping, but there is NO WAY ON GOD'S GREEN EARTH – New Zealand being as green as green as can be – that I am going to get into a car full of YOU teenage guys who are OBVIOUSLY out for a joy ride! Uh uh. No way!"

I was still rehearsing my lines when the car came to a stop directly in front of me.

Peering into the open window, I realized God had heard me after all.

"Point Number Four of Being a Nomadic Goddess," I said to myself, breathing a huge sigh of relief. "Never try to second guess the Big "G" – he knows a whole lot more than you ever give him credit for."

Staring back at me were six smiling Maori faces; all of them women.

I scanned the car, but could not for the life of me, figure out where I was going to fit myself in. The look on my face must have been priceless. They could all see me wondering, "Just where did they expect to put me when they first decided to pull over? This place is jammed!"

"Hello," I ventured, sounding more than a little hopeful. They smiled back and answered a resounding, "HELLO!" "Okay," I thought to myself, "*Now* we've established communication. We're off to a good start. But what am I going to do about finding a place to sit between these unbelievably large women? The only other time I've seen shoulders like these, they were attached to the bodies of pro-football players!"

I considered strapping myself and my backpack to the roof of the car, but then one of the women in the front seat beamed at me and said, "Throw your bag in the boot, girl and get on in!" I searched her face for hints of more specific seating arrangements and she began to laugh hysterically. Then the rest of them joined in.

I felt my face turn a bright magenta. The woman in the front stopped laughing long enough to point towards the back seat and cried out, "THEY DON'T BITE DEARIE! Just go on and SQUEEEEEEEEZE yourself in between Joanne and Murphy there. You'll be alright. G'HEAD, G'HEAD!"

I nestled myself in between my new-found traveling companions, and the woman behind the wheel stomped on the gas pedal. I felt my head separate from my shoulders. My chiropractor would probably have called it whiplash. My new female friends, however, called it driving.

We went careening wildly down the highway. I rubbed my neck and thought, "Well! I was certainly right about one thing. They *are* out for a joyride!"

One of the two passengers in the front seat turned to me and said, "Hey girl. Did you know this is your lucky day?"

I thought to myself, "Maybe she's talking about getting this ride."

Before I could reply, she flashed me a big, gleaming white smile, and with her eyes shining brightly, she proudly announced, "Why, *we've* just been to a Born Again Christian Revival Meetin' and we have a question for you: Have *you* taken *Jesus Christ* to be your *Savior?*"

An explosive went off in my head – detonating somewhere in the general region of my brain, the part of my anatomy that instantly ignited whenever someone was trying to hold me down and force-feed me religion. I decided I had better not resist.

113

"What's the use?" I asked myself, smirking. "I can't exactly shut the door in their face like when other religious groups come knocking door-to-door! I guess I'll just have to face them. No real choice, now is there?"

I looked her straight in the eye and answered back, "No. As a matter of fact, I haven't."

She looked at me – horrified, and I thought, "You know, I don't think I'm going to get a second shot at this."

As she busied herself quoting the scriptures, I asked myself, "How long can it take to cover 90 kilometers?"

My little voice piped up and gleefully answered, "An eternity, *sweet* sister!"

Curiously enough, that was exactly how long my well-meaning travelers told me I would burn in hell – if I did not take Jesus Christ as my Lord and Savior.

As I reflected on this delightful bit of news, I noticed the lines of concern growing on their sweet faces and I decided I had better say something to quell their concerns.

"I believe in a higher power!" I blurted out. "And I ask every day to be guided and protected – otherwise I'd never be out here alone."

Silence.

"There," I thought, settling triumphantly back in my seat. "*That* ought to settle their concerns about the eternal damnation of my soul!"

I couldn't have been more wrong. They looked even more worried, and one of them ventured, "Well, do you believe in the devil?"

"No," I replied.

Talk about how one word can change the lines on a person's forehead!

"Oops," I thought. "I had a fifty percent chance of getting that answer right and I blew it."

"Better luck next life!" I laughed.

Thankfully, we rolled into a gas station on the outskirts of Napier and my six traveling evangelists prepared to say goodbye. First they turned to bless me, then they handed me a blue book.

I gazed proudly down at my newest treasure and smiled. In the palm of my hand lay a royal blue, tiny as could be, backpacker-sized Bible – The New Testament.

"What an adorable little offering," I said to myself, turning it over and over in my hands and marveling at how incredibly efficient my little Lovers of Jesus were.

I looked up to humbly thank them for rescuing me from the dark, but found myself yelling at the top of my lungs, "DON'T WORRY. I'LL BE FINE!" I had to yell because the driver had once again done her fast takeoff – executing a perfect, screeching, smoking burnout on the hot dry pavement in front of me.

I smiled, waved and bent to pick up my belongings. Over the noise I could hear them calling out good wishes and caught a faint glimpse of them blowing kisses at me through the thick blue smoke.

"I'd say those girls luuuuuve to drive," I said, chuckling to myself, as I walked off into the night in search of a bed. I found one not far up the road and collapsed. I was asleep in minutes.

After Napier, my days on the road passed quite quickly. I slowly began to relax and got into the rhythm of hitchhiking. What impressed me the most about my new lifestyle, was its unspoken, fascinating way of operating.

Hitchhiking was a way of life like none other. It required immeasurable patience and trust, and it meant letting go of trying to control the outcome. I had to surrender and accept that everything was entirely out of my hands and just go along with whatever or whomever came my way.

Something else I discovered was that I needed a ton of that illusive commodity called, faith. I had to convince myself – really believe – that someone – the right one – would pick me up. Some days that was my biggest challenge; like when I was standing in the rain scanning the skies looking for signs of a let up – praying for that miracle ride; the one that would take me all the way to my next destination and not just to the next little town. The road and the next ride became my entire focus.

A yellow Mustang Cobra pulled over to the side of the road. I ran gratefully towards it sloshing through the mud and water, trying desperately not to drop my now much heavier backpack. I had stuffed an entire double load of groceries inside. I was determined not to ever get stuck on the road again without the makings of a meal.

I ran to the car window and found myself staring straight into the eyes of two Maori women dressed head to toe in black leather – their jackets sporting a Black Power emblem. I hesitated for a moment, then climbed in. I decided it was worth the risk. I was wet, I was tired – but most importantly – I was desperate. I figured that whatever adventure the ride held in store for me, it had to be far better than standing on the rain-soaked roadside strategically jumping clear of the spray that threatened to engulf me every time a big semi-trailer truck came barreling past.

My two rescuers turned out to be great educators. They taught me all about the tension and cultural disparity between the Maori population and what they called, "The white people in power." I learned more than I could ever have learned by reading the local newspapers. And even though my new-found *Black Power Goddesses* looked kind of fearsome in their black garb and colorful tattoos, the better I got to know them, the more I discovered they were just a couple of women out living their lives.

"We're out fighting for a cause we believe in," said the driver, "but that doesn't necessarily mean we're violent."

"On the contrary," the other woman added, "we steer clear of violence as much as we can. We prefer instead to use *other* forms of pressure."

I didn't get a chance to ask them to elaborate. The rain had stopped and I could begin to make out the road signs. I could see we were well within range of our destination. I say, "were," because it turned out to be the operative word of the moment. Just as we were about to enter the city limits, the driver pulled the car off the road and started heading in the opposite direction.

Dismayed, I sat up and tried to determine what was going on. I thought maybe she knew a bypass road to get us into the city a little faster. But as I listened to what they were saying to each other, I realized we were on our way to a small out-of-the-way town to pick up more of their gang members.

I started beating down thoughts of kidnapping and pain and death and thought, "Okay. Now what? First the rain, then The Black Power Gang. What else could I possibly create to make this little adventure of mine even more *adventuresome?*"

More minutes passed and I began feeling like a caged animal. "What can I really do?" I asked myself. "Aren't I, after all, a hitchhiker, and don't all hitchhikers have to go with the flow?" "Well," I said, emitting an uncharacteristically high, squeaky voice, and feeling my palms sweating profusely and my heart beating a million times a minute. "Here I am, just sitting here in this back seat – *flowing*!"

I folded my arms resolutely across my chest and watched my mind go to work on a full range of dark, twisted death scenarios – but took time out to congratulate myself for making up a will before leaving home.

We cruised straight through the hamlet and headed back in the direction of the main highway.

"Oh yeah!" I rejoiced. "Nobody home!"

I thought I was home free, but then I heard them talking in their native tongue, and all I could make out was one word: Prison.

"Hm," I thought. "They're certainly not talking about the growth in the *cell*ular phone market. What do you suppose they're up to now?"

I decided not to wait. I blurted out, "Where are we headed, guys?"

The driver turned around and replied, "We're on our way to Auckland City Prison to visit my husband. He was arrested three months ago. He's the leader of the *Black Power* movement.

I gulped.

"But don't you worry," the other big black woman interjected, "We'll deliver you to your destination first."

True to their word, they deposited me right in front of the place I was staying.

"What a couple of sweethearts you are," I said, gathering up my things – trying unsuccessfully to cover up an audible sigh of relief. They looked at me and smiled and called out, "Good-bye," and pulled away. I waved, and even though they were well out of sight, I stood on the sidewalk – stunned – with my backpack leaning somewhat uncomfortably up against my leg. I could actually hear it asking to be picked up. Maybe it thought I was its mommy.

"Pure, unadulterated entertainment," I thought, smiling to myself.

I bent down, picked up my big baby, and hauled her up the stairs to the top floor of the apartment building where a friend of my sister's lived. I had been invited to stay with her for a few days before I flew off to Australia. Living with her would be a welcome switch from my life in hostels.

FOURTEEN

Hong Kong — I Came,
I Saw,
I Took A Valium

I spent four glorious months enjoying the laid-back, leisure-oriented culture of Australia, and was completely unprepared for the frenetic, money-chasing activity Hong Kongonians called, "Life."

"Welcome to Happy Valley – Hong Kong," was the neon sign's message.

"I'll bet!" I thought to myself.

It was one o'clock in the morning and I had just left the airport with my new friend, Martin – a friend of my tennis partner back in Calgary – and we were driving through one of the city's neon-lit, heavily compressed downtown centers.

"Where's the palm trees?" I cried. "I thought this was the tropics."

Martin looked over and smiled.

I thought, "Judging from his expression, it must be a common complaint from newcomers."

We arrived at his high-rise apartment building and he got me settled in for the night. Next morning, we hopped a bus and he took me downtown. He showed me where he worked, gave a brief description of how to locate it again if I got lost, then wished me well and went off to work. I went toddling off to do some discovering.

I was excited and intent on getting acquainted with the Asian way – even though I knew Hong Kong was not exactly the best place to do it – since its history as a trading port and one of the world's centers of commerce made it more the West of the East.

"No matter," I thought. "There's much the city can teach me."

As I walked, I tried to keep my eyes focused on ground-level, but my eyes kept being pulled to look waaaaaaay up – at wall upon wall of concrete apartment buildings and office towers. I found them so incredibly obtrusive, the way they dominated the horizon and obliterated the sky. Laundry hung sloppily from every balcony, adding to the unruly look of the side-streets below, and air conditioners whirred loudly from every window. The smell of garbage and other rotting debris assaulted my nostrils each time I walked along one of the narrow streets. I was amazed at the stench – especially since it existed right alongside the perfectly-organized Central Business District.

"How can people *live* like this?" I asked myself. "There's nothing *green* here," I whined, "only gray cement and business people in suits walking the streets with cellular telephones attached to their ears. It's positively inhuman."

As I sat contemplating my surroundings, I realized Hong Kong was just an encapsulated version of business communities all over the world – including my own city of Calgary. I thought, "Valerie. Take a closer look. *This* is *your* life, too – it's just that everything is jammed into this tiny island, so the business crush is more obvious."

"Yes, my dear," my little voice piped up. "You set out on this journey to discover your truth. Well – this is *some* of it! Welcome to the world you left behind!"

After four days of hell in Hong Kong, I dubbed it The Compression Chamber, and found myself stomping moodily around thinking, "This is not fun. I want my mommy. I want my condo. I want my quiet green neighborhood. Or better yet, I want my cat. Yes, that's it. I want my cat. Now, where is that little nomadic goddess when I need her most? Colleen and Lisa and I made her an honorary Nomadic Goddess, so it's time Athena held up her end of the bargain!"

That was the one tiny problem with having nomadic goddesses for best friends; when you needed them most, they were *out*.

I stayed in Hong Kong two weeks – 10 days longer than I had planned. I got sick with a back flu from the onslaught of whirring, freezing cold air conditioners, and in Hong Kong's hot, humid weather, it was a sure-fire recipe for illness. But as soon as Martin's Chinese herbalist had me up and running, I headed straight for the airport.

I was on my way to Bangkok.

While I was waiting for my flight, I guffawed at the sight of a souvenir t-shirt in the shop window. It read, "Hong Kong. I Came, I Saw, I Took a Valium."

"Hey," I said, looking the t-shirt square in the chest, "I can relate."

Little did I suspect that my next destination would put Hong Kong's claim to shame and send it whimpering into a corner, bullying it into submission with an abusive, infuriatingly loud, "BANGKOK! I CAME. I SAW. I TOOK TEN VALIUM!"

I arrived in Bangkok a few hours later, and was stunned to find the travel guidebooks were in no way exaggerating about the insane driving methods of the Thais. I recalled the t-shirt's prescription for stress and thought to myself, "Good thing Valium can be bought as an over-the-counter item in Bangkok!"

Their driving was incredible. I willed myself to stay calm and held on for dear life.

I arrived at my guest house, hoping to settle in for a good night's rest, but I must have been dreaming. Eight hours later, after enduring the torturous heat and suffering from noise-induced sleeplessness, I emerged from my guest house absolutely bagged.

I walked out onto the street, only to discover Bangkok's streets not only had their own share of sirens going off – just like in Hong Kong – but the deafening noise of passing vehicles and infuriatingly loud boat engines of the Chao Phya river taxis assaulted my senses like nothing I had heard in Hong Kong.

It seemed mufflers were optional in Bangkok.

"Come to think of it," I said to myself, observing a cloud of sickening blue smoke billowing out from behind a passing speeding taxi, "so are exhaust systems and brakes."

"But not accelerators; no siree, " I thought. "Now *those* little babies are standard equipment. Why, they're the only things anyone ever *uses* in their cars – that and horns – which are, by the way, the *second* most-used feature in Bangkok."

Lost in thought, reconsidering my choice of countries, I leapt out of my skin at the sound of an infuriatingly loud horn blaring at me from behind. I jumped out of the way, reached into my day pack, and got out my *Lonely Planet* guidebook.

"Time to pick a tourist sight," I thought. "It'll get me off the streets."

The book told me Bangkok was by far Thailand's most famous and colorful city – once called The Venice of the East – before they started filling in some of their canals, or what they called, *klongs*. It was a city planner's desperate attempt to expand the road system, but when they destroyed the canals, they not only removed the natural drainage system, causing the streets to flood every time the rainy season arrived, but they also ended up compounding their traffic problems.

"How ironic," I thought, looking at the bumper-to-bumper traffic. "They've certainly made a mess of it all right."

I eventually found my way to Bangkok's famous Grand Palace and Wat Po (Wat means temple), and forgot all about the lunacy outside. It was so nice to be tucked safely away behind the high, quiet confines of the palace walls.

I wandered around freely, mesmerized by the sheer size and golden glitz of the buildings – impressed by the way the Thai people held their Buddhist spiritual culture in such high regard. I looked over the rows upon rows of smiling golden Buddhas and smiled to myself and thought, "How lovely. It looks like such a happy culture; a real sharp contrast to the crucifixes we have in the West which so gruesomely depict the suffering Christ. I must say I like this much better."

When the noon-day sun reached its full height, the heat was so intense, I headed back to my guest house to take a cool shower.

While drying off, I thought about how I had chosen my guest house. It had been recommended by my more experienced backpacking friend, Karen, and she had insisted the V.I.P. Guesthouse on Kao Sarn Road was one of the most popular gathering places for Western backpackers; cheap, friendly and clean. She said I would be nuts not to take it.

"I say, I'd be nuts to *keep* it," I laughed, reaching for the shampoo. "It must have been the V.I.P. part that grabbed my little Yuppie attention, because it preempted me from asking any clarifying questions like, "What's the downside?"

After five days of living on Kao Sarn Road battling the incessant din of three-wheeling, free-wheeling motorcycle tuk tuk taxis, and enduring the pounding musical cacophony of the competing cassette tape peddlers, I felt as if I had been locked in a sensory deprivation chamber and slowly – almost imperceptibly – converted into a pathetic, whimpering, raving lunatic.

It turned out I was not alone. There were a lot of other backpacker loonies out there too.

Knowing this did not improve my condition – nor my mood.

The next morning I was sitting in the open air restaurant at the front of the guest house, and began stuffing Kleenex in my ears to block out the noise from an extremely noisy tuk tuk that had pulled up in front of me. The offensive vehicle sat idling loudly, spewing blue smoke all over my breakfast plate, and I began thinking, "Maybe I should send in recommendations to all the popular travel book editors suggesting they publish a warning to keep other unsuspecting backpackers from being lured into this Kao Sarn Road Budget Den of Iniquity. What a dive!"

I began composing a letter, but my adventuresome little backpacker voice piped up and said, "Nah. And have them miss *this*? Not a chance. Isn't *this* what traveling is all about? Besides – didn't you get to meet a lot of other westerners? And didn't it help make you feel more at home in an otherwise foreign environment?"

I put my pen away and thought, "Point Number Four of Being a Nomadic Goddess: Don't ruin other nomads' chances to experience the full range of sensory perceptions – or sensory deprivations."

FIFTEEN

Get Thee To
A Monastery,
Yuppie

A monastery was the only answer. "A Buddhist meditation course would do me a world of good," I thought. "Expand my consciousness, challenge my spiritual beliefs, introduce me to Buddhism. The travel books call it, "the backbone" of Thailand's culture and way of life. What better way for me to get a first hand experience of this country? It'll be peaceful and serene and most of all, it'll be quiet."

I also knew it would give my little nomadic goddess adventure what it needed most – a good dose of culture and religion. Yep. I could round out my experiences in the big old wide world. Besides, Buddhism was Thailand's self-acclaimed Religion of Freedom and since Thailand meant Free Land, and I started out this spirit quest by calling it my Freedom Year, it seemed the perfect match.

I also knew it was time to open up and experiment with my spirituality a little more. I had met an older Englishwoman at a Buddhist temple outside of Chiangmai in the north of Thailand, and she highly recommended a meditation course in the south at a place called Wat Suan Mokh, and somewhere along the line I had read a description on open-mindedness and it inspired me. It read: "The measure of a person's intelligence is how open-minded they are."

By this point it wasn't so much that I wanted to explore how open-minded I was, or how spiritual I was, but to recognize how desperate I was. I needed to find somewhere safe and quiet to lick my wounds from the beating I had taken by staying in Bangkok for more than two days. I had slept very little because of hypoglycemia-induced insomnia, and I could not seem to keep any food down. My nerves were obviously shot.

Besides – I didn't really want to go home until I found what I was looking for. Not that I entirely knew what I was looking for. I didn't. But somehow that didn't really seem to matter. I knew I would recognize it when I found it. I kept recalling a saying I wrote down in bold pink letters on the inside of my travel journal. It inspired me to keep going whenever I was feeling defeated or scared or confused. It said: "Are you willing to give up what you are, to become what you can be?"

I wanted to know what I could become. I had to know. That was one of the main reasons I had left home. I already knew what I was – a business woman and an athlete. But certainly there was more to life than a bank account and burning up the volleyball courts. With Bangkok's craziness still fresh in my memory I traveled south to the coastal city of Surathani. On the train, I daydreamed about monasteries – picturing them as the East's answer to the padded wall asylums of the West – a safe sanctuary away from the deafening pace of the cities.

I saw myself entering into a calm, tranquil monastic retreat (as in "treat" myself) setting and having it all; minus of course, the little guys running around in their white jackets patronizingly inviting me to, "Just slip your arms into this nice little jacket with the built-in wrap-around feature." Instead of those bothersome little hospital helpers, Thailand had a delightful and colorful collection of exotic saffron-robed monks walking unobtrusively and meditatively about with their beautifully shaved round heads glistening in the bright sunshine.

I heard my adrenal glands heave a huge sigh of relief. The whole scene sounded so idyllic, so comfortable, so quiet, *sooooooo safe.*

"Even better," I thought. "Why not choose a *forest* monastery? Forty acres of bush right smack dab in the middle of nowhere, far away from the fast-paced, noisy cities of Thailand. Or say! What about choosing an *island* forest monastery?" "Nix the island idea," my little voice piped up. "That's just your adrenals talking!"

I arrived at the monastery – gingerly jumped from the bus I had caught after leaving the train in Surathani – and was shocked to see that it had somehow become pitch black outside. Night time came so fast in the tropics. Why, I could barely see the edge of the road, let alone gauge which way to go looking for an entrance to the monastery. There was not a sign in sight.

I anxiously looked around and began wondering if the Thai bus driver had somehow misunderstood my request when I told him I wanted to be let off at Wat Suan Mohk. He seemed sure enough when I first asked him, so I never thought to question him further about it.

Yet now, standing in the warm, moist night air, feeling completely disoriented and concerned, I began thinking maybe my search for a monastery wasn't such a good idea after all.

My eyes were having trouble adjusting to the blackness. I decided I may as well just head straight into it, and pointed myself in the direction of a dimly-lit street off in the distance.

As I stumbled down what I guessed to be a walkway, I spotted something that looked like a sign board. As I came closer, I was relieved to see the words, Wat Suan Mohk engraved in the wood. I kept going up the dark tree-lined path and cautiously looked around.

There was not one sign of life. I spotted what looked like an outdoor reception desk, and called out to see if anyone was home.

No one appeared. I sat down and waited. A few more minutes passed, then out of the shadows a young monk appeared.

"May I help you?" he asked. I got up quickly and replied, "Why yes. I'm here to enroll in your 10 Day Course in Silence. I heard about your offerings from another traveler I met in Chiangmai. Is it really true – that you offer this course to Westerners?"

I noticed he was very careful not to let his eyes meet mine. Instead, he stared down at the ground. At first I thought he was a little shy, but then I remembered reading about how all the Thai monks were taught to do this around women. It was one of their 250 rules and regulations for being a monk. "It's probably because of his vow of celibacy," I thought.

He looked up – being careful to divert his eyes to look past me – and bowed politely and softly said, "Yes. I will go and find the monk in charge. I will be right back." With that, he disappeared into the night.

A few more minutes passed and out of the darkness he reappeared. He pointed down a path to the right of me and said, "Please report to the Nun's Quarters. They will give you a bed for the night, and in the morning, they will arrange to take you over to the main retreat center."

I bowed and respectfully said, "Thank you," and carefully made my way down the dark forest walkway – passing what looked like an outdoor amphitheater. I squinted. I could vaguely make out about 30 or so saffron-robed monks sitting silently and cross-legged. They appeared to be listening intently to what an older monk was saying in the center of the gathering. He was sitting on a raised platform that appeared to be a huge lotus flower carved out of wood.

I was tempted to stop, but I decided to keep on going. My backpack was beginning to feel quite heavy after the long, tiring journey. I spotted a couple of women sitting in front of one of the old wooden buildings, and decided to stop and ask them for directions – just in case I had wandered off the path.

"You're already there," one of them said, smiling brightly up at me. Her skin seemed to have a translucent quality – as if it were back lit from behind her forehead and eyes. Her face was so serene and so calm – I felt touched by her presence.

She got up and offered to show me the way. We entered a small room lined with wide wooden ledges on both sides. There were straw mats and mosquito nets laid width-wise across the ledges. I set my back pack down and looked around. Just as I was about to ask her where the beds were, two Western women entered from a side door.

"Oh, hello," I said, smiling. "Any idea where we are going to sleep?"

They looked at me and smiled. "Right there," one of them said, pointing towards the ledges.

"You mean those are actually our *beds*?" I exclaimed.

"Yes," she replied – looking amused. "But they're not as bad as they look, especially if you're really tired!"

With that, they both started spreading out their bedding. I turned to my back pack and felt tears beginning to well up in my eyes. I asked myself what was wrong, and realized I was tired and hungry – and there wasn't a scrap of food in sight, save for a few bananas off in a corner of the room. I looked longingly over at them and asked whose they were. One of the two women told me they belonged to the nuns. My heart sank. I had already experienced that it was not right to ask for food unless I was at a restaurant or at a street vendor. I had to be willing to pay for it. The Thais were very poor people, so it made sense. I instantly began feeling sorry for myself and chastised myself for not planning ahead. I decided I may as well just lay down on my bed and try to ignore the wood's hardness, and will myself to go to sleep – empty stomach and all. I knew my weary body desperately needed the rest. Even though I was dead beat, it took me more than an hour to adjust to my new sleeping quarters. When I finally did manage to fall off to sleep, I found myself waking up every hour in order to turn over on my other side. My body had gone numb from the hardness. A few hours passed and suddenly the lights came on. I looked at my clock and it was only 4:00 a.m.

"What on earth is going on?" I thought, as I blinked into the bright light. People were moving all around me. They seemed to be getting ready to go somewhere.

"What's happening?" I said to the woman lying next to me.

"It's time for meditation," she answered.

"Oh," I said – then rolled over and fell back to sleep.

Morning came quickly, and at 7:00 we were told to get into the back of what looked like a big dump truck, and we were hauled to the retreat site two and a half kilometers up the road. I felt like a cow loaded up to be taken to market. It was not a nice feeling.

THAILAND'S WELCOME WAGON AIN'T MUCH OF A WELCOME

As I entered the women's dormitory, I realized I had gotten much more than I had bargained for, because staring me straight in the face was a cement wall that said, "PLEASE PLACE SCORPIONS, SPIDERS AND STINGING CENTIPEDES IN THE BUCKETS PROVIDED AS SOMETHING ALWAYS DIES."

"So, *this* is how the Thais break out the Welcome Wagon," I thought. "How *very very* quaint."

The comforting warm words of welcome were written boldly in capitals in thick white chalk on the center of the entrance wall. I couldn't believe my eyes so I read the notice again, and recalled what the Buddhists believed about refraining from harming living beings and I thought, "Does that rule still apply no matter how many *legs* the beings have?"

Sirens started going off again in my head.

"It's those darned limiting beliefs again," I said to myself. But then I surrendered and admitted to myself, "Limiting beliefs Valerie, or just plain fear?"

As I considered my options, I noticed the frequency and volume of the sirens were starting to increase and my brain was busying itself screaming out thoughts like, "SCORPIONS? AS IN LETHALLY DANGEROUS SCORPIONS? BBBBUT. I'M ABSOLUTELY PETRIFIED OF CREEPY CRAWLY THINGS. IT JUST NEVER OCCURRED TO ME THAT A FOREST MONASTERY WOULD MEAN THERE WOULD BE THINGS ACTUALLY LIVING IN IT! I MEAN REALLY, I COULDN'T POSSIBLY..."

Then, while I was still reeling from the shock, an even more bizarre thought came rushing frantically into my mind, waving its arms in the air, and yelling, "THEY CAN'T BE SUGGESTING WE ACTUALLY CATCH THOSE THINGS AND THEN SET THEM FREE IN THE FOREST SO THEY CAN CRAWL BACK IN AGAIN? BBBBUT..."

I stood frozen with fear. A short, dark-haired western woman came up to me and identified herself as the course coordinator and handed me what she called, "Standard Issue." It consisted of a mosquito net, a blanket, a straw mat and a six-inch-high, hard-as-rocks, square pillow.

"Follow me and I'll show you to your room," she said. When we reached the end of the walkway, I critically surveyed my new abode, and thought, "Room? That's a pretty liberal term. It looks more like an inmate's cell to me!"

I couldn't help noticing one of its most endearing, *Welcome*

130

To Your New Home features, was six iron bars inside a two-foot-square window. She followed my gaze and smiled sympathetically and said, "The bars are only there to keep your valuables safe – nothing more."

"Well," I said, feeling myself noticeably wincing. "It's obvious they're not there to keep out the scorpions, spiders or stinging centipedes, since there's at least two *inches* between each of those bars!"

She smiled ever-so sweetly, then offered what I am sure she thought were some helpful and comforting words of advice. She looked me in the eye and said, "The cups to trap the scorpions are at the entranceway. Feel free to help yourself. All you have to do is slide a piece of cardboard underneath, trap the scorpion in the cup, and then deposit it in the pails provided."

My jaw dropped open as I watched her turn on her heel and walk away. As she disappeared down the sidewalk, thoughts of escape began running rampant through my mind. I quickly caught hold of myself and thought, "Hold on! You're *not* leaving – no matter what. You're a Personal Best graduate – remember? You've *got* to take the challenge. Besides – Point Number Five of Being a Nomadic Goddess, is: *Never* let a puny little scorpion or any spider bigger than your two hands put together, *ever* keep you from reaching your goal. Get in there and fight, fight, *fight!*"

There I was, standing stunned and up to my eyelashes in "standard issue", staring blankly into my 15' X 9' cement room, and I could not help but notice how it featured this delightful large slab of cement which looked kind of like a raised platform. I could only assume it was my bed.

I looked around and sighed deeply. I could faintly detect the notes of a familiar song beginning to drift through my consciousness. It sounded something like, "You're in the army now"– only with a slight change in lyrics.

I recalled a passage from the Buddhist Meditation Course outline, and thought about how they said they would teach us to meditate while sitting and walking. I was not at all surprised when my little voice bounced straight away into a resounding, rabble-rousing chorus of, "HUP TWO, THREE FOUR...."

"Walking meditation here I come!" I exclaimed.

MEDITATION – THE EARLY DAYS

After a filling breakfast of brown rice and curried vegetables, I sat contemplating Nirvana, considering such meaningful questions as, "Do you suppose mosquitoes get their consciousness raised by the transference of energy as they suck our blood?"

Slap, slap.

Or, "If monks shave their heads, faces and eyebrows, what *else* do they shave?" Scratch, scratch.

Oh, and one of my all-time favorites was, "If the Buddhist philosophy teaches there is *no* self or *no* soul, then *who* gets liberated?"

"Ten days of silence," I thought, smirking to myself. "It's going to be like being locked in a torture chamber. All I'm allowed to do is sit here and listen to my own mind as it dances and prances and darts all over the place. *Sheesh!* What a mind! It's all over the map. Still – I know it's going to be tough, but it's what I volunteered for, and I'm going to see it through no matter what."

"It's only 10 days," I told myself. "How *hard* can it be?"

The answer arrived instantly, as I adjusted the cushion under my bottom.

"Hard," my little voice said. I reached around and rubbed my sore back. "But you've got what it takes, dear Valerie!" it called out. "What with your orange socks and your Personal Best course under your belt, this will be a *cake*-walk."

"I wish I felt as confident as *you* sound," I replied. "And I wish I could *eat* cake. Darn hypoglycemia."

I mumbled on and on about my hardships, but somehow got through the first day. The day consisted of spending hour after hour alone with my own mind, surrounded by 99 *other* silent volunteers alone with *their* own minds. It made for a pretty strange and eerie scene.

It was odd observing all of us Westerners sitting impassively on our cushions in a rock-hard cement meditation hall undergoing instruction in Buddhist Meditation Made Easy – which was not easy. And it was all made possible by a team of Thai monks and nuns who spoke with adorable, often incomprehensible accents. I was constantly straining my ears to make out exactly what it was they were saying. They were so gentle, and so soft-spoken. Most of the time I understood absolutely nothing at all. But it didn't seem to matter. I kind of liked withdrawing from the world of sound and not having to speak. As I looked around at my fellow classmates, I was amazed at how many of us had left our comfortable homes and affluent countries – to make our way to a monastery in the south of Thailand, where we sat hidden away in a forest, sleeping on cement slabs, enduring the oppressive heat of the tropics, while battling fighter squadrons of mosquitoes, anxiously searching the night for scorpions and other little do-no-gooders. All of this – so we could earn the privilege of sitting and walking in silence while learning how to calm our minds by focusing on the subtleties and circular movement of our breath. The monks called it, "Vipassana Training" or "Mindfulness Through Breathing."

"Incredible," I thought. I could think of only one explanation for such ludicrous and insane behavior. It was something called Enlightenment. For me, the word translated into, Trying To Get A Handle On The Meaning of Life.

"After all," I reasoned, sitting lost in thought. "Life can't *just* be about choosing good mixed doubles tennis partners or buying sports cars, or selecting the next holiday destination or even doing the coffee thing with my closest friends."

"Or *could* it?" my little doubting voice piped up.

"In my heart of hearts," I replied firmly, "I hope the answer is no. Otherwise, I'm putting my mind and body through all of this for nothing. But I do know one thing. I have to know. I have to know what IT is. I have to know what The Meaning of Life is."

No answer.

On the second day I found myself sitting diligently trying to locate my breath and calling out, "Yoo hoo. *Here* girl. Come *on* now, I know you're *in* there somewhere; otherwise I'd be dead!"

While I searched for my breath, a catchy tune sprang to mind, and I started singing (silently of course) "Getting to know you........getting to know ALL about you......."

Thoroughly amused by the meaningless meanderings of my mind, I began thinking about all of the titillating little tidbits one could entertain oneself in a ten-day course of silence.

My mind started doing a little two step, tipped its "top hat" and executed a perfect *That's Showbiz* bow, suddenly switched channels – then began reviewing the behavioral guidelines of the course.

Buddhist Summer Camp was the thought that jumped to mind. "That's what this is!" I exclaimed. "Boys in the Boy's Dormitory and girls in the Girl's Dormitory. Fraternizing is discouraged. The teachers informed us that they wanted us to get the full benefit from the course – which meant focusing on ourselves, rather than on each *other*."

Another part of my mind retorted, "But how do you fraternize when you can't talk?" That was when another of my more mischievous little thoughts started looking seductively around on the dark stage of my mind, and covertly fluttered its tiny, dainty eyelashes – then sweetly answered, "Why, with your *eyes*, sweet sister, with your *eyes*!"

I read later on that that too was off limits.

More time passed as I sat impassively on my cushion, squeezing my eyes shut while willing myself to follow the sound of my breath, when I suddenly realized mind training was really very serious business. If I didn't start paying attention, I would never figure out how to gain the peace of mind I was searching for. For that matter, I would never be able to discover how to access that illusive treasure; my intuition.

I decided I'd better start focusing more closely on my breath again. My cat Athena appeared in my mind.

"What now?" I thought, feeling myself beginning to lose patience with my erratic mind. But then I smiled again once I saw what she was up to.

She was writing me guilt-induction letters; expertly outlining her case for why I was a bad mother. She said I had done the unspeakable and quite possibly the unforgivable; I had deserted her to go on this world journey. One of her letters was in the form of a newspaper want ad. It read, "Sweet, loving, adorable black cat abandoned by wanton, uncaring mother. My name is Athena, and I need a home. I am willing to beg for food, but only if my backpacking Happy Wanderer *mother* is willing to beg for my *forgiveness*! I mean, how *could* she? If this call for help tugs at your heartstrings, and if you *really* love me (I recognized that as her Jewish Mother routine) you'll call 283-LOVE."

I giggled at the ludicracy of my thoughts, then marveled at how a funny little cartoon character face had suddenly taken her place. It looked kind of like a combination of a *Bugs Bunny Tweety Bird* and *Athena the Cat.* Together, they formed a most perfect *All-Innocence* look, peering back at me from inside their sweet little pookie face; a face so cute and so precious, I swear it had the power to melt even the heart of the most treacherous, psychotic criminals – or worse – that of the most irresponsible traveling mothers. I'm sure in her mind, they constituted the same thing. I watched the little pookie-faced character go darting off into the distance of the dark recesses of my mind, but it stopped long enough to cast me a furtive, over-the-shoulder "Come and Get Me" look. I called out, "Stop!" As I did, I looked inside and suddenly realized I had been drawn into playing the role of the mother of this little cartoon character. And as a mother would call after a mischievous, misbehaving little child, I found myself yelling, "HEY! JUST WHERE DO YOU THINK YOU'RE GOING, MISS? NOW YOU GET BACK HERE RIGHT NOW. I MEAN IT! I WON'T STAND, (but recognizing that I was sitting, I quickly corrected myself and yelled), I WON'T SIT FOR THIS BEHAVIOR. NOW YOU BEHAVE AND DO AS I TELL YOU."

After I caught on to her tactics, I began to wonder what this scene was really about. Then it dawned on me. The misbehaving little "child" was actually my intuition talking to me – and it was the very first time it had ever talked to me in my entire life!

"Oh God," I thought, laughing. "I'm having my very first vision and it's a cartoon! Why – this is hilarious! I would *never* have guessed my intuition was so playful! Yet here it is, acting out the role of my run-away breath – doing all kinds of disappearing acts – trying to entice me into searching for it on the playground of my own mind. Why – it's actually asking me to follow it, just like when kids play *Hide and Seek!*

I felt staggered by my realization. I suddenly started giggling and reflected on how my ego – my self-imposed arrogance – had actually gotten in my way all of these years. I guess I thought I knew everything. It seems all these years, my ego had made me believe that meditation and the abil-

135

ity to tap into my intuition would take a great deal of effort – and that I needed a super serious attitude in order to find it.

"Well," I thought, grinning widely to myself. "My intuition sure put my ego in *its* place – now *didn't* it?"

"This is ironic," I thought. "Didn't Oscar Wilde once say: "Life is much too important a matter to ever be talked about seriously?" Well, I think it's time to rework *that* one and call it, "Point Number Six of Being a Nomadic Goddess: Playfulness ceases to serve its purpose when it takes itself too seriously. So stay light! "

I turned to my new-found intuition and exclaimed, "Okay little fella! Who's turn is it to be IT?"

A WESTERN BARBIE

During the second evening lecture, I started thinking about Paul Hogan – Australia's goodwill ambassador from the fabled *Land Down Under*, and I thought about how Australians were known the world over for their barbies.

The Thai teacher standing in front on the raised platform, was in the midst of talking about barbecues and I thought, "Yes. Most other parts of the Western world refer to this favorite past time as a barbecue, but in Thailand they simply call cooking over open coals, *Daily Life*."

One time when I was in Australia, I had been invited to "Throw a steak on the barbie," as my host put it. I was visiting some new-found friends in Brisbane. At first I was horror-struck when I saw them place a griddle over the open grill that was already straddling the smoking hot, aromatic coals. Thinking they must have made a mistake, I offered to remove it, explaining how the smoke couldn't penetrate the meat if they did that. They all looked at me quizzically – but then my host's face lit up and he cast me a big toothy grin, and he slapped me gamefully on the back and replied, "Why, *that's* the idea, mate!"

I was stunned. I quickly crawled into a corner of the yard and kept my mouth shut. It seemed the art of barbecuing had taken on a completely different meaning here in the Land of Oz (Aus.) I discovered I was still pretty much an unseasoned nomadic goddess.

As I reflected on my time with the Australians, I had to admit that when they slapped those huge pieces of meat on the coals, something about eating a part of an animal upset me. It suddenly felt grotesque and barbaric – and here I had been a meat eater all my life. So now, sitting on my cushion in the monastery, I could see why it was easy for me to accept the Buddhist principle of being careful not to harm any living beings – although I must admit sparing mosquitoes was a huge challenge – especially when I was meditating. Most of the time my reflex action got the best of me and another poor little mosquito unexpectedly found its way to Nirvana.

Barbecues and hot coals were still leaping freely about inside of my mind, when the Thai instructor started describing how Westerners sit. Or rather, how they did *not* sit down.

"A peculiar thing about Westerners," the monk offered, "is that when they sit down it is as if they sit down on a bed of hot coals. They immediately jump up as a thought comes to mind, then launch themselves into action within seconds."

I smirked and let out a guffaw.

"That is so unlike the East," he continued, smiling at my reaction. "To sit still and reflect is an important part of our culture, but this approach to life is absent in the Western world. All your thoughts seem to spur you into action. They produce a need to fulfill a want, and instantly propel you out of your seats. You suddenly have a burning desire to *do* something."

I laughed and looked self-consciously down at my hands. I didn't say a word.

The next day, as lunch time was approaching, I found myself thinking more and more about what he had said about how hard it was for us to sit still. I realized this 10 days of meditating would really stretch my patience and tolerance levels. I was an active and hyper individual at the best of times.

"A relatively inactive period could prove to be a humdinger of an endurance test," I thought to myself, frowning. "Ten days without swimming! What'll I do? One thing I do know, is the prospect of taking baby steps in what they call, Walking Meditation does little to alleviate my concerns. Even thinking about a nightly dip in the hot sulfur spring running alongside the retreat site does little to satisfy me; but at least it pleases my sore back muscles. Sitting and meditating for so many hours each day is really starting to take its toll."

All of a sudden the course requirements started looking tougher than ever. Not only did the monastery require complete silence and an early wakeup call, but there was no exercise – except for morning yoga lessons – which looked to me more like the stretching I did before I got into a *real* workout, like say – a three hour volleyball practice. All things aside, what I was really struggling with, was frustration. Their breathing exercises and meditation sessions really challenged me. Half the time I thought I was going nowhere fast. I felt more impatient every day, trying to locate and follow my elusive breath. It didn't help that my back was frustrated as well. It seemed to constantly cry out for a reprieve from its misery.

I started thinking about what it would be like to leave the course early. As I did, the instructor seemed to have read my mind. He jumped straight-away into a topic he called, Loving Kindness, the essence of which was to learn to be kind and patient with ourselves.

"Show some compassion when you deal with others," he said, "but also give that gift to yourselves. Give yourself mercy from time to time. Otherwise, you will give up before you even start."

I realized how hard I was on myself. I was so darned achievement-oriented. And as he kept talking, it became obvious to me that if I wanted to survive the next eight days, I needed to make loving kindness an essential part of my meditation practice. If I didn't, I would have to consider going AWOL –Away Without Lunch.

"Hm. Tough choice," I pondered, smiling to myself. "Eating is my favorite thing to do, next to being active." I knew Mrs. Bethoun and her little Thai kitchen helpers were busy preparing yet another fantastic vegetarian feast of curries and noodles and brown rice.

As I thought some more about her army of little kitchen helpers, I thought, "But Valerie, everybody in Thailand seems little to you. They have the *littlest* doorways to fit their *little* bodies through, and those same *little* doorways represent big challenges for you, because you're a six-foot-tall Nomadic Goddess. The doorways are so short, you walk around unconsciously hunched over because you're afraid you'll knock yourself silly when you fall prey to yet another tricky *little* doorway."

I decided to wait. "Food first," I told myself. "I wouldn't want to chance running into anything out there in the jungle. No sense in trying to navigate the perils of the forest without at least filling up my body with some of Mrs. Bethoun's nummy fuel!"

I sat back and listened intently.

"Do not use momentary lapses while training your mind as reasons to go around beating yourself up because you think you've done something wrong," the monk continued. "*Love* your mind," he said. "If your thoughts go wandering off, *praise* it. Love it for its capacity to recall and feel. Then, gently bring it back to your point of focus. Do not get angry at it. Instead, be patient, loving and tolerant. Then, you will see just how well it responds."

I thought about it for awhile, and I had to admit he had a point. Problem was, my first few days I couldn't quite get past the point of berating my mind. Clenching my teeth, I would scream things like, "YOU CALL YOURSELF A MIND? WHY, YOU CAN'T EVEN FOLLOW SOMETHING AS SIMPLE AS ONE SINGLE BREATH! HA! YOU'RE PATHETIC!"

I thought about how when I was a child, and my mom asked me to do something, if she asked me sweetly, I would happily comply; but if she made it sound like a command, I would always get angry and resist.

"It's the same with this mind of mine," I thought. "If I'm not kind and sweet to it, it simply refuses to serve me."

I decided to opt for the loving-kindness approach. It was easier on my teeth.

ENLIGHTENMENT – WHAT, NO SPECIAL EFFECTS?

On the fourth night, it was hot and muggy and the teacher was offering his insights on the New Age movement in the West.

I sat up and adjusted my damp seat cushion. My legs were sweating so badly, the cushion was soaked almost clean through.

"The West's idea of enlightenment," he said, "is something we here in the East call, Spiritual Materialism. From what we can see, people in the West equate spiritualism with New Age concepts like physical demonstrations of psychic power, or channeling spiritual insight from the other side, or healing people by placing crystals on different parts of their bodies."

"In essence," he continued, "the West focuses on spiritualism only as it relates to the material realm, rather than something purely spiritual; something non-material in nature. More often than not it implies that by having the gift of psychic abilities, one can conjure up dreams of winning the lottery or choosing horses at the horse races. In other cases, mediums or psychics make claims about having highly-evolved spiritual entities having selected their bodies as instruments – saying no one else's will do."

I nodded in agreement. I had seen a lot of that sort of thing when I was doing my New Age research – before I launched my spirit quest.

"Well," he said, wiping away some beads of perspiration which had gathered on his brow, "do you not think it all seems to boil down to an issue of ownership and ego – and is that not what is becoming more and more prevalent in spirituality today?"

He looked expectantly around for an answer, knowing he would not get one. It still felt strange to me to be totally silent – even after spending four days in the program. A lot of the time I found myself desperately wanting to call out an answer – or just raise my hand to ask a simple question.

I silently agreed with what he was saying, and thought about how my last six years had been spent enrolling myself in a variety of New Age esoteric classes searching for the elusive goal of enlightenment.

As I sat looking back at it all, I thought about how the more metaphysical books I read and the videos I watched portraying psychics channeling reams of fascinating and illuminating information, the more I came to believe enlightenment had something to do with a blinding flash of light – the Realization To End All Realizations. I had somehow convinced myself that Ultimate Truth was something that would come soaring through to me in a vision, a blast of color, the Universe, no no, the *galaxy* speeding towards me. Or better yet, *me* to *it*! I had been exposed to too many special effects movies in the Stephen Spielberg and George Lucas style.

I kept discovering enlightenment was not the stage entertainment I expected it to be – nor was it a one shot deal. I began to accept that no one just *became* enlightened; every step and every new realization meant enlightenment.

I remember how shocked I was when I figured it all out. But from then on, every time I heard myself exclaim, "Aha! So *that's* it!" – whatever "it" was that I was concerned with at the time – I understood I was finally becoming enlightened.

As I sat contemplating the New Age movement some more, I realized how much I took exception to its heavy emphasis on money. Throughout all of my experiences at home, and even during my travels throughout Australia and New Zealand, I noticed how New Age practitioners charged exorbitant prices and made big money packaging and merchandising all kinds of offerings to help us poor pilgrims along our *Road To Enlightenment*.

"Heal your inner child and have a playmate for life," I thought to myself. "Open your third eye and say 'Bye Bye' to your bifocals!" One of my all time favorites was, "You were *born* psychic, don't you *remember?*"

I thought about how every course was designed to raise our level of consciousness and help make us more aware. I had to admit they *did* help me understand a lot of things about my life. They also showed me how to accept the different aspects of myself. But I still could not quite get over the hefty price tag.

The esoteric courses I had taken in the past had not always raised my level of consciousness, but they did raise my level of expectation. In my very first psychic development class, virtually every one of my classmates succeeded in communicating with disembodied entities in the spirit world. But not me. Uh uh. All I managed to do was annoy myself. I got more and more frustrated and felt more and more inferior every time I observed my classmates doing it right. Then – class after class – I'd perform my "Woe Is Me" routine – lamenting things like, "Nothing like *that* ever happens to *me*. I must be doing something wrong. Geez!"

It seemed that instead of achieving what I began calling the "Hollywood Effect of Meditation," I would follow the teacher's guided visualization, do all the right breathing exercises – only to find I had managed to reach a blissed out, peaceful state – emerging from the meditation looking like some kind of a space cadet; eyes shining and thoughts of peace, love and brotherhood dancing in my mind. Funny thing was, I never considered my peaceful state of mind to be something of value. Instead, I would whine and complain and get all exasperated and proclaim to my teacher, "I must be *missing* something. You said we were all *born* psychic. Where was I when they handed out the special powers?"

I wanted some of what they had.

I suddenly thought, "With all this talk of spiritual materialism, could this be what they mean by *possession?*"

MEDITATION; MORE FUN THAN A BARREL OF MONKEYS
During my first few days at Buddhist Summer Camp, the teachers constantly made a point of reiterating how the natural, original state of our minds was one of restfulness – in a sense, peacefulness.

"You can discover the mind's original state by meditating," the monk explained. "And to help you experience what it feels like we will show you a range of techniques to help focus on your breath. You will begin to see everything else fall into place once you start following the length and direction of your breath."

"Originally peaceful?" I repeated to myself. "He's *got* to be kidding. Does he have any idea how noisy and out of control my thoughts are? Blah, blah, blah, blah. That's what they're like – an endless and aimless parade of desires and doubts and passions and repressed fears and aversions and I don't know what else. Even if I *had* noticed how noisy my mind was before coming to this summer camp, I'd never have thought there was anything all that odd about it. I had just assumed that was the nature of my mind – doing what it does best – thinking."

The more I sat observing what was happening inside my mind, the more I noticed my incessant, inane mind chatter was simply jumping from thought to thought to thought, then back again. After a short while, I noticed I felt kind of overheated, like a car radiator – spurting and sputtering all over the place.

But the more I concentrated on following my breath, the more I could feel its calming effect. I discovered I could actually cool my mind by focusing on my breath.

"Wow!" I exclaimed. "I had no idea it was that simple to cool off the fire of my thoughts! Why, I just cooled off my mind like a radiator cools off a hot engine!"

The next day the instructors showed us how to use the same breathing technique to help us reign in what they called, The Monkey Mind.

"Monkeys," I thought, "Yeah. What better way to describe it?" As soon a thought entered my mind, it triggered an unending, inexhaustible string of other thoughts, sometimes even seemingly unrelated thoughts. They really were just like naughty little monkeys, clinging and grabbing and grasping at each other, then chattering away at each other and instigating a fight. They'd maniacally go darting off in all four directions – then disappear. One thought would lead to the next, and to the next and to the next – ad infinitum.

It all became very clear to me. If I focused on my breath, it was like giving my monkey mind something else to do. And if I didn't, it simply went gamboling wildly about, getting into all sorts of trouble – and dragging my peace of mind right along with it.

The first four days turned out to be quite a struggle. I had trouble adjusting to the 4:00 a.m. wakeup call and then lights out at 9:30 p.m. But then, in an odd sort of way – I was really beginning to enjoy my new way of life. I was getting up a good two and a half hours before the sun even poked it's head up over the horizon. It felt like I was experiencing the world in a whole new way.

One morning we did a 4:00 a.m. hike – walking silently along the palm-lined road for two and a half kilometers to the main monastery. We had been invited to listen to a talk by the head of the monastery – a highly revered, soft-spoken 84-year-old monk.

I looked up into the sky as we were walking and I noticed the moon was almost full. It was so incredibly bright, it lit our way as we walked quietly up the forest path.

The monk's name was Buddhadasa Bhikkhu. He had established the monastery in the early 1940's by hacking his way through what was then a dense and dangerous forest – complete with cobras and scorpions and malarial mosquitoes – and probably a whole host of other dangerous critters I knew nothing about. "Gee," I thought. "With the cobra sighting they told us about the other day, things have not changed much in 50 years – except that the forest is no longer as dense and there is a main highway 100 yards from the entranceway."

We all took a seat and waited for him to begin. "You are asked to rise early," he began, in a slow, deliberate tone, "so that you can feel what it is like to have your cup empty." He was speaking in Thai, but his words were being translated simultaneously by one of the young English-speaking instructors sitting off to the side. A huge white rooster suddenly jumped up to the top of the marble bench where the Buddhadasa was sitting, and began strutting around aggressively – swelling out its chest and making chortling noises. The Buddhadassa looked over, smiled, then continued on with his talk.

"The early morning is the only time of the day when your mind is relatively new and fresh and empty," he said. "It is also a time to begin to fill your mind as if you are filling a cup. You must fill it with positive, peaceful thoughts. That way you will be sure to have a calmer, more stable day."

"Well," I thought to myself, shifting to get comfortable on the hard, cement seats. "I wouldn't go so far as to say my days are exactly stable. Matter of fact, they're far from it. I'm experiencing all kinds of mood swings. They seem to come out of nowhere! First I have a high, joyous feeling which totally overwhelms me for a moment and sends me into a state of utter euphoria. Then – just as quickly – a thought or feeling comes in, and I drop into melancholy or anger or just plain, old-fashioned frustration."

I sat scowling for a moment, shifted again, then willed myself to listen to what he had to say. After the lecture was over, we fell into single file and walked silently back to the retreat center. The young monk at the head of the line explained that the walk was designed to be a meditation. He encouraged all of us to be aware of our every step – aware of our every footfall. He told us to walk as softly as if were walking on a bed of lotus flowers; to be that focused, and that gentle – concentrating our thoughts on the simple, lovely action of walking.

I found the exercise to be quite fascinating. It was a whole new way of walking. I felt serene, calm and happy. I noticed how great it was to be out in nature; exploring its early morning gentleness and seeing the soft mists off in the distance. It provided a magical backdrop for the simple bamboo farmers' huts in the foreground – smoke rising slowly from their outdoor fires, as they prepared for their early morning meal. At one point, I felt as if all of nature was totally enveloping me, revealing its secret self to me. I smiled and walked on.

We put in another full day of classes and meditation sessions, but by around 5:30 that afternoon, my stomach started to grumble. We had had lunch at 12:30 but I was hungry again. I was not entirely sure what to do about it, since we only got two meals a day – breakfast and lunch. Dinner consisted of a couple of bananas and sweet soy milk.

"Hooh boy," I thought, "neither of those two selections are going to do my hypoglycemia any good. And there's no more food until eight o'clock tomorrow morning."

I decided I had better go to the women's coordinator. I thought maybe she could make special arrangements for me. I had lasted all the other days no problem, but this morning's hike had been more exercise than I was used to, and with my fast metabolism, all the food had been used up. It turned out she could do something about my dilemma. I was given some rice and vegetables left over from the previous day's lunch.

Over those first few days, the strict food regime was my toughest battle. Quite often I would end up eating food which caused quite a reaction. I really had no idea what they put in their food, but I suspected there was a little sugar in the sauces and maybe even some MSG in the texturized vegetable protein chunks they used as meat replacements – judging from the headache and stomach ache I experienced from time to time. My mood swings proved it.

Even with such unexpected food surprises and temporary hardships, I was amazed to see that I was still enjoying myself. In the deepest part of me, I knew it was a once-in-a-lifetime experience, and I was determined to make the best of it. When would I ever get to withdraw so completely from the outside world again? I was fascinated with learning all about the hidden aspects of myself. I also got a lot of benefit out of watching my classmates. By looking at them, I realized I was not alone in my trials. It was obvious from their faces that they too were going through a lot of emotional and physical stuff.

"We're all in this together, alright," I thought, smiling compassionately. "Silence or no silence, we can all *hear* what's going on for each other."

One day I entertained myself by observing all of our different sitting positions. Some of us were sitting forward on our knees, others were kneeling with their buttocks resting on a small wooden stool, and still others had chosen to sit in chairs. The instructors had shown us a wide range of sitting positions, and had encouraged us to find the one which was most comfortable.

"Don't worry about whether you are doing it right," one of the monks had advised. "And do not allow yourselves to get sidetracked by seeing what others are doing. There is no right way to sit. What is important is that we sit – that is all. Because if you think about it, most people in this world never even take time out from their busy lives to sit still for even one minute – *not one minute* – in order to listen to their thoughts. The fact that you are willing to subject yourself to this discipline means you must be seeing some value. Otherwise – you would not still be here!"

We all smiled. One of the younger monks sitting beside him gave us a big, toothy grin.

"He's right, you know," I thought, smiling to myself. "I would have been out of here days ago if I hadn't seen any benefit."

I realized how much I loved the instructor's simple, no nonsense approach to meditation postures. I remembered how relieved I felt when I first found out they were not going to get us to twist our bodies into that infamous pretzel position – the one Eastern meditators so delicately called, The Full Lotus. I had seen my first live lotus flower offered at the temple of the Emerald Buddha in the heart of Bangkok, and as I sat reflecting on that beautiful, delicate flower, I could not help but wonder how something so soft could be so hard – when put into position.

I remembered for the first few days of the course, I tried sitting cross-legged on the floor with a cushion tucked underneath my buttocks, but the pain was excruciating. Then, when the instructors told us to make sure we were comfortable – even if it meant sitting on a chair at the back of the hall – I was not one of the first students to jump up and grab a chair. I wanted desperately to sit cross-legged just like all the other expert yogis I had seen on the front of meditation books. But my back was not there yet. I decided it was time to surrender my ego. I got up and claimed a chair.

"Just sit comfortably," the monk said, smiling, as he watched me reach for the chair. "That is the most important thing. If you are in pain, how can you possibly concentrate?"

I got settled in, but my back still screamed at me. It was going to be a long haul. During particularly frustrating moments at trying to concentrate my thoughts on my breath, my mind would also join in and yell, "I AM SO BORED! GET ME OUT OF HERE!" I started daydreaming about my Dutch backpacker friends. I had left a group of them to come to the monastery. I imagined them lounging around on a nearby island; doing a little bodysurfing – maybe the odd bit of partying – bronzing their bodies in the warm, tropical sunshine, and partaking in Thailand's broad selection of mind-altering substances. I thought, "The drugs are probably part of their own individual search for enlightenment. It was certainly part of mine, although the opium I tried up north of Chiangmai with the hilltribes people made me so ill, I've sworn off drugs for good. I've never *been* so sick."

I thought about how people in the '60s used to talk about raising their consciousness through drug-induced highs. I remembered trying it a few times in university, but it never really did all that much for me. Now, holed up here in a monastery, I realized I was now looking for ways to alter my mind "naturally" – whatever that meant. Half the time I was not entirely sure what I was doing. I only knew I was curious about what meditation had to offer, and I wanted to give it the old college try. Being an athlete, I was no quitter. I was going to keep practicing until I got it right. I also knew all of us meditators were really no different than any of my friends who were out there enjoying the island life. We were all discovering ourselves in whichever way was right for us.

"Travelers are seekers," I thought to myself. "How *else* could you explain a traveler's behavior? We would never have left the comforts of our home, or given up our jobs and families and friends to head off and travel the world unless we were *looking* for something.

HOW NOT TO CATCH A SCORPION

As I settled into the daily routine, I found myself enjoying the early morning meditations and class readings the most. The mid-morning lectures on Dhamma – which was the Pali/Indian word for The Laws of Nature – were interesting, but not as lovely as the morning's offerings. Everything eventually began to make more sense; the meditations, the knowledge. I even started feeling more at home, even though I had the odd unwelcome visitors come to my room at night. I didn't really mind, because they were only spiders; and non-biting spiders at that. But their size did take some getting used to. They were the size of my two hands joined together. I had never seen anything quite like it. It was absolutely astounding.

One night I became totally absorbed in the magic and tranquillity of the beautiful full moon shining above our dormitory. Its brilliance and soft cool light through the masses of coconut palms had me positively enraptured. We had completed a group walking meditation earlier in the evening and all of us had looked up in stupefied silence. We were witnessing the moon pass behind another planet. It was a spectacular, unforgettable lunar eclipse; my first ever.

I ended up staying out well past my bedtime, wandering out amongst the swaying coconut palms. I felt a bit like a naughty little child. I managed to get into the dormitory grounds just before they locked the gates. I had to tiptoe in very quietly. Everyone was fast asleep.

When I got to my room, I shone my flashlight around, searching the dark corners for scorpions. It had been my nightly regiment since I had arrived. The thought of it made me positively writhe in discomfort. I hated it.

Nothing showed up in the glare of my lamp. I breathed a huge sigh of relief – happy not to have to do any house cleaning.

I turned off the flashlight and crawled into bed, but could not seem to fall sleep. Something did not feel quite right. My little voice piped up and agreed with me.

"Look in the corner behind your discarded fruit skins," it said.

That was when I saw it. Exposed in the light of my flashlight, I could see it was tiny, translucent and looked incredibly tenacious. I had seen one the day before when it was trying to climb up the side of one of the disposal buckets at the entranceway to the dormitory. It made my skin crawl. And here was one right in front of me – untethered and about to reek havoc in my humble little abode.

I felt frozen to the spot.

"What to do," I thought, feeling panic beginning to rise in my chest.

"It's time for your initiation, little Nomadic Goddess," my little voice said. "You haven't yet had the privilege of entertaining one of the monastery's famous prized guests!"

"Oh yeah?" I retorted, scowling. "I can assure you it's a privilege I would like to live without – for an eternity!"

I shone the flashlight on the scorpion for the longest time, debating whether I should do something with it, or just leave it there.

"Fat chance, " I said to myself. "You know if you don't catch it, you'll never get any sleep."

I stood and stewed about it for a moment longer. I knew I could sleep with spiders in my room, but not scorpions. I had already seen what a scorpion bite had done to a Dutch woman a few doors down. I was not willing to take the chance.

I looked at the clock. It's little green LED read-out said 11:10. "Everyone will be sleeping," I thought. "I can't exactly call for help. Besides – I've taken a vow of silence."

It was just me and him. Someone had to leave, and it was not going to be me. I filled myself with firm resolve, but that didn't stop my knees from shaking uncontrollably. I walked outside and grabbed a cup. There wasn't a piece of cardboard in sight, so I got two photographs out of my backpack – then moved nervously towards my unwelcome house guest.

It took me a full three minutes to will myself to make my move. When I was ready, I lunged forward and managed to trap it underneath my cup. A creepy chill crawled up my back. My first instinct was to let go of the cup. But I knew it was now or never.

I carefully began sliding the photos beneath the cup, but the scorpion moved suddenly and I lost it.

I let out a screech of terror and jumped back from the cup. To my utter horror, it crawled out from under the cup and started coming towards me. I screamed again. This time it was one of those long, drawn-out blood-curdling screams reminiscent of a *Freddy's Back* – *Halloween II* horror movie. I lost all self-control. I lunged for the cup and slammed it down. Unfortunately, my aim wasn't as good as the first time; I only managed to get *some* of his little body underneath. His tail was writhing around on the outside of the cup – dangerously close to my fingers. It was all I could take. I ran screaming from the room, only to find myself standing in the middle of the grass courtyard looking around at all of the help I had been wishing for earlier.

"Oh goodie," I thought. "I'm glad I never learned how to scream silently."

Most of the women were from the neighboring cells – looking very concerned and confused, and calling out, "What? What's happened?"

Some of them were standing around wrapped in sarongs, others were in their nightgowns. All of them were demonstrating the various stages of wakefulness and dishevelment one would normally expect from people who had been tossed from their beds by an ear shattering scream in the middle of the night. I pointed towards my room and performed a pantomime of the horror I had just endured. I was too stunned to speak.

One of the women confidently stepped forward, walked nonchalantly into my room, and handily removed the scorpion. It looked like she had been doing it all of her life. You would think she had just rescued a ladybug. I watched her coolly walk the scorpion to the pail placed at the dormitory entrance. I gaped after her, muttering to myself, "Point Number Seven of Being a Nomadic Goddess: Never slam a cup down on a scorpion's tail if you don't want to get him royally riled."

THIS IS YOUR LIFE
The next morning we talked – or rather, the instructors talked – about the changing nature of things, and one of the teachers emphasized how meditation was not something we did to achieve anything or to get rid of something. Instead, he said, we should use it to help realize the true nature of things.

"If you understand the true nature of things – or what we call the conditions of the world," he said, "you will be less likely to be dragged around by the conditions."

As I listened to him expand on the concept, I envisioned a caveman with his club raised high in the air, looking mean and tough – a real rugged individualist type. Emblazoned across his forehead I saw a stamp which read, "Conditions," and he was mercilessly dragging around some poor woman by the hair. When he turned to go the other way, I caught the woman's name. Indelibly tattooed across her forehead were the words, "This is Your Life."

I smiled. As I brought my attention back to the speaker, I heard him saying something about how one of the conditions of the world was nature's indisputable Law of Change or Law of Impermanence. He said everything that arose in life, ceased.

"There really is nothing to get rid of," he elaborated. "You just have to be patient and allow things to take their natural course. They will eventually end of their own accord. To experience this, just sit and listen to your own thoughts. I guarantee you will see how true it really is. Go ahead – try it."

After meditating for 40 minutes, I noticed he was absolutely right. A thought came up, then just as quickly disappeared. I was very pleased with my new insight. It made sense.

As a wrap-up to the morning lesson, he pointed out, "If you apply the same principle to other things in your life, you will soon see that when conditions are right, things come into your life and when conditions are right – they leave. Conditions appear or disappear according to their cause."

"How positively astounding," I thought. "If I think about events in my life this way, I can teach myself to be less upset when things change. I can choose to see that it was all perfectly natural."

TO BE OR NOT TO BE. THAT IS THE ANSWER.

As the course progressed, whole new vistas began opening up for me. Every day was filled with fresh information and fascinating new insights, and it all seemed to pour in virtually non-stop.

Every day the notice board outside the meditation hall had a selection of sayings – kind of like a "food for thought" approach. We were told that behind every saying lay a deep and incredibly profound meaning, but somehow it always eluded me. I usually left the board shaking my head and walking away feeling kind of "hungry". It was a spiritual hunger – a craving for the truth.

I had known very little about Buddhism before entering the course, but the one thing which had always stood out clearly in my mind, was the way Buddhists – especially Zen Buddhists – often used riddles to teach spiritual concepts. A lot of people called Buddhism, "Mental Gymnastics." Not me; I called it, "Wide World of Wrestling." If I could not figure out the sayings the first go-round, I would just make a game of it. I imagined them to be a little group of tag-team wrestlers issuing a silent challenge for a mental wrestling match. I would picture the bulletin board as a brightly-colored marquee, and underneath it an announcer was climbing into the center of a ring and boldly calling out, "Valerie – The Buddhist Novice versus The Sayings."

On the sixth day a Shakespearean adaptation appeared on the notice board. It said: "To be or not to be. That is the answer." I was ready for a good fight. I had had no luck wrestling the other brain teasers to the ground, so by the time this little baby made its debut, I was hungry for a victory.

I threw everything I had at it.

The crowd looked on in hushed silence as my Shakespearean rival and I entered the ring. Then the crowd went wild. I felt the blood beginning to pound in my temples, and I mentally willed the butterflies to stop wreaking havoc in my stomach. I stepped forward. I was determined to win the match – no matter what.

Round Two ended quickly. Nothing happened. It was a pathetic showing. I had not made one small dent in my opponent. But I refused to give up. By the time the bell rang to end Round Six, my Shakespearean rival was still fresh as ever. And me? I was wiped.

I trudged over to my corner, wiped the sweat from my brow and sat down to lick my wounds. Again, the referee signaled to us to take our places in the center of the ring. Five seconds into the round I let my guard down. It seemed only a split-second – but it was long enough for my opponent to take the upper hand.

He pinned me face-down on the mat.

As I lay admiring the lovely shade of blue, I thought, "He's good! *Darn good!*" I looked up at the crowd and cried out, "Touché, mes amis, but *most* uncomfortable."

I turned to get a better look at my adversary. I was shocked to see it was not my Shakespearean opponent who had me in such an unenviable, infinitely humiliating position, but my own intellect. It had been trying to get my attention all along. I had been so busy struggling, it had no choice but to incapacitate me. It simply wanted to say, "Hey, Bucko! It's not a riddle. It just is what it *is*. You're wasting your time."

"Oh," I answered, sheepishly. "You mean the answer *is* the answer? I guess it was just so darned obvious, I missed it completely!"

NO REALLY – WHEN *DOES* THE FUTURE ARRIVE?

I had heard the saying, "The future is now," many times in my life, but I had never quite grasped its full meaning.

Its true essence came to life one day as I sat in one of the classes.

The teachers were taking great care to show us how to live in the moment by focusing on our breath. What flabbergasted me, was how such a simple little exercise could bring it all into perspective.

I realized most of my thoughts focused on past events or future happenings. They seldom focused on the present moment, even with words like, "The past has left you and the future has not yet arrived" still ringing in my ears from the morning lesson.

I discovered staying in the now took every ounce of awareness and discipline I could muster. The more I practiced being mindful of my every thought, the more acutely aware I became. It took me only a few days to realize that not only did present moments instantly become past moments, but my anticipated future moments quickly became present moments. None of it was exactly new to me, but what shocked me was how they were not all that much different from one another. I was so disappointed. Here I had been sitting rubbing my sore buttocks, readjusting my seat cushion for what seemed the 100th time in the last 30 minutes, and thinking it *had* to get more comfortable – yet it never did.

"Rats," I thought, glowering. "What bad news."

As if that wasn't bad enough, I suddenly realized that most of my life I had unknowingly sacrificed all of my present moments for dreams of a better future. I thought, "What a waste!" I suddenly felt a wave of melancholy surge into my consciousness. I thought, "Why have I been spending so much time thinking about the future, when it was really the present all along? Is this what philosophers mean when they say, "Being in the moment"? Being here and not there, because *here* is *there*?"

As I continued to mutter away to myself, I began thinking, "If I keep on talking like this, the little guys with Men With a Mission name tags and trendy little wrap-around jackets are bound to rush in and make me an offer I can't refuse."

"I guess there really *is* no future," I thought. "I guess it's time to throw out *that* little belief as well."

I somberly began humming the dark, sorrowful funeral march – picturing a huge glorious procession of mourners following respectfully on the heels of a tiny, shiny black hearse. I watched my, "The future has got to be better" illusion being lovingly lowered into a waiting grave, and I could hear the words, "Ashes to ashes, dust to dust," wafting gently over the scene, filling the cool night air with their essence.

MENTAL DEVELOPMENT IS THE HIGHEST FORM OF EDUCATION

The next day the instructors talked about feelings.

"Feelings," said one of the younger monks, "are thoughts. A thought springs into our minds and we instantly react. Sometimes they are pleasant thoughts and they make us smile, but most of the time they worry us, pull us back and forth, and tire us out. Eventually, if left on their own, they can destroy whatever feelings we have of happiness and peace of mind. Take anxiety for instance. What comes up for you when you think of anxiety?"

I didn't have to think about it for long. "It's certainly something I've gotten really familiar with since I started backpacking," I thought. "Looking for a cheap, clean bed; a proper meal; and the day to day challenges of finding my way around foreign countries has really tested my nerves. I guess you could say anxiety and I are well acquainted."

As I reflected on the concept a little more, an older monk stepped in.

"Worrisome thoughts burn us up all day long," he said. "They create a vicious fiery circle of thoughts. Then – when it is time to go to sleep, they change from "fire by day" to "smoke by night" and we toss and turn and look anxiously at the clock and think, "Anxiety is hell."

"Well, meditation can help you stop all this," he said, sitting up confidently. "It can teach you to train your mind and thoughts and help put yourself back in charge. You can use your thoughts to serve you – rather than unknowingly putting yourself in the position of being a slave to them. All you need to do is be aware that you *thought* the thought, so you can *change* the thought. That way, you will see the feeling will change. It is like teaching yourself to think before you think," he said, grinning.

He happily showed us a number of ways to try out the concept, but by far my favorite one was where he explained, "Rather than trying to stop your thoughts, see them as visitors and your minds as a living room. The thoughts come knocking on the door expecting to be invited in for a visit, but you send them on their way. The key is to simply refuse to entertain them. As you have experienced, the mind has an endless parade of thoughts coming and going all of the time. It gets all caught up in them. It is a veritable feast for the intellect. But what you need to do is see thoughts like worry and fear as uninvited guests. And everyone knows what uninvited guests are like; they drain your energy and leave you feeling tired. Just send them away and you will find your peace of mind and energy will return once again."

"Try it," he said, eyes sparkling. "I assure you it will work."

"Scat, skidaddle," I called out – laughing to myself as I meditated – watching negative thoughts jump into my mind.

"Yes indeed," I thought, "chasing away unwanted thoughts is kind of like when a cute little fluffy wide-eyed kitten spots its victim, leaps out from some ambush-style hideaway, and adeptly attaches itself to your leg as if you were it's long-lost mother. Kittens – like thoughts – are very tenacious. They return like a boomerang."

"Ouch," I cried, as my adorable, harmless little kitten dug its tiny but unbelievably sharp little claws into my leg.

"Well," I thought, "if my thoughts are anything like this cute little kitten I've just envisioned, this is definitely not going to be an easy exercise!"

We rehearsed for a short while, then the teacher took the concept a step further. He suggested that even though we may not be able to control when or how our feelings arise, we can always control how we react to them.

"Begin to see them for what they truly are," he said. "See them as always changing. They come and they go. If we take time out to watch how they just fade away, you'll probably ask yourself, "What was there to cling to or attach to, if everything just changed anyway?"

"Wake up," he said. "Wake up to the essential nature of everything happening around you. Start to become more accepting of the way things are."

From that day on, I made a point of practicing his helpful hints. It made sense to me. It was fascinating, really. The more I practiced this new awareness, the more I began to view my life realistically.

The next day, the monk told us the true meaning of the word Buddha.

I was flabbergasted. He said Buddha meant, "The one who is awake; the one who knows".

"Here all of my life I've believed the word Buddha was the name of a rotund religious founder," I thought, "when all along it was nothing more than a wake-up call!"

On the morning of the eighth day, I was sitting with my eyes closed – back straight – daydreaming about the myriad of ways they had been showing us to concentrate and train our minds; ways I never ever imagined.

"Yep," I thought, smirking. "This is definitely the most difficult thing I've done next to my Personal Best course. And they're so similar – especially the way they work on getting through my emotional barriers."

As I sat contemplating how much patience and tolerance was needed to train my mind, it struck me that maybe mental development was the highest form of education.

"From what I've seen here," I thought, "it stands head and shoulders over a Masters degree or a Ph.D.– kind of like the way I look standing next to a Thai monk!"

"Higher education?" I said. "Look waaaaay up, Valerie – way up towards your mind."

I left the meditation hall watching my mind skip merrily along as it jumped from idea to idea, and I noticed what tickled my fancy the most, was one of the monk's earlier insights on worry.

"When you worry you die," he said. "When you don't worry you die. So – why worry?"

HOW TO BRAINWASH YOURSELF – TIPS ON MENTAL HYGIENE

On the second last day, the instructors took turns talking about ways to make meditation part of our daily ritual. They recommended we begin by seeing it as important as eating or sleeping.

"Meditation is a way of developing your mind to become firm and strong," they said. "It helps make an unhealthy mind, healthy. It is like gardening, in a way. Meditation studies the nature of the mind, so it provides ways to cultivate what you want in your garden. It shows you how to pull up the weeds, which are your negative, destructive thoughts, and helps you to plant more positive, happy thoughts; or what you could call, flowers."

They suggested we look at our minds closely; to begin to see what was wholesome. "Now look at what is unwholesome," they said. "Out of everything that comes up in your mind, pick out what is clean and what is dirty. The dirty things – those things that are already in your mind – throw them out. Now, out of all of the wholesome things that are in your mind, begin to stretch them – nurture them. Make those the ones that occur in your mind most often."

"Seems a simple enough method," I thought, smiling at the analogy which had jumped to mind. "We just need to do the laundry!" I thought. "Wash out what's dirty and create more clean things!"

As I watched my mind hit the spin cycle, the next instructor took the bench and sat down cross-legged. He took the concept a step further. He called meditation, "Brainwashing". Then he jokingly called the ten-day course, "How to Brainwash Yourself – Tips on Mental Hygiene."

"I love it," I thought. "So *that* is the true meaning of brainwashing. Finally an answer to one of my most long-held questions!"

Another helpful hint he passed along was: "Remember," he said, "the only brainwasher in your life is you. Nobody else can do it for you."

That afternoon we were treated to a rare moment in religious rites. Two monks from the morning sessions asked us to look at how serious we got about things in our lives.

"Check in with yourselves every once in a while to make sure you are not totally lacking in joy and happiness," one of them cautioned. "Be careful not to lose your sense of humor and just repress things. If you do, you won't last long in this method of meditation."

Next they both took the stage and began telling monk jokes. It was obvious they enjoyed letting their hair down; their big white smiles and glowing eyes bore testimony to it.

I looked around at my classmates. I could tell from their gaping mouths that I was not the only Westerner surprised at such an impromptu stage show.

"Hey!" I thought. "Who would expect a bunch of Thailand's holy men to get up in the front of a meditation hall full of Western visitors and take turns doing *comedy* routines?"

We all broke into raucous, not-so-silent laughter, when a relatively senior monk performed a hilarious Helpful Hints To Hum By magic act. I thought he was going to break into a round of "Let Me Entertain You," a la Shirley Temple style – minus the ringlets, of course.

Once the laughter had died down, he smiled at all of us and said, "Life in itself is serious enough – you certainly don't have to make meditation into something serious too."

The same monk lead our 5:00 p.m. chanting class, and afterwards, advised us to, "Let go of your expectations. Stop making meditation into some burdensome task where you feel you have to achieve something. Instead, see it as an opportunity to be peaceful and at ease with the moment. Think to yourself, "Nothing special, nothing to attain, no big deal."

My High Achiever Yuppie Antennae shot high into the air. Riding arrogantly atop my upwardly mobile noggin, they zeroed in and cried out, "WHAT, NO GOAL SETTING? AREN'T WE SUPPOSED TO BE AIMING FOR SOMETHING?" "YOU CAN'T BE SERIOUS," they yelled. "IT CAN'T BE THAT SIMPLE!" I decided to ignore them. They had been driving me crazy for years. The more I thought about the monk's words, the more I realized it was that simple.

"All you need to do is relax," one of the monks went on. "Enjoy yourselves – see meditation as an opportunity to give your mind a rest. Realize you are doing something good for yourself. *Gladden* your hearts."

Their big white smiles lit up the entire meditation hall. Theirs was a clean, resonant energy. It was positively enchanting.

"Smile," they said. "Lighten up."

We all broke into a wide grin. We couldn't help ourselves.

After that, whenever any nasty little thoughts would come stalking me, trying to drive me mad with anxiety; or whenever I found myself beginning to get frustrated because I was still trying to achieve something, I would simply stop and recall nature's Law of Impermanence and calmly smile to myself and sing out, "This too will pass, cause the monks they told me so" – to the tune of "Jesus loves me this I know, cause the Bible tells me so."

"I like the paradox," I thought. "Bizarre, yet fitting."

"Why does the Buddha smile?" I thought, chuckling to myself. "Because *he* knows *he's* in *charge!*"

IF YOU DON'T LIVE IN THE MOMENT, WHERE WILL YOU LIVE?

On my next to last day, a quote of a famous philosopher appeared on the bulletin board. It said, "Life is what happens to you when you are busy planning for the future."

"How very true," I thought, reflecting on how deep and profound its meaning was. But then – I felt a little sad.

"It sure holds true for *my* approach to life," I thought, frowning. "Much as I hate to admit it. But at least I'm here trying to learn ways to fix it. It could be a whole lot worse. I could have learned the lesson when I was 85 years old, instead of when I was 35. At least *this* way I get a fresh new start *early* in life."

I smiled for a brief moment, but then found myself frowning again. "So, is *that* all there is?" I said to myself. "They're saying if we don't live in the moment, where will we live? The mystery of life and nature has been revealed, and it's all wrapped up in nature's Law of Change and How To Live in the Moment?"

I suddenly felt shortchanged. But then I began marveling at the simplicity of it all and said to myself, "Thanks to the course, I now see the world in a whole new light – and I don't *ever* want to lose sight of the ways of the world again. This *works* for me, as hard a pill as it is to swallow."

I began thinking about how I could make a commitment to working with this meditation method every day. I knew it would fade into oblivion if I didn't.

"Use it or lose it," I thought, "that's what they say. And I know my mind is a slippery little thing at the best of times. It is unruly and erratic and a creature of habit, and if I don't keep on reprogramming it, it will just go running right back to its old ways."

"It's like anything else," I said to myself. "If I do it often enough; it sticks. If I don't; it disappears."

The more I looked at my ordeal of silence over the last nine days, the more I began laughing about how deprived I felt – or maybe I should say depraved. After all, it was no easy task being away from a nice soft bed, and having to eat the food they served, rather than being able to eat all the food I liked, how I liked, when I liked. I also found it tough being inactive for so long. My body was crying out for exercise. I longed for the chance to stretch myself to my fullest length – to feel my muscles pull me through a warm, glistening emerald sea.

I began picturing my impending escape from my self-imposed prison – or what I liked to playfully call, The Voluntary Sensory Deprivation Centre – Welcome to Buddhist Summer Camp. Suddenly, I couldn't wait for the course to finish. I wanted to run off to the sandy beaches of Koh Phangan, a quiet little island I had heard about – only two hours away by ferry boat.

I brought my thoughts back to the present moment and suddenly exclaimed to myself, "You *know*, this camp really took a lot of *courage*! And that's something I've been identifying more and more with – ever since I first donned my fluorescent orange socks after my Life Reading with Troy. It is amazing, really. It has been almost four years since I met him, and it has been quite a journey. The first half of this Walkabout I was sightseeing and exploring in Fiji and New Zealand and Australia, and now the last half of my trip I have started exploring the inside of my mind. Sightseeing has taken on a whole new meaning!"

I realized all of my life I had been exploring outer space – that is, the world outside of myself. Whether it was through school, or sports, or playing with my friends or going to dinner parties, it was still all outer world exploration. But working on my beliefs and thoughts – now that was definitely exploring the inner world reality – or inner space.

"What's happening to me?" I thought, suddenly feeling alarmed. "I hardly recognize myself! Wasn't I the one who used to make fun of people living a monastic life? And didn't I tease them about how they were hiding out from life – running from intimate relationships by taking a vow of celibacy – retiring to the jungle? Yet now, here I am – sitting in this monastery, trying out life on the other side; sitting still and quietly meditating on what it is like to live in the moment, discovering the inner nature of things for 10 challenging days. And even though I'm constantly being bombarded by my fears and doubts and neuroses and anxieties and responsibilities and successes – my life – I can't believe I'm actually *enjoying* it!"

I realized all of us meditators were like spiritual warriors. We were taking up our swords of courage and going inside to see what was really happening – instead of just going through life saying, "That's just how it is", or, "I've always been like this", or, "Can't teach an old dog new tricks," or, "It runs in the family".

I realized it took courage to let go of our beliefs, to try and truly see the way things were; not to hide from the truth any longer, but to confront it. By getting to know and accept that things had to change – simply because it was their nature to change. And we were now finding ways to cultivate a true honesty within ourselves. It meant the end of the words, "Ya but."
"Ya but, this is different", or, "Ya but, I thought I could make it work – I thought I could make *them* change."

"We also now recognize that everything in life is impermanent," I thought. "We no longer have a reason to go stomping around angrily for days muttering, "Why can't it stay the same? What's the problem? How can they *be* like that?"

"Now we know better," I thought. "We've experienced the truth about change first hand, by doing our moment to moment meditations. I used to pay lip service to the word 'change'. I always knew things had to change, yet I still got emotional and resented it every time it happened. Now, by remembering what I've learned here in the monastery, I will be able to soften my mind – to let go of some of my hard-headedness. It will make it a whole lot easier on myself and others."

THE ANSWER

I sat reflecting on how when I was traveling through Australia, I came across a magazine article featuring a collection of entertaining ideas for retail marketing, and how one idea had stuck with me. It was one about a woman planning to open a shop called The Answer. I could not recall what she was selling, but I liked the name of the shop.

The Answer jumped to mind the day I was preparing to leave the monastery to rejoin what the monks called The School of Life.

It was Graduation Day – or some sort of Thai monasterial equivalent.

"What joy!" I thought. "I actually made it! I kept my mouth shut for 10 whole days! Unbelievable."

The Dome of Silence had finally lifted, just like in the *Get Smart* television reruns I loved to watch, where Special Agent Maxwell Smart tried to keep secrets from the enemy – Chaos.

By leaving the monastery and re-entering the world of Chaos – otherwise known as Daily Life in Thailand, I was about to rejoin the masses. But I was going to try to keep my special agent identity – and not let the ups and downs bother me so much. And now that I knew how all situations changed anyway, all I had to do was to go out there and practice, practice, practice. I also knew I would have plenty of opportunities to try out my new loving-kindness approach to life. Thailand would be as noisy and exasperating as ever.

But before leaving, I had a promise to keep.

Everyone was busy loading up their back packs onto the waiting taxi, which was actually a tiny Toyota truck with a handmade wooden bench precariously perched on either side of the truck box. I threw my bag on the roof rack and went sprinting down the road. I leapt high into the air, clicked my heels together and yelled out, "YES! I'M FREE. I MADE IT!"

It felt great to express my feelings. It was such a rush just to be able to talk, let alone *yell*. My feelings had reached their boiling point about six days into the course. I had been sitting quietly day after day, following their directions and paying attention to my breath and practicing. But by the seventh day all I could think of was escaping. On that day, I promised myself I would let out a huge cry of victory.

I ran madly around the truck yelling, "YIPPEE EIO KAYAY!" A few people turned to see what all the commotion was about, but when they spotted me, the look in their eyes showed me they could relate. We had all gone through so much together, and it was only now that we realized just how much. Trouble was, the monks were not quite as understanding. They cast scolding looks in my direction. It was early morning and they were eating their breakfast. It seemed my loud theatrics had jarred them out of their silent reverie.

"Ah well," I thought. "Sorry, my friends, but I just had to get it all out. I've been waiting 10 days for this opportunity!"

I skipped to the back of the waiting taxi to go to Koh Phangan, and realized why I had remembered the shop called The Answer. It was just so darned obvious. It was absolutely and unequivocally the most perfect theme for my Nomadic Goddess – Gone Walkabout adventure.

I was on a quest, wasn't I? Well, I was looking for The Answer, right?

"That's the beauty of nomadic goddessing," I thought to myself. "I can find out parts of The Answer as I go along. It doesn't happen all at once. Why else would I be traveling around the whole world?"

"Besides," I thought, "I wouldn't be much of a nomad if I stayed in one place, now would I? It is indeed time to hit the road again. No telling what other parts of The Answer are waiting for me out there."

I climbed on board, and as I covered my mouth with a hand-kerchief to block out the suffocating exhaust fumes, I thought about how my time in the monastery helped me tap into my intuitive sense of knowing. Now I knew for sure, that all I had to do was pack along my intuition and trust everything would come along as I needed it. The Law of Nature said things would appear when the conditions were right and disappear when they were right again; not before and not after. And every book I had read talked about intuition as an untapped and magical resource – something right 100 percent of the time. I would be silly not to use it.

Now that I was eight months into my backpacking adventure, I was convinced intuition and trust were the cornerstone of nomadic goddessing. If I was not convinced of that, I would probably have packed up my Yuppie/Nomadic Goddess Backpack my first day of hitchhiking and hightailed it home.

I thought more about why I was so determined to uncover my intuitive sense, and ended up recalling something I had heard from a keynote speaker. He was addressing an audience at a Successful Businesswomen Seminar I had attended in Calgary just before leaving on my spirit quest.

He was one of the most colorful gentlemen I had ever run across. He was an entrepreneur from Kansas, and he was giving pointers on how to start a new business. I laughed to myself as I recalled his humorous personality.

"As entrepreneurs," he had related, with a long, Kansas drawl, "we never know everything we need to know before starting out. If we did wait to know everything, we would never open up a business. All we know is where we are right now. Then, all we can do is take the first step and begin, then trust we will be shown everything else as we go along."

When I first heard him relating his experience, I remembered beaming with recognition. "What faith he has," I thought. He had started his first business using his wife's Mastercard as capital. His golf accessories business had soon become a multi-million dollar going concern.

I remembered his closing remarks most clearly. He had paused and looked down as if searching for something to say. It was a good, long pause, and all of us shifted around in our seats, waiting expectantly for his next words of wisdom. More time passed, but still – he said nothing. Then without warning, he looked up and burst out in an evangelistic fire and brimstone fervor, and shouted at the top of his lungs, "GO FORTH! PICK A DIRECTION AND GO FORTH!"

The rafters shook with his words.

As I watched him step down from his 'pulpit,' I sensed the audience was not quite certain whether to yell out, "HALLE-LUJAH!" or "AMEN!"

"What a great motto for my nomadic goddess adventure!" I thought. "Go forth!"

His words often inspired me on my journey. They helped me see how important it was to trust my feelings and stay true to myself. All I had to do was get out there and do something I believed in. It all boiled down to one thing; a nomadic goddess had to simply show up. It was like in school when the teacher took attendance before beginning class. Whenever she called out my name, all I had to do was raise my hand and say, "Present." Well, traveling was really just like going to school. If I showed up, I got a present. And all kinds of marvelous gifts popped up from out of nowhere. A lot of the time, it was a veritable treasure chest full of goodies. Whether it was finding good, safe food, or a comfortable bed, or even miracle of miracles – locating French fries in the heart of Asian rice country; bonuses abounded everywhere. One of my all-time favorites was finding Haagen Daz ice-cream. I sat singing, "Heaven, I'm in heaven, and I can't believe..." while I watched my ice cold ice-cream bar steam away in the hot noonday sun in Hong Kong.

I smiled to myself and said, "Presents. What better reason to be a nomadic goddess?"

SIXTEEN

If I'm Going To Search My Soul, Shouldn't I Know Where It Is First?

The taxi pulled into Surathani, southern Thailand's commercial center, and we piled out and boarded a tourist bus bound for the ferry terminal. We were hoping to catch the 2:00 p.m. express boat to the island of Koh Phangan.

It was a relief to escape the sickening smell of exhaust fumes from the taxi, but now we found ourselves trapped in a multi-colored bus at the mercy of Thailand's version of Mario Andretti of Indy 500 fame.

The young bus driver careened through the traffic with a vengeance. I got out my motion sickness pills and downed a double dose. Then, as if his driving wasn't bad enough, Thai hit-parade music started blaring from his stereo – assaulting our sensitive, silence-trained ears.

I got out my silicone earplugs.I wanted desperately to escape.

I started reflecting on how I'd gotten here and began to laugh.

When I first started talking about going on my Walkabout, the faces of my friends had registered amazement. It wasn't so much that they couldn't believe I was leaving a successful business to travel the world, it was more the part about "a year" that astounded them. In their mind, a year's absence from work was utterly incomprehensible.

At the time, I too felt a little ill at ease. I remembered thinking, "You know, they're absolutely right. I really don't have any experience at this sort of thing. What *on earth* am I going to do out there for an entire year?"

My little voice replied in a second.

"Enjoy yourself, Valerie!" it said. "Have a taste of freedom; relax; go and see what's out there. Remember how you dreamt about calling in sick when you were an employee in the oil industry? Then along came an excellent little book bold enough to raise the thought-provoking question: Rather than call in sick, why not call in well? It would go something like this: you'd get your boss on the line and say, "Listen, I've been sick ever since I started working here, but today I'm feeling well and I won't be coming in anymore."

"You know, you're right," I replied. "When I first read it, I remember how my heart jumped."

"Well, you *did* it!" my little voice replied. "You called in "well" to all of your clients, and went off to look for The Answer.

"But they kept calling it a Soul Search," I said, "and I thought, how absurd. Why, I don't even know what a soul *is* – how am I going to search for it if I don't what "it" looks like?"

"Pretty likely prerequisite," my little voice remarked.

I sat and thought about the concept some more, and realized I found the whole idea of a Soul Search rather confounding. I really didn't have a clue about "it," because "it" was a complete mystery to me.

I first started searching for "it" in my Sunday School classes. I was the only one in my class to insist on attending school for an extra three years. All of my other classmates, or should I say, cellmates, finished their compulsory Sunday school sentence and gleefully broke out in Grade Nine.

Not me. I was going to keep right on doing time until they gave me some answers. I refused to leave until they did. But I wasn't going to settle for just any old answers. I wanted The Answer.

It turned out I was wasting my time. They didn't know either.

Years later, I found myself enrolled in New Age philosophy classes. What really surprised me was how much I comprehended it all. I thought, "Oh, oh. I can feel another alarm beginning to sound."

"Didn't you jeer and taunt Patrice and Troy whenever they talked about Woo Woo Heebee Jeebee concepts?" my little voice piped up. "Well, aren't those the concepts you readily accept now? And didn't you call them Space Cadets behind their backs, and point and laugh and taunt them by moving your index finger in a circular motion beside your temple?"

"You're right," I replied, laughing. "And look. Now I'm one of them!"

"Well at least these concepts make sense to me," I said, defensively. "Unlike the meaningless mush they served up to me in Sunday school! At least the stuff I've been learning fills in some of the blanks, or should I say, gaping holes, which have been left recklessly unguarded by the unarmed battalions of conventional religion."

"Ooh, that's dangerous," I thought, chuckling to myself. "Mighty dangerous. And I don't mean Almighty. If religion keeps on failing to cover all of its bases, people might just start thinking for themselves. Heaven forbid – what's to become of the world, then?"

"Yep," I thought, rubbing my chin and smiling and looking out the window. "The answers came in hard and fast back then – kind of like the way this bus-driver's driving. Trouble is, my New Age teachers kept on interchanging terms like the Higher Self, the Light, the Life Energy, the Chi, the Kundalini Serpent Fire, Intuition, Natural Knowing and the Third Eye to signify that elusive being called, The Soul. But to me, it all seemed way too complex. I thought the truth must be something simple."

I reflected some more, and thought about my time in the monastery.

"I've figured it out," I thought. "Man is equipped with a fascinating tool called, The Brain. And because he happens to have one, he feels compelled and even somewhat obliged to make simple things – complex. That way, it gives The Brain something to keep it busy; kind of like throwing toys into a toddler's playpen – it keeps The Brain amused while man goes about doing the really important things in life; like – looking for simplicity."

"The soul," I thought dreamily, looking out at row-upon-row of rubber trees whipping past my window. A sudden jolt took my thoughts off my soul and tossed them onto the road. Our Kamikaze bus driver had just bullied some poor motorcyclist off the road.

I managed to catch a glimpse of the unfortunate victim as he was struggling to regain control of his bike. I could see his startled wife and two children clinging to him for dear life.

"Unbelievable," I thought. "This world is so vicious!" I leaned back in my seat and folded my arms resolutely across my chest. "I *swear* that because these bus drivers are hired to drive, they drive – and that means right through the middle of onrushing motorcycles and cars and cement mixers and water buffaloes and roosters and horse carts, and whatever else gets in their way."

My blood began to boil. I could feel my adrenal glands lighting up. I scowled to myself and thought, "There certainly are some pretty ugly human characteristics out there. And yet everybody seems to accept such meanness and continue on their merry way as if nothing untoward has happened. Is this world getting *worse*, or is it just my imagination? Oh, how I long for the peace and tranquillity of the retreat center. The noise and the hustle and bustle of this School of Life is completely overwhelming. I want desperately to yell out, "RECESS!"

I pondered my situation for a while, then started thinking more deeply about my peaceful time in the monastery and willfully decided to let the ugly thoughts pass.

"Why not just enjoy living in the moment?" I asked myself. "Don't put your mind on it. Let it go. This too will pass."

Surprisingly, I instantly started smiling again, and I set my mind to taking in the lush green countryside flashing past me.

We arrived at the express boat dock and I jumped into line. By the time I got to the island, all I could think about was finding a quiet little beach. I had only been absent from the monastery for four hours, yet it seemed like an eternity.

I discovered a wondrous spot at the opposite end of the island from where the ferry had docked; a peaceful little haven called Tong Nai Pan – a long way from where most of the tourists seemed to be going.

It was perfect. There wasn't a soul around. And because it was nearing the end of the season – just before the monsoon winds hit the Gulf of Thailand – there would only be a few locals around and the odd backpacker.

I was ecstatic.

"Yippee!" I yelled, dancing down the beach.

I found a quaint little bungalow under a huge palm tree and lay down on the hammock. Looking out over the blue-green bay below, I thought about how so many changes had happened to me over the last two weeks. I breathed deeply. I could feel my body and mind slowly begin to relax.

The next morning I jumped out of bed at 4:00 a.m. – set myself up to meditate, and happily breathed my way into a beautiful, blissful state – serenaded by the constant, heavenly sound of the waves far below.

In the first few days that followed, I found I had absolutely no trouble finding ways to maintain my meditation practice. I expected it to be a lot tougher outside the monastery, but somehow it had become a part of me – the silent sojourns into the world of my mind were so rewarding, and so revealing, that when I didn't do it, I felt like I had lost something of great value.

One day I was sitting meditating and I looked down at myself in my cross-legged position, and I thought, "You know – in the monastery I sat on a chair most of the time. My back got too sore if I didn't. Yet look at me now. Here I am sitting cross-legged – and it doesn't even hurt! Why – this is a major coup!"

Some mornings I would go out for what I called Buddhist Beach Walks. I would walk along the sand practicing the mindfulness of my movements – honing my concentration and focusing on the moment – and thinking about how useful my new skills would be in a tennis game.

"You're a riot, Valerie," I exclaimed to myself. "Leave it to you to come up with a worldly way to use your new-found spirituality!"

I laughed and walked back to my bungalow.

After two weeks of swimming and cross-legged meditation,

I felt as if my body was becoming more supple. I was more flexible than I had ever been in my entire life. What was more, my back pain never returned.

I was euphoric.

"Victory at last!" I cried, speeding down the beach, recklessly kicking up the sand and splashing the seawater all over the place. I had finally conquered my back ailment after suffering for almost ten years.

I noticed the gulls stopped scavenging for food long enough to look up and see what all of the excitement was about.

"FIRST THE BACK!" I yelled at them, raising my fist in the air, "THEN – THE WORLD!"

They answered me with a blank expression, then went back to picking at the shells which had washed up in the early morning tide.

"I guess gulls don't have back problems," I said, chuckling to myself.

I knew I had turned a new page in my life. Now – there was nothing holding me back.

SEVENTEEN

Nomadic Goddess Treasure Map

My time on the beach filled me with a sense of wonder and awe. I felt like I accepted things more as they were, and enjoyed each moment more than ever.

Finally, after a long journey through life of wondering "how to," I was becoming fully aware of each moment's specialness and beauty.

I took a boat back to the mainland and hopped a train from Surathani to Bangkok, then flew to Singapore for a few days – then on to Bali.

It was definitely time to go to Bali. I had always wanted to go – ever since I had first heard about it from a professional photographer I had met while working in the oil business. Out of the 110 countries he had visited on his commercial photography adventures over his thirty-odd years, none had compared to the idyllic paradise of Bali.

"I've been to some of the most magical lands known to man," he said, "but the Balinese have something very special. I can't quite put my finger on it, except to say that maybe it's connected to something quite mystical."

He had me so enchanted with his promise of paradise, I vowed to see it some day – no matter what.

Problem was, the "no matter what" proved to be quite a challenge. As soon as I had spent two hours in the country, I wanted to leave. I discovered all too quickly I had waited far too long. Eleven years had gone by, and tourism had completely destroyed Bali. Paradise had vanished.

It took me a full six days to even begin to let go of my disappointment. Everywhere I looked, there seemed to be greedy hawkers waiting to pounce on me – especially in the seaside town of Kuta. They kept relentlessly harassing me – trying to talk me into buying their tourist trinkets.

I felt attacked and invaded, and found myself wandering around moodily longing for the gentle manners of the Thai people.

It wasn't so much the Balinese who were causing the problems, but the business-minded Indonesians from Java; they were the pushy ones ruining it for everyone else. The local Balinese said the Javanese were too greedy.

I had to agree.

As we drove through the little wood-carving village of Mas in the central, high country of Bali, on our way to what was to be my new home-base of Ubud – I willed myself to remember the Buddhist's teaching on the Law of Impermanence. It stated that everything that comes – goes. "So even though it looks pretty bleak right now," I told myself, "It's got to get better. But for now – just look for the good in people – that's the best you can do."

When we pulled into the artist's town of Ubud, I felt like I had been dragged through an emotional keyhole. My spirits picked up considerably, though, when we pulled up alongside where I was staying. The address of my newest Nomadic Goddess residence read: "Nick's Pension – Monkey Forest Road."

"Good Greek name for an Indonesian homestay," I remarked, chuckling as I got out. "I love it. It's eclectic – just the right resting spot for a Nomadic Goddess. It'll help me adjust to the realities of Bali.

I walked up to a stone statue of a fierce-looking monkey god guarding the entranceway to one of the neighboring homestays. I looked him straight in the eye and said, "I *ask* you – what more *perfect* location could there possibly be, than Monkey Forest Road to practice training this little old monkey mind of mine?" He didn't answer. He kept looking as stolid as ever, hand extended – waiting for another offering of incense and rice. In Bali, the homeowners made offerings to the gods – asking them to protect their homes and to bring prosperity to their household.

Something else about the synchronicity of it all occurred to me, and I recalled a favorite saying of one of my zany friends back at home. Whenever something particularly coincidental happened, she would always exclaim, "Why of course! It's karma, it's Zen, it was meant to be!"

I later found out Ubud's Monkey Forest Road was aptly named. It had a real live forest with real live monkeys.

THE GODFATHER SCREACHER FROM HELL

One sunny day I decided to venture into the monkey forest, and ended up climbing to the top of a jungle knoll where I discovered a dense collection of vines and an irrigation canal. As I looked further down the canal, I could see rice paddies in a cleared area beyond, then heard the familiar quacking of the ever-present ducks as they fed on the left-over grain from the past season's rice harvest.

My chest was heaving from the exertion of the climb. I wiped the sweat from my brow, and looked around. It was then that I spotted them.

"Look no further, you little monkey scout," I said, patting myself proudly on the back. Much to my delight, I counted 60 or so monkeys sprinting and jumping and cavorting all over the place – generally doing what monkeys do best – monkeying around.

"I've hit pay dirt," I proclaimed, eyes gleaming.

I pictured the rest of my fellow tourists down below in another part of the forest, entertaining themselves by watching a small handful of monkeys greedily grabbing peanuts from their hands. Yet here I was – multi-million times more fortunate – being treated to an entire tribe of the little gaffers.

No sooner had I finished congratulating myself, than I had to duck out of the way of an oncoming, screaming, airborne, Kamikaze monkey.

When the coast was clear, I stood up.

"Yes!" I gleefully exclaimed. "This is *definitely* where they all hang out!"

A bunch of monkeys were swinging confidently from vine to vine, chattering boisterously and curling their tails around one another's throats or ankles – whichever was the easiest to reach. They were either playfully pretending to choke the life out of each other, or attempting to dislocate each other's limbs – all in an enthusiastic bid at one-up-manship.

"Better yet," I chuckled to myself, "make that one-up-monkeyship."

When they tired of the sport, they dashed maniacally off to execute a perfect dive into the nearby canal.

I ran after them to get a closer look. I was surprised to see how they could swim underwater with their eyes open. Alert and determined, they menacingly looked around for an unsuspecting prey. Suddenly, one of them spotted his target, noiselessly glided up to one of his "teammates" – and quickly reached out and grabbed him; then mercilessly dragged him into the water.

"What a grand spectacle," I thought. "These guys are hilarious! More than that – they're positively adorable." Positively adorable, that is, until I became the prey. It seems my bright red back pack had not gone unnoticed by one of the older monkeys.

I heard a little sound, and when I turned to see what was up, I saw a mammoth-sized monkey adeptly snatch his prize. Shocked, I lunged towards him in a desperate attempt to retrieve my valuables. He easily dodged my hand, demonstrating as good a form as any expert running back on *Monday Night Football* , and deftly jumped clear – running off in the direction of the dense forest – with my back pack in tow.

I leapt up from the edge of the canal and started giving chase.

Suddenly he stopped and curled back his lips, exposed his long sharp yellow teeth, and let go a blood-curdling battle cry.

I dove for cover.

As I lay peering out from under the dense jungle foliage, a solution jumped to mind.

"Hey," I thought, "I can always *buy* another back pack. I don't need my passport *or* my cash! I'll manage, I'm sure. Besides – the day pack kind of goes with his outfit. I'm sure color coordination is an important facet here in the jungle. The back pack's red; he's brown with gray whiskers. Perfect! Just forget about the back pack, Valerie and concentrate on staying out of range of those fangs."

As I looked at him some more, I couldn't help but notice how he bore a striking resemblance to a cross between John Wayne and Marlon Brando. He was, in fact, a comic look-a-like.

As I watched him strut his stuff sporting a swaggering gait that he could only have mastered by watching late-night John Wayne television classics, I began observing his mind at work. Behind those big bushy eyebrows, I could see that he thought he was a safe distance away, and so he really started prancing arrogantly around – exuding an air of superiority as if to say, "I'm in charge here, Lady" – puffing out his cheeks and serving me a triumphant stare.

Our eyes locked. It felt like one of those old fashioned show-downs – reminiscent of a scene from the movie, *The Godfather* – combined with a bad hombre scene from a cheap spaghetti western.

As I sat contemplating my options, a Buddhist analogy went swinging through my mind. The Thai monks had taught us about clinging, grasping, naughty little monkeys and how their antics related to our own thoughts. One thought would pop up, then another, then another, and before we knew it, our mind would be raging out of control, and we would be in a panic.

"Problem is," I thought, "not only are my thoughts behaving like a monkey, but real life action has taken over – right here on the Monkey Forest floor!"

While the Godfather Screecher From Hell continued attaching himself to my back pack, I reflected on the Buddhist concept of Detachment. They had taught me that all source of suffering comes from our desires and attachments. "But if we really think about it," they said, "whatever we think is ours – isn't. We can own nothing, we can simply use it – so why attach to anything?"

"Say bye bye back pack," I said to myself, as I started thoughtfully humming the tune to *Bye Bye Blackbird*.

It seemed the most appropriate response. What else could I do? People had warned me about rabid monkeys, so I certainly wasn't going to risk safety for the sake of retrieving a silly old passport. I knew I could always get more traveler's cheques once I got to Kuta. I sat back on my heels and started calculating the amount of money and time it would take to go cross-country to Jakarta in search of a new passport. Another Buddhist concept leapt to mind. It was the Law of Impermanence saying, "Hold up Pardner. Wait a minute. This *too* will change." And by golly it did. The Screech and Run Running Back soon lost interest in his latest victory, dropped his prize, and bounded off towards the crest of the hill – all the while sounding his heart-stopping *Battle Cry of the Backpack Battalions.*

"What a consummate warrior," I thought, smiling. As he faded into the distance, I noticed he had stopped screeching long enough to sink his yellow teeth into another monkey's calf tendon.

"Good thing he was only after my belongings," I thought, running to pick up my day pack. I clasped it gratefully to my chest, and thanked my lucky stars for having such a lovely Nomadic Goddess red decoy.

"You see?" my little voice called out. "Not only did your little back pack provide you with an excellent diversion, but it also helped you practice the Buddhist Law of Detachment and the Law of Impermanence!"

"Yeah," I replied, playfully feigning a heart attack.

I pulled out my water bottle and thought, "I can hardly wait to find out what's next!"

EIGHTEEN

Step Right Up, Folks.
Free Meditation Lessons

The Meditation Shop. The sign hung above an ornately-carved Balinese style wooden door – the entranceway to a small, tastefully designed white-washed building on Monkey Forest Road.

"Strange sight to behold," I thought, furrowing my brow as I walked by. What was obviously a Western-style house was nestled unobtrusively into a spot normally reserved for Balinese tourist shops and restaurants. On closer scrutiny, I began thinking it could have been someone's home, but then I wondered, "Why would anyone choose to live on such a noisy street? Motorcycles and cars are roaring by from morning until night, and shop owners are constantly yelling out, "COME INSIDE MY FRIENDS. MASKS, BATIK PAINTINGS, CLOTHING!" I must say, it's not exactly my idea of a location for a home."

"Besides," I thought, "if it were someone's home, why would they call it The Meditation Shop?"

"Such a strange name," I thought. "Every other shop on the street has a Balinese name. Either its Jaya's Warung, or Made's, or Wayan's, or something equally ethnic. None of them are as Western-sounding as – *The Meditation Shop.*

"How odd," I pondered. "I've been walking down this street so many times over the past two weeks and I've never *once* noticed this place." Then I realized why. The nondescript little house was virtually incognito – upstaged by the surrounding buildings and imposing structures of the lavishly-designed Balinese stone entranceways leading into the myriad of shops. Plus, all of the shops were spilling over with the usual ostentatious, brightly-colored Balinese masks and large, multi-hued Ramayana wooden string puppets – not to mention massive collections of gaudy giant wooden fruits. On top of all that, was the endless collection of rack-upon-rack of paisley-designed batik clothing. Of course I hadn't noticed the house before. So much else was happening all around it.

"Shops, shops," I kept thinking. "That means they must be *selling* something!"

A host of New Age images flew to mind and I pictured a marquee reading, Meditation Merchandising – Come one, come all. Step right up to Monkey Forest Road. Tarot card readers, Angel card readers, Card card readers and Do-it-Yourself Enlightenment Kits. One stop shopping. Just follow the yellow brick road and watch for arrows that say, Wizard."

I decided to see what was inside.

I walked up the path leading to the entranceway, but as I did, I failed to see a large white sandwich board advertising, Free Meditation Lessons. Sign Up Here. As a matter of fact, I was so intent on solving my little mystery, I probably wouldn't have noticed it, even if it had stuck out its leg and tripped me. It seems I was not yet a Masters student of Buddhism. If I had been, I would have been more awake. The fact that I had missed this little clue did not surprise me one tiny bit. A Buddha I was not – at least, not yet.

"Point Number Eight of Being a Nomadic Goddess," I thought. "Remember to read the signs – all of them."

I passed quietly through the doorway. My ears were met by strains of soft, sweet-sounding music. I peered suspiciously around, surveying the collection of brightly-colored posters and hand-painted sayings tastefully arranged on the walls. Each poster showed a variety of Indian personages dressed dramatically in long flowing gowns, with golden halos shining out from around their heads. They were all smiling beatifically, exuding rays of tranquility and peace.

I assumed they were Indian, because each of the subjects were sporting a small colored dot in the middle of their foreheads. Because I knew absolutely nothing about Hinduism, all I could think was, "For a New Age meditation place, they sure have some weird drawings.

Most of these places display images of flying white unicorns and pointy-eared dancing fairies – or fantasy drawings depicting Merlin's spell-binding wizardry.

When I traveled through New Zealand and Australia, these kinds of shops almost always portrayed New Age philosophy as something esoteric and etheric and cosmic. Usually there were symbols like the Yin and Yang draped generously around the premises, and aisle upon aisle filled with books and meditation tapes and fortune-telling cards.

Looking incredulously around, I thought, "What *is* this? No *goods*? How can that be possible?" But then I spotted a tiny cabinet of pamphlets and tapes tucked away in the corner of the room. Feeling totally vindicated, I marched triumphantly towards the cabinet and exclaimed, "Aha! They *are* selling something!"

The sign above the cabinet announced the tapes were not for sale – and neither were the booklets.

Feeling completely dumbfounded, I started thumbing through the materials looking for more clues.

"If not sales, what?" I asked myself.

"Raja Yoga," was the title on all the booklets – and in five different languages no less.

"What could *that* be?" I wondered, scratching my head.

Out of a corner of the room, a voice softly said, "May I help you?"

I jumped out of my skin. I thought I was alone in the room. I looked around and was startled to see a smiling young woman sitting on a small white floral-patterned love seat sofa off in the corner. The love seat had been positioned unobtrusively in a small recessed area – which explained why I had not noticed her when I first entered.

I quickly recovered and replied, "Why, yes. What's this place about, and what is Raja Yoga? Is it an exercise program or something?"

181

"Why no," she answered with a slight English accent. "It's purely meditation – open-*eye* meditation."

"Really?" I replied, cocking my head to one side. "I always thought the eyes had to remain closed to help shut off the outside world – to make it easier to focus on calming the mind. Besides, I figure if I close off one of my most distracting senses, it would help minimize all the diversions coming at me – to help me concentrate."

"Actually," she said, gracefully rising from her seat, "what we teach is the opposite. We believe in stimulating the mind – giving it positive things to busy itself with – like thoughts of well-being and peace. After all, you go through life performing actions with your eyes open, why not meditate that way too? Besides – it is a really practical way to apply the things you experience in your meditations, to take it with you as you go about your daily life."

"That makes some sense," I replied. "I've often wondered how to apply some of the new knowledge I've just received in a Buddhist course, to real life. For one thing, I'd like to know how I can keep myself from becoming downright indignant whenever harsh street noises or the demands of day-to-day living leaves me longing for the quiet, peaceful, protective premises of what I call Camp-Getaway – The Monastery – in southern Thailand."

She gave me a knowing smile and told me she had also sought something similar. I thanked her for her help, and she suggested I feel free to look around some more, then sat back down and picked up the book she had been reading.

I was secretly glad she hadn't gone on. I didn't want to have to tell her that I already had a perfectly good meditation method, and I really wasn't interested in changing it – at least not just yet. I wanted to give it a good shot before wandering off to a new one – just like the Buddhist monks had suggested.

I wandered over to the next wall, and spotted a few words on a large poster that talked about souls and points of light, and something they called a Supreme Soul. I stood reading for a while, then turned to leave.

As I did, she came over and announced that they were offering an introductory class in Raja Yoga, and would I be interested? That was when it registered. It was a shop – after all.

I felt an immense wave of disappointment overtake me. She was attempting to make a sale, and that bugged me. I had really enjoyed our little talk, but now I thought, "Yep. Everybody's out to sell me something. Oh well. End of story. I guess that's life."

"No thank you," I said, looking her in the eye, as I headed for the door. As I stepped outside, I heard her call, "It's free!"

I stopped and turned around and stepped back in and said, "Pardon me?"

She smiled back at me and said, "We offer the seven lessons free. There is no fee. We have one starting tomorrow morning at 8:00 a.m."

"But how can they be free?" I replied. "*Nothing* is free!"

When I heard the words come tumbling from my mouth, I cringed and looked down at the floor – then promptly scolded myself for being so cynical. I didn't like seeing such unattractive qualities in others, and yet here they were – in me. I recalled reading something which said, "Skepticism without cynicism is beneficial."

"Guess I missed the point," I said to myself. "I just covered both of them in one foul swoop!"

Feeling somewhat embarrassed, I looked up to see her reaction.

Surprisingly – it had not fazed her. I guess she had had a similar reaction from other people. She simply smiled and replied, "It's actually quite simple, really. We believe every human being has a right to truth and knowledge and there should never be any strings attached – financial or otherwise. There is also something else I would like to share with you. The gentleman who started Raja Yoga in India in 1937 offered it free because he believed people thought spirituality was so cheap, they could actually buy it for money!"

I burst out laughing, and said, "How true. How true and yet how very sad. But how can you afford to run your center?"

"All the Raja Yoga teachers offer their services voluntarily," she explained. "We donate our time. And the people who attend meditation classes on a regular basis sometimes choose to make a donation anonymously – based on the value they feel they have received. That way it gives us a clean beginning right from the start, and everybody benefits. There is no hidden agenda."

I recalled my time in the Personal Best course and thought about how they too had used a similar approach.

I smiled broadly back and replied, "How very lovely. A New Age offering free from the profit motive. I'd say things are looking up!"

She smiled and bid me farewell and I set off down the road. Passing by the tourist shops, I was still reflecting on the free aspect of the course, when I heard an alarm beginning to sound in my head.

"Not again," I thought. "Now what?"

It was another one of my beliefs yelling, "PAY ATTENTION!"

I could feel my eyes suddenly turn big as saucers and I thought, "Oh my God! It's a cult. *That's* why it's free. Wasn't she a Westerner, after all? And didn't she have a gleam in her eye? Yes. Yes. Of course. Shiny eyes. That's what I've been warned to look for. They say watch out for groups of people who befriend you, make you feel welcome, put you at ease, get your guard down – and then whammo kabammo. They steal you away, brainwash you, gradually take away your free will, then reprogram you to make you a part of a group consciousness, and life as you know it is over. You become a slave for an eternity."

My mind went dashing off, creating all kinds of elaborate schemes and imaginative venues to carry them out in. But then my little voice popped up and said, "You're paranoid, Valerie. Not only are you paranoid, but you've lost all sense of trust."

My little voice had a point. The word free did not necessarily mean dangerous – or dishonest. And it did not necessarily mean people had ulterior motives. It could mean just what it said – free. Problem was, living in the western world, I was harassed almost daily by door-to-door-sales people and advertising sales flyers and telephone solicitations by carpet cleaners offering free goodies like, "Cat hair a problem? We demonstrate the ultimate in *Cat Hair Removal.* Your carpet worries will be over forever. Allow us to come into your home and vacuum your cat."

I laughed as I envisioned a warning written in minuscule, almost indiscernible words on the back of the vacuum cleaner warranty which read: "Cat guaranteed to survive. However, prolonged use may be detrimental, resulting in nerve damage or behavioral disorders – i.e: severe distrust of master, clawing of the skin. The company is not responsible for any loss or damage to cat – or master."

I walked down the street debating whether or not to enroll in the course, when I recalled the unbelievably low price I had paid for my Buddhist Summer Camp. The monks asked us to pay the equivalent of what it would cost to buy two candy bars in the West. They explained they only used the money to cover the cost of the food.

"But that was the East," I objected to myself. "That was different. I trusted them. The people at The Meditation Shop are from the West, and with all the media coverage of strange goings-on and stories about charismatic leaders and naive followers, I feel justified in my strong reservation. Besides – one of my friends was stolen away by a cult in California and after hearing his story, I really question such strange offers. Why do you think I ask so many questions up front? It's a way to avoid surprises."

I opted to bide my time and think about it a little later. I decided to read my travel journal instead.

I sat down on my beautiful stone deck outside the quaint little brick bungalow I was renting, and started flipping through the pages of my journal. As I turned a page, a piece of paper slipped out and floated gracefully down – executing a beautiful four point landing – ending up smack dab in the center of my lap.

I picked it up. My little mystery floater was a letter from my dear friend Patrice – The Whacko Wicca Of the West. For years we had been faithfully keeping in touch. After she had helped me with recipes to help cure my hypoglycemia, we developed a really loving and caring friendship. Whenever an important issue came up in my life, I knew I could always look to her for advice. So it did not surprise me one bit, that I was a half a world away, and here she was – traveling under the guise of a special delivery from the heavens above – her six-foot-five essence wrapped up in a little piece of paper just begging for my attention.

"She'll help me solve the cult dilemma," I thought. "I can just feel it."

I picked up the paper and noticed it was one of her more recent letters. And true to form – it contained a passage giving me a fresh new perspective on the Raja Yoga decision.

She had written a few months earlier telling me she was pulling up stakes and moving from Canada's west coast to Ottawa – Canada's capital. In the letter, she was sharing her experiences about what it was like to trust and venture into the unknown.

"In older cultures," she wrote, "an initiate would go on a Vision Quest, often naked and completely unguarded except for a basic tool she was allowed to fashion for herself. The complete reliance on self was a part of the birth of the new adult or spiritually-awakened person, and the deprivation was in fact a way of taking existence to its barest bones in order that there might be maximum room for new growth. That way, when your hands are empty, you can catch the golden apple when the goddess tosses it to you."

I liked the passage instantly. It appealed to the soul-searching nomadic goddess within me. Besides – I knew I could not go on ignoring how I had read some things on the posters at The Meditation Shop which had touched me deeply. I liked their philosophy about the nature of the soul and its relationship to a Supreme Soul or a Supreme Being. All through my travels, I had believed that some higher being had been protecting me and guiding me, but somehow that fact had slipped my mind since I had entered the monastery and started learning about Buddhism.

"Oh my God!" I thought, laughing to myself. "I forgot *God!*"

I sat reflecting, and realized all the more how Buddhist philosophy made little or no reference to the concept of God or souls. Thai Buddhism spoke of there being no self – which I took to mean no soul. Whether or not I understood it correctly, I have no idea. But I do remember it left me feeling empty. Thai Buddhists also believed all beings and all things of the world were simply a part of nature, and no one part was more or less important than the other. A belief in a Higher Power or a personal God did not appear to exist – and that troubled me. I really enjoyed all the other aspects of their teachings, but somehow I could not help feeling something was missing. I got a clue what that something was, when I stepped into The

Meditation Shop. It was the concept of God and souls.

"This feels right," I thought. "And when something feels that right, I know that's my intuition talking to me – and I'd better heed it. It's been right 100 percent of the time."

I suddenly felt filled with a sense of renewed optimism and adventure. I decided to take the plunge.

"Oops," I thought. "Wrong word. Patrice's Golden Apple story was not about *bobbing* for apples, now was it?

"Lunge," I thought," Yes, yes. That's it. *Lunge* for the apple."

"Point Number Nine Of Being A Nomadic Goddess," I said to myself. "Never miss a chance at a free snack. When they offer – lunge."

NINETEEN

Nomadic Goddess Turns Out To Be A King

Walking into The Meditation Shop, I still couldn't help feeling a little ill at ease.

I walked in the front door, fully expecting Liz to greet me, but was surprised to find a handsome young dark-haired man approaching me. He extended his hand and said, "How do you do. My name is Robert" – rolling his "r's" as he spoke.

"Hello," I replied.

"He sounds very Frrrrench," I thought.

I looked around the room. He followed my gaze and answered, "I'll be teaching you the course today. Liz and I take turns and she had an earlier advanced class. She is off eating breakfast."

I looked at Robert a little more closely. He seemed to emit a warm, peaceful glow, and his voice possessed an effervescent quality mixed with an uncharacteristic calmness. I also noticed his eyes shone – just like Liz's.

Feeling somewhat touched by his presence, I fumbled to compose myself.

"Nice to meet you," I finally said.

He kept looking at me with his big brown glowing eyes,

and I started feeling somewhat uncomfortable. They were so penetrating.

I desperately wanted to get out of what was fast-becoming a staring match, so I decided it would be best to divert his attention and hastily exclaimed, "So! *Where* shall we begin?"

He did not seem at all taken aback by my nervous, high-pitched, staccato question. He led me around to a small area behind a white room divider, and offered me a cushion. Sitting cross-legged on the floor, he positioned himself directly in front of me, and prepared to begin the course.

I looked around the room and thought, "But there is one thing missing. Where are the other students?"

I decided to ask.

"Point Number Ten of Being a Nomadic Goddess," I thought. "When in doubt – ask."

Never one to wait for an appropriate opening, I interrupted him in mid-sentence, and nervously blurted out, "I assumed when Liz first recommended I take the class, she meant there were other classmates. But as you can see, we are here *alone.* Where *is* everybody?"

Robert smiled indulgently and replied, "The other students opted for a later start time. They will be coming to the afternoon class."

"Funny," I said. "Liz didn't mention there was another class."

As I reflected on it some more, I realized I may have been too anxious to leave, and did not get all the details on the class offerings. But with Liz nowhere in sight, and feeling suddenly alone with this strange man, I began questioning the Raja Yoga motives again. Cult-kidnapping episodes started racing madly again through my mind.

However, this time I surprised myself. I thought, "Golden Apple Tosses are rare. I'm not about to miss this golden opportunity to become more spiritually enlightened. Besides – I can handle whatever comes up. I handled Hong Kong and Bangkok. I can certainly handle a little uncertainty here in Bali."

"Besides," I thought. "It's free! It fits my budget!"

"Point Number Eleven of Being a Nomadic Goddess," I recited. "Never look a gift horse in the eye."

"Or is it in the teeth?" I thought. Suddenly I felt confused over body parts.

"How ridiculous," I thought. "It's such a common saying. How could I possibly forget?"

Robert had already started his introduction again, and was talking about the soul being like a star and I suddenly heard an announcer's voice start talking excitedly over a loudspeaker inside my mind. He was yelling out, "THEY'RE AT THE GATES, FOLKS. STEADY. STEADY NOW. STAR OF FORTUNE IN GATE NUMBER SEVEN IS HAVING A LITTLE TROUBLE SETTLING DOWN, BUT I THINK SHE'S FINALLY READY. YES, YES.... AND – THEY'RE OFF!"

I watched my thoughts go racing at breakneck speed neck-in-neck down the 20 or so furlongs of my mind and I began to laugh. With all the excitement going on, I missed the first three minutes of Robert's introduction. But what I *didn't* miss, was the tremendous finish as my thoughts went crashing headlong through the tape – a photo finish if ever there was one.

"What a race!" I thought, marveling at the drama of it all. I began reflecting on my horse-racing days in university, and how I had worked in the Parimutuel Department calculating the prices paid to the winning ticket holders, and how I had lost my first summer paycheque betting on the horses. By the time I returned my attention to the scene at hand, I had missed Robert's entire introduction.

"Point Number Twelve of Being a Nomadic Goddess," I thought. "Pay attention."

Robert looked inquisitively at me. I knew that he knew I had not been listening. But somehow that did not seem to matter to him. He simply continued on, saying, "In Raja Yoga, we believe the original religion of the world is peace."

"I like that," I replied, beaming. "It's sounds so simple."

"Well, Valerie," he said, "did you also know the root of the word, religion is the Latin – religare – to reconnect? And yoga – in its truest translation means link, or union?"

"No," I replied. "I had no idea. I always thought yoga meant stretching, or exercise."

"Yes," he said, "most people do. But Raja Yoga means connecting with the Supreme. Raja means Supreme."

"Is Raja Yoga a religion?" I asked.

"No," he replied. "That is what attracted me to it. We have no religious dogma, no gurus, nor do we prostrate ourselves in front of stone images."

"Now *that's* different," I piped up. "I just came from Thailand where I watched people bowing in front of Buddha statues as a show of respect, but I saw it as giving *up* their self-respect. I guess that's why I never felt right doing it. Then when I learned Buddhism was about seeing we were *all* Buddhas – that we simply needed to wake up to our own true nature – it resonated with me instantly."

"You're right," he replied. "People in virtually every religion bow down to all kinds of stone statues as if they are bowing down to a God or a king. But in Raja Yoga we have another viewpoint. We believe *everyone* is a king!"

"Well *that's* certainly different," I said.

He ceremoniously tipped his crown and flashed me a royal smile.

"What you say does make a lot of sense, Robert," I replied, smiling. "The Thai monks did say meditation taught us how to put ourselves back in power. Could this be why you call everyone a king?"

Straightening his 'crown', Robert chuckled and said, "You are absolutely right. The raja in Raja Yoga also means king. We show you how to become self-sovereign – to not only become ruler of your sense organs, but also to become king over your own thoughts. That is the true nature of the soul."

"Sounds romantic," I said. "It reminds me of a story of a damsel in distress, and a king rides to her rescue. Only I'm the damsel *and* the king. I rescue myself! I like it. So – where do we start?"

"Okay," he said, adjusting his position. "Let us begin with the soul. The true nature of the soul is peace – pure and simple – peace. Maybe you have heard the saying, "Everyone is crying out for peace – just as soon as we win this war?"

"No," I laughed. "But nothing could be more true."

"Today's religions are at the heart of most wars," he continued. "Countries everywhere are fighting over the belief, "My God is better than your God." They spend most of their time looking for ways to rub each other's faces in the mud just to prove a point."

"And isn't it also interesting," he went on, "that since World War II and the beginning of what they call the Age of Peace, we have had over 160 wars?"

I laughed.

"Ironic, isn't it?" he replied. "What's funny, is we are all souls! But we forget, and we identify ourselves as a body – to say "I am Muslim, I am a leader, or I am black – we create a dangerous illusion."

"Even to say I am a boy or I am a girl creates all kinds of false beliefs," I added. "My mom wouldn't let me play the really fun games with my brothers – like football – because she said girls don't do that. I thought, "Horse ca ca. Who says so?"

"Right," he replied. "So if you consider yourself a soul, it changes everything."

"Yeah," I replied. "I like that."

"Okay," he said, "let me help you picture what a soul looks like."

He placed his index finger on the spot between his eyebrows.

"In divine visions," he explained, holding his finger in place, "the soul is seen as a shining micro-star radiating light from right here in the center of the forehead. It is a point of light, tinier than an atom, but infinitely more powerful. You cannot touch it, you cannot see it with your physical eyes. It is the Third Eye people talk about."

"Bingo!" I said. "That strikes a familiar chord! Is that what my metaphysics teacher, Troy, meant when he talked about opening the third eye through something he called, the Third Eye Initiation Ceremony?"

"Possibly," he replied.

"The reason I ask," I said, "is I took his course hoping to find out more about my intuition, but just ended up in tears. Everyone in the class had a lovely vision of their higher self, but all I saw was blackness. I can't tell you how crushed and humiliated I felt. I cried for an hour."

He listened intently, his eyes shining with compassion.

"What you think of as being a failure," he said, "was actually a victory! You see, you already knew your third eye was open! The day you began questioning the truths in life, was when your eye opened – the eye of awareness."

"Wow," I said, scratching my head. "You mean, I didn't have

to wear the orange socks after all?"

He looked at me. His face was a total blank.

"Oh," I said, laughing. "Let me explain. I spent years trying to learn to meditate. I thought it meant I had to see something – or hear a voice. But nothing ever happened, so I built up a real inferiority complex. When I met Troy, he explained that colors represented different characteristics, and if I wanted to rid myself of feelings of inferiority, wearing orange would help. So – I chose socks!"

"Fancy that," Robert said. "Did it work?"

"Yes," I replied, "and it is still working. I think about them whenever I hit tough hurdles in life. It gets me through. You see, orange also stands for courage and change."

"Glad to hear it," he said. "If it works, why not? Okay. Now let us get back to the soul, shall we?"

"Only if I get to bring along my orange socks!" I teased.

He smiled.

"Okay," he said. "Here it goes. The soul is an eternal spark of light and life – a self-luminous star. Your body can be destroyed, but your soul cannot."

I looked down at my body and tried to picture what my soul would look like riding around inside of it.

He watched me and motioned towards the ceiling and turned his eyes upward. Looking somewhat wistful, he went on. "If you are ever wondering what you really look like," he said, "pick a lovely clear night and go outside and look up at the magnificent shining constellations up above. Your soul is like a bright, radiant star. A pin-point of pulsating light. You are a dot, and I am a dot!"

"I love it, " I said, feeling all dreamy-eyed.

"Come to think of it," I said, "your star analogy reminds me of one of my most favorite special songs from childhood. The title of it was *Twinkle Twinkle Little Star, How I Wonder What You Are.* And now I know!"

"Right!" he replied, smiling.

I thought about it for a moment, and something else struck me.

"Oh my God!" I exclaimed. "You'll never guess what else I've been doing all my life! Why, I've been drawing star after star after star. I'm a doodler. Whenever I'm on the telephone or just sitting around contemplating, out comes my pen and no piece of paper is safe within a five-mile radius."

"That is very funny," Robert replied. "Do you suppose that maybe, just maybe – the soul I've been looking for all these years – isn't as elusive as I thought?" I asked. "Maybe it's been there all along, jumping up and down, doing somersaults and impossible contortions on the parallel bars and performing every stunt it knows just trying to get my attention – enticing me to draw it on pieces of paper?"

Robert smiled. The look in his eyes said it all.

"I can't believe it!" I exclaimed, dumbfounded. "It's just too amazing to think the star drawings I like to call doodles were actually my little soul calling up to me, "Hey! *You* up there! Here I am! Yoo Hoo. Looking for me? Why, I'm right here in front of you! Can't you *see* me? I know I'm *short*, but this is ridiculous. I've covered three pages of note paper in the time you've taken to make a three minute phone call. Puuuuulease. Give me a break!"

"And do you think when I failed to notice it," I continued, "it simply threw its tiny little "hands" in the air and yelled, "Sheesh! Guess she's just too busy looking for me in her psychic awareness classes and meditation retreats. That's okay by me! I've got all the time in the world – I'm *eternal* dontchaknow. I'll wait. She'll come around when she's good and ready."

Robert laughed.

"I guess it just ran off on its merry way," I said, "while I ran off to see the world."

Robert looked at me, smiling. He was obviously enjoying watching my lights go on.

"Darndest thing!" I exclaimed. "Here I am, halfway around the world, thousands of kilometers from home, and this itsy bitsy little star followed me all the way here because it wanted me to remember who I am! Amazing! Absolutely amazing!"

I scratched my head and sat back.

Robert got up and went to put on a tape.

He suggested I get comfortable, and said, "Just enjoy yourself. Have fun, and simply follow the guided visualization. It will give you a taste of the way Raja Yoga stimulates the mind with positive, uplifting thoughts and help you gain a sense of the peace we have been talking about."

I shifted my position to make sure my legs did not fall asleep. While I did this, Robert said, "Oh, and remember. Just let your eyes feel cool and relaxed – then – simply focus your attention on a point of light as if it is radiating out from the middle of your forehead."

At first, meditating with my eyes open felt more than a little strange. For one thing, I didn't know where to look. I asked Robert, and he suggested I look straight ahead at the image of a point of light radiating out from a red center, or at the wall – whichever I preferred. I chose the red center.

"Having your eyes open," he said softly, "actually makes it easier to meditate. The wall, or the image, never moves. It makes it a nice stable image to focus on. But if you were to close your eyes, your imagination would create all kinds of distracting images."

"That makes sense," I replied.

"As you follow the taped commentary," he went on, "you will begin to relax even more and picture yourself as light. Then, with more practice, you will be able to reach a heightened state of awareness, or something we call soul-consciousness, and you will begin identifying less and less with your body, and start to feel a natural sense of ease and detachment."

We were only gone six or seven minutes, but it was so incredibly powerful, it left me feeling wonderfully relaxed and peaceful – like I had been gone forever.

"Hm," I thought, drowsily. "Maybe I'll just go off and have a little nap."

I got up and thanked Robert for his introduction and toddled off, feeling like I had come out from a kindergarten class.

I decided it was time to track down some milk and cookies.

"Taking up the challenge of a Golden Apple Toss sure does make a goddess hungry," I thought. But then I reminded myself hypoglycemics did not eat cookies, so I opted to buy some sweet mangoes instead.

"Besides," I thought, as I walked towards the open-air morning market, "didn't orange socks provide the impetus for this entire Nomadic Goddess soul searching adventure? Well, why not skin a nice, bright *orange* mango and salute their memory?"

I arrived home with one large, beautiful mango – quickly got out my Swiss army knife, and proceeded to cut into its bright orange flesh. No sooner had I started, than I found myself standing helplessly by – and watching it slip handily out of my hands to slither silently and relentlessly down the front of my white t-shirt."

"Of course!" I exclaimed, smiling sardonically. "What *other* color would I be wearing?"

"HOW ABOUT ORANGE?" my little voice blurted out.

"Oh yeah?" I retorted. "Why do you say that?"

"You're in for some *big* changes, my friend," it replied.

"You're going to need all the help you can get!"

"Uh oh," I thought, grimacing. "Here we go again!"

TWENTY

Nomadic Goddess
Uncovers A Jewel

The next morning I arrived for class still smiling to myself about the*Twinkle Twinkle Little Star* discovery. "I love the way Robert tells stories," I thought. "It really appeals to the child in me. Most of my life I've spent being such a grownup."

As I thought about this, Robert came out from behind the room divider and smiled and said, "Welcome back! How are you after Lesson One? Do you have any questions?"

"Not really," I replied. "And that really surprises me. Normally when I take a new course, I have a million questions."

"Oh really," he replied. "What makes this time different?"

"I guess it's because what you've told me makes perfect sense," I answered. "And it jives with what I've learned in the Buddhist course. The only difference is, they never talk about a soul – and they certainly *never* talk about a Supreme Soul."

"Well," Robert replied, "as we go along, you will see there are many more differences – but it doesn't mean the two philosophies are incompatible. "

"Now, that's an interesting thought," I replied.

"Yes, I suppose it is," he said. "But just wait – you will see what I mean. So – are you ready for Lesson Two?"

"You bet your sweet stars!" I exclaimed, following him around to the classroom.

"For years I've been looking for my soul," I said, as I selected a cushion. "So when you told me my soul was a star, I felt like I'd discovered a precious lost jewel."

"That is beautiful!" he exclaimed. "Because that is what you are – a sparkling, flawless jewel – like a diamond. You just have to remember. And that, as it happens, is what today's lesson is about!"

"Great!" I exclaimed.

We sat down and he began. "Today, Valerie," he said, "I am going to ask you to remember your childhood. By that I mean, remember where you came from. Before you ever came into a body, you lived in a world of golden-red light; a timeless world filled with silence and peace; and all around you were other little star-souls – all tiny pin-points of light – twinkling away – radiating qualities of perfect peace and purity."

"Is that what that image represented that I meditated on yesterday – the point of light with the red background?" I asked.

"Why yes," Robert replied. "Precisely. And that world of light was your original home. It is what we call the Soul World."

"It sounds like such a lovely place," I replied. "Maybe that's where the sayings, 'Home Sweet Home' and 'Home Is Where The Heart Is' come from."

"Could be," Robert answered, smiling.

"Imagine that," I said, sparkling.

I liked the warm feelings I was getting. It had been eight months since I had left home.

"Well, if you think that is interesting," Robert continued, "you will be even more interested to know that you lived there with your parents – the mother and father of all souls. Christians call him God. In Raja Yoga we call him the Supreme Soul, or Shiva."

"Shiva," I repeated. "The name rings a bell, but I can't quite place it."

I searched my memory banks, while Robert went on.

I kept contemplating the name, but finally decided to bring my attention back to the lesson. I did not want to miss anything. Even so, I could not help feeling I was forgetting something very important.

Robert saw my dazed reaction, and his eyes twinkled. He gave me a knowing smile and said, "I can see we hit something. Anything you would like to share?"

"No, not really," I replied. "Just something from the past. I'll let you in on it when I figure it out."

"Okay," he replied, "but just let me add one more thing to the concept of God as a spiritual parent. Not only do we call him Shiva, but we also call him, "Baba". In Hindi, Baba means Dad – it is a term of endearment that helps us experience the closeness of that relationship."

"That's very sweet," I replied. "Only now I *really* can't relate. You see, I grew up with my Ukrainain Baba – my grandmother – so God as my Baba is just too weird!"

"Yes, I can see why," he said, smiling. "Okay, then let us go back to the Soul World, shall we? Do you suppose the soul enjoyed such complete peace there, that it would explain why people the world over yearn so much for the elusive quality they call peace and quiet?"

"Why yes," I replied, sitting up straighter. "That's precisely one of the reasons I went traveling."

"Well, let's take it one step further," he said. "What if we forgot the details of that world, but had such a deep sense of loss and longing, we felt compelled to search for it. Plus, we have lost our mom and dad – that is, God. Wouldn't you say it would make us orphans?"

"That's funny!" I replied. "Maybe that's where the term 'lost souls' comes from! It reminds me a lot of the Peter Pan story."

"Oh really," Robert said. "How so?"

"I just watched Hollywood's *Hook* update in Thailand," I answered. "It was a take-off on the Peter Pan character. *Hook* portrayed Peter Pan as a grown up – a high-achiever Yuppie-type corporate lawyer consumed by the hectic world of mergers and takeovers."

"Sounds entertaining!" Robert replied.

"You've got that right!" I exclaimed. "I felt as if I was watching my own life. The grown-up Peter Pan's life gets thrown into complete turmoil when his children are kidnapped by the vicious and vengeful Captain Hook – his archenemy from childhood, and he launches himself on a quest to rescue them."

"Sounds like a marvelous adventure," Robert observed.

"Yes it was," I replied, "because in the movie, he had to go back to the Land of Never Never – a land where children never grow up – a wondrous land of magic and freedom. But when he arrives, his comrades-at-arms, the *Lost Boys* – a battalion of orphan boys – come out to welcome him back, but are utterly horrified when they discover their fearless leader has not only grown up, but he has also lost all his special powers!"

"He doesn't even remember how to fly!" one of them cries out, and they all stand back in utter horror and yell, "Why, *he's* been gone so long he's forgotten everything!"

"How extraordinary!" Robert exclaimed. "That is exactly what we are talking about."

"Well, Robert," I replied, beginning to feel excited. "Maybe *that's* why I've been so intent on searching for the Meaning of Life – I knew there was something missing, and from what you're telling me – the missing ingredient is *peace!*"

"Yes," Robert answered, "that and maybe a sense of belonging. And did you know peace is the real oxygen of the soul?"

"Why is that?" I asked.

"If you think about it," he said, "when we do not have it, we choke and we gasp and we look for it everywhere."

I laughed.

"How would you like me to tell you a fairytale?" he said.

"Oh, goodie!" I exclaimed. "I love stories. Let the show begin!"

I shifted around in my seat and got comfortable. I felt like an eager young child awaiting a special treat.

I looked expectantly at Robert. His eyes were gleaming.

"Once upon a time," he began.

I began laughing and he said, "No, no. Just teasing."

He winked back and said, "First of all, Valerie, let us set the stage. Think of the intellect – your deciding power – as the king, and then picture your soul's characteristics and thoughts as the subjects. Then, look at the mind as the kingdom."

"Okay," I replied. "I'm set."

"Okay, now. Imagine how, in the beginning, there was complete and natural control of the thoughts. The soul was full of love and peace and power. But then, unbeknownst to the king, impure tendencies and thoughts began entering the kingdom and before long, they master-minded a perfect coup d'état and handily deposed the intellect king and began ruling the self – running rampant over the kingdom, and forcing the king to surrender. The king felt utterly defeated and totally despondent and went into exile. He knew he was no longer fit to rule. He had lost all his power."

Robert stopped talking and looked straight at me.

"What kind of a fairy tale is that?" I blurted out. "I thought fairy tales always had a happy ending. You know, 'And they all lived happily ever after.' *That* kinda stuff."

"Aha," he said, smiling mischievously. "That is where Raja Yoga comes in!"

"Oh," I blushed.

He winked and said, "Yoga means to connect, Valerie. When you connect with the Supreme – or Raja – you draw power from him and you become king (Raja) over your senses and over the parts of your character you would like to change."

"Is that like recharging your battery?" I asked.

"Well, yes," he replied. "You feed in that super-charged power of positivity and goodness and discard all your negative habits. That way, your intellect 'king' can once again claim its rightful place on the throne. It can decide what is the right thought to think and what is the right action to take."

I smiled. I liked his concept of the battery charger.

"Have you seen the television commercial for Duracell batteries?" Robert asked, as if he had read my mind. "You know, the one where they show a little toy soldier drumming?"

"Yes," I answered, smiling. "It's one of my favorites."

"Well, do you remember," he inquired, "that as its batteries wore down, he reached a point where he could drum no more?"

Before I could answer, Robert fell over on his side and promptly "died." Then, seconds later, he miraculously came back to life.

I laughed. He smiled back at me and straightened himself up and said, "Well, that is the case with people today. All of us souls are like little drummers who have run out of energy and fallen off our thrones. Now it is the Supreme Soul's job to come and introduce himself and teach us how to recharge our spiritual batteries."

"That's a blast!" I exclaimed. "Are you saying God comes and plays the role of a Super-Charger – that he jump-starts the soul?" "Precisely," Robert replied, smiling.

"And you say that God – or who you call Shiva – gives his *own* introduction?" I queried.

"Yes, well," Robert replied – suddenly looking a little nervous. For the first time since we had met, he pointedly avoided my gaze.

"I'd be interested to know how God *does* that," I ventured – choosing to ignore his discomfort. "It sounds pretty bizarre."

"Let us just leave that for now, shall we?" he replied. "We will talk about it later."

With that, he smiled tightly and I thought, "What's he hiding? How could a guy like God introduce himself, anyway? I mean – would he come and extend his hand and say, "Hello there. My name is God – and what might your name be, sweet soul?"

I thought about it for a bit, then laughed, and quickly turned my attention back to Robert.

"By focusing on the soul's original virtues," he said, "we build a life based on virtues – pure values, if you will."

"Your idea about virtuous living," I remarked, "is similar to what the Buddhists called, "The Noble Eightfold Path of Right Living".

"That's right," Robert replied, "and by building virtues, we not only experience a more pleasant side of ourselves, but we also experience it in others too. We remember it is also their original attributes – they have simply forgotten them."

"That makes sense, too," I responded.

"Well," he said, leaning back, "since I started Raja Yoga seven years ago, I have changed dramatically – even my friends and family say so. I am easier-going, more tolerant – even more patient."

"Really?" I said. "Well, I like the idea of it, but what I don't understand is, how do I meditate on God? I don't even know who or what he is!"

"Oh," Robert said, looking a little surprised. "I guess I forgot to mention that he is is also a point of light – just like us – only his light shines the brightest because he has never lost his purity and power by coming into a body."

"But that doesn't make sense!" I exclaimed. "For one thing, I was taught God was limitless – which to me, means huge!

How can he possibly be just a tiny point of light?"

Robert laughed and said, "Good point!"

Then he laughed again and said, "Oops! No pun intended! What I mean is, God is limitless – but limitless in virtues. Power really has nothing to do with size – just look at the atom. And did you know that atmah, in hindi, means the soul, which sounds just like atom?"

"Hm," I replied, rubbing my chin. "I never thought about it that way. Tell you what, let me consider what you've said and I'll get back to you. But right now, there's something else I want to ask you. You said God's power never decreases because he never comes into a body. What mystifies me, is – why do we lose our power and virtues in the first place? What is it about coming into a body that de-energizes us?"

Robert's eyes twinkled and he shifted his cushion.

"Quite simply, Valerie," he said, settling into his new position, "it is the Law of Entropy. It is a scientific law that says every time energy – in this case – our soul – changes form – which means we take a new body – there is less available energy for the next go-around."

"You mean if I believe in reincarnation," I replied, "your theory would explain why the world has changed and become so much more violent and out of balance over the last few centuries?"

"Exactly," Robert said. "That is because we were more pure, then. We had more spiritual power – a stronger sense of right and wrong. That is why you see more anger and hatred and possessiveness in the world today. Not only that, but it is increasing."

"Okay," I said, "so how do we reverse this trend?"

"Well," he replied, "things get topped up by God and we all begin the cycle of time again!"

"That's weird!" I piped up.

"Well," Robert said, smiling. "Think about it. Who but God could recreate the lost energy? He is the only one who has never been caught in the state of entropy – unlike the rest of the universe."

"You've got a point, there," I said, scratching my head. "But it's still pretty unbelievable."

"Okay Valerie," he said, smiling even more brightly. "Think of a full moon. It slowly decreases in degrees, only to become completely full again; a circle – which is, by the way, the symbol of perfection."

My face lit up and I exclaimed, "Wow! Now you've hit something I can relate to! I've been fascinated with the full moon for some time now. When I was at home, before I started traveling, I was totally mesmerized – magnetized – by the soft white moon perfectly outlined in the dark blue sky. Then – when I started my spirit quest – I started tracking it – charting the length of my journey by its phases."

"Well," Robert said, smiling, "maybe it is your soul waking up to its own memory of wholeness and perfection!"

I did not respond. I just gave him a blank look.

Robert looked at me and laughed and said, "I can see you have gone into overload!"

"Is it that obvious?" I replied, playfully rolling my eyes back into my head.

"I would say it is time to relax and let things flow," he said, his eyes sparkling. "What do you say we do a little meditation?"

"Okay, I'm game," I replied.

"What I would like you to do," he said softly, "is to listen to the words on the tape and try to imagine yourself in your original state of perfection. Relax, and try to keep your eyes open. And remember – enjoy yourself. That is what meditation is all about."

"That's a new concept," I replied. "My time in the Buddhist monastery wasn't all that enjoyable. As a matter of fact, some days it was actually quite stressful – trying to follow my breath and attempting to stop my thoughts."

"Well," Robert replied, "our method is not about stopping the mind, so it should be easier. But there is also something else I would like you to try. It may help you to detach from your surroundings more easily."

"Okay," I said. "What's that?"

"Begin to see your life and your journey of self-discovery," he said, "as one big dramatic play created purely for your own enjoyment and entertainment. Just allow yourself to sit back and enjoy the show."

"Sounds fine by me," I replied.

He dimmed the lights and I shifted my legs into a comfortable position.

I prepared to focus on the woman's soft voice drifting imperceptibly towards me from somewhere off in the corner of the room, and I could hear her saying, "Picture yourself as a soul. I am a tiny star...I have no size. I am really just a pin-point of light...I can easily detach from the world around me..no longer does the physical world pull my senses...on the screen of my mind, I picture my destination...a world of light beyond the sun, moon and the stars...a region of soft, subtle golden-red light..on the wings of thought I fly there...I experience my natural original qualities of peace, love, power, joy....I recognize this world...my sweet home...total silence..."

Before I knew it, the meditation was over. I felt like I had been on some etheric vacation – transported to some long lost world.

"That was lovely," I said, trying to refocus my eyes to take in the whole room. "And your technique worked very well. I did kind of feel detached from my body – like I was glowing from somewhere deep inside of myself. I also had this incredible, overwhelming sense of peace."

"That is fantastic!" Robert said, smiling. "It is exactly what Raja Yoga is all about. You know, Valerie – even if you forget everything else I teach you – all you really need to remember is that you are a soul – and that peace is your original religion."

"I like that," I replied. "It's nice and simple."

"Yes, " he said, eyes sparkling. "Isn't it though?"

The theme song from the Wizard of Oz popped into my head and I started humming the words, "I'm off to see the Wizard, the wonderful Wizard of Oz."

"That's strange," I thought. "Where did *that* come from? And what's Dorothy got to do with Raja Yoga?"

Before I could answer myself, Robert got up and stepped forward and asked me how much longer I would be in town.

"One more day," I replied, getting up from my cushion.

He smiled back at me and said, "The reason I ask, is I just want to let you know that we have covered most of the basics already. There is really just a little more left."

I stepped out onto the road, and no sooner had I waved goodbye, than the *Wizard of Oz* song jumped back into my head. I suddenly thought, "You know, old Dorothy was a nomadic goddess just like me. She left home to go off on an adventure as well."

I instantly began mimicking Dorothy's most memorable line of the entire movie. "There's no place like home," I sang out, "there's no place like home!"

"Dorothy buddy," I thought, "you certainly hit it big on that one!"

I stopped dead in my tracks.

"Oh God!" I thought. "Could it be that Robert's tale about the Soul World, and how it's the home of the Supreme Soul is actually about Dorothy's real home – *all* of our real homes? Could it be that the infamous golden yellow brick road really leads to the golden world of light? And if that's so, I guess that makes God the real Wizard!"

"Holy Toledo!" I exclaimed.

"Well, if it is," I said, suddenly laughing. "I think it's a brilliant analogy!"

"And suppose, just suppose," I continued on – my mind racing – "all of the characters were combined to make up just *one* Nomadic Goddess! How utterly symbolic! Why, the whole story is actually about the journey of every soul on its road to enlightenment!"

I stopped walking and stood staring out over the nearby rice fields. I felt in that sudden, golden moment, everything had become perfectly clear.

"All of us are here to discover who and what we really are," I thought. "We're all digging deep down inside ourselves and finding the courage to confront our fears – just like the Lion. And we're looking inside our minds and learning ways to use our minds more effectively – hence the Scarecrow who's looking for a brain – and most of all, we need heart – just like the Tin Man. Otherwise, if we didn't have heart, we'd give up before we started."

"That's incredible!" I exclaimed.

I ran down the stairs and over the little swinging bridge and into my bungalow at Nick's Pension and waved and called out, "Good morning," to Made, the young man managing the homestay.

"Breakfast in a minute," he yelled, as he ran off towards the kitchen.

"What a sweetheart," I thought, "and what a dynamite cook. His banana-coconut pancakes are out of this world."

"I may never leave this little piece of paradise," I thought, settling in to await my feast – wondering what adventures the next day would bring.

TWENTY ONE

Nomadic Goddess
Hits The Spin Cycle

Walking to class the next day, I found myself completely preoccupied with thoughts of leaving Ubud. What surprised me the most, were my thoughts of leaving Robert.

"I'm actually sad about it!" I exclaimed. "I never even expected to *like* the course, let alone find it so fascinating!"

My little voice popped up and retorted, "You never expected to find such an entertaining teacher, either – or so many mysteries; unveiled or otherwise."

I laughed and thought, "You've got that right, sweet little Nomadic Goddess!"

I walked into the Meditation Shop. No one was around, so I stood reading an 8"x10" framed write-up – the same poster I had read the very first day I entered, when I was on my reconnaissance mission.

But this time it hit me in a totally different way. I felt drawn into the words, as if someone was saying them directly to me.

It read:

You call me God, Jehovah, Allah and Shiva.
You have built churches, temples, mosques and statues to Me.

You have waged wars in My name and made sacrifices to Me.
You say that I am in nature, or in the sky. You say that I am every-
where. When you suffer, you call out to Me for help. When you are
happy, you forget Me.
You have worshipped Me in human form and yet you do not know
Me.
Prophets and Teachers have tried to point the way to Me, but no-
one has found Me.
I am your Father, and I am the one with whom you can have all
relationships.
I am not born and, like you, I can never die.
I am light. My form is a tiny invisible point. You too are a subtle
point of light. My world is the world of silence and peace. You used to
dwell with Me there, in that golden silence.
Then you were born into a body and began to create your story.
You forgot your home and you forgot Me.
I have come again to remind you of who you are.
I have come again to reveal to you the secrets of Time.
I have come again to fill you with all of the Love and Power and
Peace that you have missed for so long.
Remember.

"Remember," I repeated to myself, "remember."

It was as if something had been lying dormant inside of
me for a very long time, and by reading that one word, I somehow felt "awakened". I felt suspended in time, imagining myself as Sleeping Beauty, and the word was like the kiss of a
prince. I smiled to myself as I pictured a shiny red apple, and
thought, "Of course. The whole reason I'm in this course is
because of the Goddess's Golden Apple toss. What else would
I expect!"

Robert stepped quietly into the room. His silent entrance
startled me. I abruptly turned to face him. Bemused by my surprised look, he smiled sweetly back and softly said, "Hello."

"Hello, yourself!" I exclaimed. He smiled again and excused
himself and disappeared around the corner.

I turned back to the poster and reread the part about, 'I have
come again to remind you of who you are,' and thought, "is
this what Robert keeps going on about? But then, why is he
being so evasive – especially if it's all right here in this poster?
What do you suppose he's up to?"

Just as I thought this, Robert reappeared and smiled at me sweetly. He noticed I had been reading the poster, but didn't say a word. Instead, he motioned graciously towards the classroom and said, "So – shall we begin?"

I went behind the room divider with thoughts of princes and princesses and shining red apples and the poster's words about how God had come to pay us a visit, still dancing in my mind.

"Remember Shakespeare's famous words?" Robert began. "All the world is a stage and we are but actors playing out our roles in a world drama?"

"I sure do," I replied. "It's one of my favorites."

"Well," he went on, "instead of seeing ourselves as people, or bodies, picture yourself as a soul acting out a role. You adopt a body like an actor adopts a costume, play out your role, and then – when your role is over – you simply shed your body or costume and go on to adopt a new costume and play out a new role."

"You know," I said, "that sounds like a great way to detach from my whole life!"

"Think about it," he said, eyes all aglow. "Not only are you an actor-soul, but so are all the other five and a half billion people on the planet – and our stage is the earth, and the sun and the moon and the stars are our lighting system. And what is more, it is an eternal world drama."

"Bravo! Bravo!" I called out, applauding excitedly. "Who would have thought something as serious as metaphysics and spirituality could be so entertaining? Is this what they mean when they say, "The show must go on?"

"Why – yes indeed," he replied. "And if you like that, you'll enjoy this next example. Let us go back to the costume angle for a moment, shall we?"

"You know, Robert," I interrupted. "All along when I thought I've been putting on my wardrobe, I've actually been putting a costume over my real costume – over my body! That's hysterical!"

"Yes, isn't it?" he replied.

"Okay Valerie," he said, nodding, "yesterday I touched on the possibility of a world cycle and I promised I would have some thought-provoking ideas for today's lesson. Well – it is

211

time: time to raise the curtain on what we call the Eternal World Drama."

"Oh, goodie!" I cried. "You mean you're finally going to help me solve all the great mysteries you've been promoting?"

"Yes indeed," he said, smiling playfully. "I made a promise and I am going to keep it. So here it goes. Remember how we talked about the symbol of the circle?"

"Yes," I replied. "I remember you saying something about that."

"Well," he went on, "it represents infinity – or if you like – eternity – because as I said yesterday – we believe time is cyclical. It never begins, and it never ends."

"Isn't that interesting," I said. "In my high school mathematics, I knew infinity meant without end, but I never entertained the possibility it also meant no beginning!"

"But everything else in life is an unending cycle," Robert replied. "Why not time? We have got economic cycles, the changing seasons, day and night, the phases of the moon – even our lifetimes are a cycle of birth, growth, decline and death."

"Yes," I replied, "but cyclical *time* seems way too bizarre."

"Well, if you think that is bizarre, wait until you hear the twist," he said, smiling mischievously. "Not only is it eternal, but the world drama cycle also repeats identically."

"Hey, wait a minute Robert," I said, springing into action. "Are you saying what I think you're saying?"

"Maybe," he replied, eyes sparkling gamefully.

"Are you saying I've lived this lifetime before," I retaliated, "exactly the same way that I'm living it at this very moment?"

He smiled innocently, watching my mind do leaps and somersaults.

When he surmised I had finished doing my mental gymnastics, he laughed and said, "Yes indeed, Valerie. You are quite correct. You and I have met before, and we talked about the very same things, and you wore the same clothes you have on today, and you had the same astounded look on your face, and you said exactly what you are going to say."

"This is a real shocker!" I exclaimed. "Does that mean that whatever I do this very next moment will be indelibly recorded and replayed over and over again for posterity? God! That means that whatever I do will echo throughout eternity!"

"Now don't go getting all upset about this," Robert said, observing my look of growing concern. "Just take it slow. Give it some time; let it settle into your intellect for a while."

I looked at him – dazed.

"Let me point out one more thing," Robert said, carefully choosing his words. "Look at the upside of all this. It helps make sense of some of the world's biggest puzzles. Take the saying, "History repeats itself."

"Bingo," I said, pulling myself together and sitting up straighter. "Maybe that's why psychics are able to see the future, because they're actually seeing the distant past!"

"Exactly," he replied. "If you picture time as a cycle, it makes sense of the three aspects of time; past, present and future. That is why we say all three are the same. What was the past was at some point the present, and what is the present, will immediately become the past, and the future becomes the present."

"That's just too weird," I replied, scratching my head. "But what's even weirder, is it's the only explanation I've ever heard that actually makes sense! But I can't say I like the idea."

"Yes," he replied. "I felt the same way when I first heard about it."

"Yeah?" I answered. "Well, I can't say that I like the concept of making the same stupid mistakes I've made in the past, and enduring the same kind of pain. Yuch."

"Think of it another way, Valerie," Robert replied, smiling brightly. "You also get to do all of the things you have enjoyed again and again."

"Oh yeah," I answered, feeling my mood brighten considerably. "I never thought about that."

"So tell me," I said, imploringly. "Is this role-playing stuff compulsory, or can a soul opt out? I mean, can I choose an easier elective and get out of playing a part in this Eternal World Drama of yours?"

Robert smiled.

"Guess that's a 'No,' then?" I ventured.

Still no answer.

"Okay," I replied. "I get it."

As I thought some more about Robert's Merry-Go-Round of Life, I recalled my childhood days riding the merry-go-round at St. Andrews park. My brothers – being the bullies they were – and sibling rivalry being what *it* was – I invariably found myself face down on the pavement. Then I would turn over, look down at my scraped, bleeding knees and go running home crying, "I'M GOING TO TELL MOMMY AND BOY ARE YOU GONNA GET IT!"

I was – after all – the only girl in the family at the time, and my two brothers certainly kept me going in circles.

"Nothing new under the sun, alright," I mumbled to myself. "Just more of the same old silly stuff. Well, dear brothers – see you *next* cycle. Same time, same place."

I laughed and applied a few mental bandaids and brought my attention back to Robert.

"Something else you may be interested to know," he said, "is that the original meaning of the word, universe is "the turning of one."

"Wow!" I exclaimed. "That's incredible!"

"Yes," he replied, "isn't it though?"

"But what I don't get," I went on, "is this concept of "a deja vu that won't stop vu-ing!" I mean – what's the point? Why bother to do this life again and again? Wouldn't it make more sense to create a new role each time – so it doesn't get boring?"

"Actually, no," Robert answered. "Every event appears to be new because we do not remember what happened the last time around. Remember how I said we lose our spiritual power and suffer self-forgetfulness?"

"Oh, yeah," I said, smiling back at him. "Ironic, isn't it? And you know, something else has just come to mind with this eternal repetition idea of yours; a joke a friend of mine told me – or rather the punch line. It says: "Please God. Don't let me die doing something stupid."

Robert laughed.

"What do you suppose something stupid would look like, Valerie?" he asked, smiling amusedly.

"I'd rather not think about it, thank you very much," I said, beginning to feel a little irritated. "Could we just go on?"

"Okay," he said. "Let me just finish up on the World Drama idea. Once all the actor souls leave the Soul World and come onto the stage, the World Drama reaches its climax and all the souls go backstage – back to their home of golden-red light. God removes everyone's sorrow, and takes them all home." I listened intently and thought, "But where does he get all this information? So much of it seems impossible and even a little bit bizarre." I decided it was time to go fishing again.

"Okay," I said, adjusting my position for what seemed the fiftieth time. "I give up. You've been telling me all about souls and God and the Soul World, and now you tell me there's a climax and all the souls go backstage. But what does that mean – exactly? Does everybody die and return to the Soul World and we start the game over again? And if that's the case, who says any of this is true?"

"Whoa, whoa," Robert said, motioning like he had been run over by my stampede of questions. "I can see I have stimulated your intellect!"

I looked obstinately back at him.

He smiled and said, "My answers are; Yes, Yes and God!"

With that, he sat triumphantly back on his cushion, crossed his arms in front of him, and laughed at his little game of Chess.

I grinned and thought, "I think he fancies 'God' as his checkmate!"

"Are you saying *God* told you this story?" I said, incredulously. "Oh, I get it – you're still talking about this 'God's introduction' bit. Well, I say it's utterly impossible."

"Well," he said – in a gentler voice, "if you will bear with me until I finish the story, you can decide for yourself!"

"Well," I replied, rather hesitantly, "tell me something else – how long is this play?"

"Five thousand years."

It was all I could take.

"That does it," I thought. "I was willing to try and handle his God answer, but now he's challenging Darwin's Theory of Evolution! Teachers and newspapers have been feeding me this stuff since I was a kid! I've been nursed along on the Ape Becomes Man story, like a mother feeds pablum to a baby. He certainly can't be serious to think the world is only 5,000 years old!"

"Now that's where I draw the line!" I piped up. "What you say just isn't possible!"

I put my hands on my hips and glared at him.

215

Robert smiled back and asked me ever-so-innocently, "So! Have I pushed any buttons yet?"

I laughed and feigned a frown.

"Well," he said, "did you know that virtually all the world religions put the age of the earth at between 4,000 and 6,000 years old? It is only since the advent of science – say, the last 100 years or so – that we have been talking millions and billions of years."

"Yeah, but what about Darwin's Theory of Evolution?" I retorted.

"Well, Valerie," he answered, "many scientists argue against it, because there have never been any documented cases of the transmutation of one species into another – and that is at the very heart of Darwin's theory. A monkey is still a monkey, and an amoeba has not become a human being!"

"Hm," I said, rubbing my chin thoughtfully. "I've never thought about it that way."

He laughed and replied, "Consider that maybe, just maybe, our ancestors were neither monkeys nor cave-dwellers, but human beings who possessed a deep and natural understanding of the world they lived in. For the sake of a better term let us call it the Golden Age – a time when everything was at its highest level of purity."

"A Golden Age," I repeated. "My my, Robert. Do you mean to say you believe there really was a time when people where totally happy and there was no suffering and people lived in complete harmony?"

"Why, yes Valerie," he answered. "Why not? We were self-realized, fully soul-conscious divine beings."

"Sounds positively *divine!*" I joked. "Is this Golden Age like Heaven on Earth? The Garden of Eden, shall we say?"

"Why yes, as a matter of fact it is," Robert replied. "It is also called the Kingdom of Heaven."

"But my Sunday School training taught me the Kingdom of Heaven was somewhere up there," I said, pointing towards the ceiling.

"Well, there is actually a very simple explanation for that," he answered, his eyes following the line of my finger. "Words like Heaven and Hell are symbolic. Heaven is not a place up in the sky – nor is Hell a fiery pit where we are punished for our sins. They are merely periods of history that are referred to when our consciousness is either high or low. You see, we were once gods and goddesses – self-realized beings. Then, we slowly became self-forgetful and became what we are now – living in Hell, or what we call the Iron Age."

"You know," I said, "I have to admit your description about gods and goddesses makes some sense to me. I've recently been studying goddess mythology, and I've even gone so far as to create a whole new class of goddess I jokingly call, The Nomadic Goddess – in honor of my solitary journey."

"Good for you!" he said, smiling. "If you consider the Golden Age is indeed where today's mythology originated, you can see why they were called gods and goddesses – they were God-like with their qualities of peace, power and purity."

I sat and quietly contemplated what he was saying. It really was amazing.

He could see I was quite taken with it, so he went on.

"In the cycle of time," he continued, "we are now in the last quarter of the cycle, the Iron Age. Everything has become totally degraded. Our air, water, and food are becoming more and more toxic because we have reached our lowest point of power. Our thoughts are focused mostly on the negative, and we are affecting the nature all around us."

I suddenly began laughing – even though I knew it was no laughing matter. I had recently seen a poster showing a photo of the earth floating around in space and the caption read, "Save The Humans."

Robert looked on in amusement.

"Can't argue with that," I replied, as I related scenes from my travels which were flooding into my mind. I described how my journey through the third world countries had shown me the rain forest devastation and the extraordinary amount of pollution running rampant over the countryside, and how I flashed back to the people who were literally drowning in their own waste in Bangkok.

"We self-forgetful human beings," Robert went on, "have gone millions of miles into space, yet we have not advanced one millimeter into understanding the self! As you can see, we have lost our moral strength and spiritual health, and now we are faced with cleaning up the mess."

"Well, Robert," I answered, "I've always believed scientists would magically invent something to save us. But if I'm reading you right, you're saying it's not going to come from some source outside of ourselves. Rather, we have to clean ourselves up, first."

"You are right, Valerie," he replied. "That is why so many people are turning to meditation and spirituality; they are waking up and seeing the old ways are not working."

"Yeah," I piped up. "They've realized science isn't delivering the goods like happiness and security, or freedom from disease. I guess you're right, Robert. It *is* up to us, as individuals, to do something."

Robert nodded.

"And the New Age, as it is called," he said, "is simply a time of heightened awareness and accountability. But what is funny, is humankind is recycling products, when indeed it is the whole world and all the souls that get re-cycled and made new again! Even the symbol we use on the recycled products shows arrows pointing clockwise in the direction of a circle, so the recycling programs are actually a memorial of the eternally-spinning world cycle!"

"You're crackers," I said, smiling. "What's more, you're positively outrageous!"

"Well, if you think that is funny," he said, laughing, "you will like the story behind the swastika. It is also a circle pointing clockwise – a symbol for wholeness – just like a circle represents completeness. In the East, it is considered to be an auspicious symbol – one of prosperity and great wealth. Businessmen place it in the front of their accounting ledgers to bring good luck."

"Imagine that!" I replied. "I thought it was something evil."

"Actually, no," he replied. "If you look at it closely, you will see the top right quarter actually represents the Golden Age – a time of happiness and prosperity, so the insignia is really about spiritual perfection – when we reach our purest, most powerful stage.

"I've had enough!" I exclaimed, leaning back and stretching my legs. "These concepts are unbelievable. Not only is what you say mind-boggling, but I've just had the most incredible revelation!"

"Yes?" he said, smiling. "And what might that be?"

"Would you believe that as a child," I said, sitting up straighter, "my twin brother and I designed tiny swastikas from wood, then put a link chain through them and sold them to our classmates in Grade Four? Boy, did *we* get in trouble. What would a couple of nine-year-olds know about Nazism? We just thought it made a pretty neat piece of jewelry!"

"Isn't that fascinating!" Robert exclaimed, glowing.

"Yes," I said. "So tell me Robert – were we tapping into our intuition and recreating the world cycle or were we simply two young, aspiring Yuppie capitalists out to make a profit by cornering something called, The Elementary School, World War II Personal Adornment Memorabilia Market?"

Robert smiled and answered, "I believe it is the former! You see, children are more in touch with their original qualities of purity and innocence; they have much cleaner intellects – even though we argue they are "underdeveloped."

I chuckled and said, "Well, Robert. On that note, I'll take my leave. You've managed to turn my whole world upside down – and I still don't know much about your mysterious source of information. You keep saying God delivered this news, but I've seen nothing about it any of the newspapers. So...what's the scoop?"

Robert smiled and replied, "Tell you what. There is a whole lot more to it than I can explain to you as you walk out that door. Do not worry about the source; just try out this knowledge. See if it rings true for you."

"Okay," I replied. "I'm going up to Tulumben to do some snorkeling for a short while. There's a pretty neat shipwreck I want to check out. While I'm there, I'll spend a few days thinking about what you've said. Then, I'll be back for more answers."

"Okay," Robert replied. "But I must say, I am surprised that you have stayed this long. Liz told me you had a Buddhist meditation method and philosophy you were happy with. Yet – you are still here!"

"That's because I have a good sense of humor!" I remarked – winking.

"Well," he said, winking back, "I am a firm believer that humor is a key ingredient in spirituality. If spirituality was not so much fun, I would not do it!"

I stepped thoughtfully onto the front steps and into the blinding morning sunlight. I had to shield my eyes for a moment. Once they adjusted, I looked around, and began to take in the scene in front of me. The streets were awash with tourists and shopkeepers and motorcycles and tour buses. It was absolute chaos.

"Just another day in Paradise," I remarked, stepping onto the road.

"*Lost* Paradise – that is," I added, as I dodged an oncoming motorscooter.

I turned and waved good-bye and promised to return in a couple of days.

A van went by with a bus board advertising shampoo. The slogan read, "Remember."

"That's strange," I thought. "Didn't I just read that on the poster inside before class?"

I smiled to myself and walked thoughtfully down the road. I found myself observing every motion and thinking, "You mean 5,000 years ago, I was actually right here on this very street, at this very same time of the morning, walking down this very same Monkey Forest Road and thinking about the very same fantastic coconut banana pancakes I know are just waiting to be devoured back at Nick's Pension?

"How very very weird. Somehow it seems impossible to believe, and yet..."

As I was busy considering the possibilities, I failed to lift my foot and stubbed my toe on the uneven pavement. Cursing, I looked down at my toe, now throbbing with pain, and exclaimed, "I can't believe I get to do something as stupid as stubbing my big toe every 5,000 years for the rest of eternity! Who wants to do something that nerdy, that embarrassing, and that stupid – *forever*?"

"*You* will," my little voice piped up.

"OH YEAH?" I yelled back, belligerently. "WE'LL SEE ABOUT *THAT* LITTLE MISS SMARTYPANTS!"

"Darn," I thought. "Everytime that little voice of mine pipes up, it's been right. I hate that!"

TWENTY TWO

But What Will
My Family Say?

The next day I packed up and headed north – my mind swimming with all the things Robert had related to me.

Sitting at the front of the bemo – a converted Volkswagen van that served as a public bus on Bali, a thought occurred to me. Shivers of recognition ran up and down my spine.

I recalled how Robert had talked about God being called Baba and how we could experience the closeness of a father, or a dad – someone we could go to for comfort or advice or protection. I thought, "Hm. That is so strange."

The shivers intensified and I covered my bare arms with my sarong – even though it was a hot, humid morning.

"Baba," I thought.

For the first 15 years of my life, my Ukrainian grandmother – my Baba, lived with my family. How I loved her. She was the kind of a grandma every little girl loved.

"Every little *Ukrainian* girl, that is," I thought, getting out a snack.

She was rotund and soft and loving and fiercely protective, and she smelled of perogies and cabbage rolls and paska – fresh-baked Easter bread, my three most favorite foods in the whole wide world. My Baba and I would spend hours working together in the garden, cutting cabbage and making sauerkraut in huge crock urns. We would mend clothes on the verandah, or she would let me help her roll the dough for perogies, and sometimes I would sneak off into my mom's bedroom and pinch a bit of my Baba's raw sweet bread dough which was sitting out on the bed rising in the morning sun. On Sundays I would take my Baba to the Ukrainian Greek Orthodox church and endure three painfully long hours of unintelligible mass delivered in Latin or Ukrainian – I was never really quite sure which was which. The words all seemed to run together.

"Baba," I thought wistfully, as I looked out the window of the bemo, watching smiling young children lovingly being given fruit by a wrinkled old woman bending over them on the roadside.

"Must be their grandmother," I thought, smiling.

They saw me smiling and smiled back.

The grandmother looked up, saw me, and held up some fruit and motioned for me to take some. I waved and mouthed a "Thank you" and thought, "My sweet Baba. Where are you now?"

Suddenly I could feel the sensation of her warm, pudgy hand move over mine and her smiling eyes looking softly down at me.

I broke down and wept. I finally understood what unconditional love really meant.

The van sped by yet another village filled with families sitting alongside the road watching the traffic. I looked at them through my tear-filled eyes and thought, "You know – I really miss you Baba. You were the best friend I ever had. You gave me everything I ever needed."

I dried my eyes and reached for another tissue.

"But you know what's really weird Baba?" I said. "I have the strangest feeling you really are here with me – right now – holding my hand and encouraging me to meet another kind of a Baba. There are no accidents, they say (*they* being the guys with the free advice). And if what *they* say is true, and I take Robert's explanation of the word Baba, and add it to my other list of coincidences like the swastika jewelry and my star doodles, it's really quite incredible. So many of the pieces fit together – yet if I stand back and take a good look at it, I double over in fits of laughter. The whole story is so bizarre! I mean – really. Who'd ever *believe* such a story?"

"Why, *you* do, Valerie," my little voice popped up.

I sat up defensively and said, "*Look*, little voice. I do not! If I ever told anyone this story they'd toss me in a loony bin." The little voice persisted.

"Do so," it teased back.

I retaliated and answered, "Do not!"

"*Do so*," it answered.

I set my jaw and yelled, "DO NOT AND THAT'S THAT!"

The thought hounded me the whole time I toured the island. I could not seem to get it out of my mind.

Eventually I gave in and laughed to myself and exclaimed, "Self! You are in *mighty* big trouble, sweet Nomadic Goddess, if you buy this story. I mean, what will your family say?"

Right then the same little voice I heard a year earlier popped up. It was the voice that worried about what other people would think when I spent time in Lisa's company. It said, "What are you? An Approval Suck or a fearless Nomadic Goddess? And what about that saying you heard? The one that says, "Be daring and fearless and don't be afraid someone is going to criticize you; if your ego isn't involved no one can hurt you."

I frowned and thought, "I hate when my own well-meaning sayings are thrown back in my face – particularly when I don't want to hear them."

To make matters worse, I found myself longing for the peace and serenity of the Raja Yoga center, while at the same time watching myself questioning the sanity of such a longing.

One afternoon I tried my own form of open-eye meditation, but it did not work the same as when I was in the room with Robert – especially without the voice of the woman on the taped commentary.

I decided to stop trying because I was getting frustrated. Instead, I gently closed my eyes and went back to following my breath.

A few moments passed, then ten minutes passed, and I found I was having a tougher and tougher time following my breath and stopping my thoughts.

"Geez," I thought. "I can't stop thinking about my soul, and the soul world! I guess I never realized it, but somewhere along the line I really began to like the idea of feeding positive thoughts into my mind. The few times I've tried it, it's given me such a lovely sense of peace. It works even better than my Buddhist method."

"What does *that* tell you?" my little voice beckoned.

"It tells me I've got more research to do!" I answered, haughtily.

Noticing my own testiness, I thought, "I guess this Raja Yoga stuff has had more of an impact on me than I'd care to admit."

For the next few hours, I foraged around the beach of Tulumben, but all I could hear was the war of conflicting thoughts raging relentlessly inside my head.

I spent a few more days there, and also at Lovina Beach – a black sand beach on Bali's northeast tip, then went off to explore Bali's famous, exquisitely-sculpted terraced rice paddies at Tirtananga. Then I started back for Ubud.

I had made up my mind. I was an adventurer, and it was time to experiment some more.

"I want to know everything," I said to myself, "the works!"

As I contemplated what 'the works' meant to me, it struck me how I used to love to order a foot-long hot-dog with everything on it. I flashed to how I had given up meat and seafood to become a vegetarian and thought, "A hot-dog is definitely out of the question!"

"Raja Yoga advocates vegetarianism on moral grounds," I thought, "and so do so many other spiritual groups I've run across during my travels – like the Hare Krishnas in Perth, Australia."

I had struggled to become a vegetarian many times in my life, but after starting my journey, I figured I was trying everything else new in life, why not vegetarianism? However, being the poor misguided soul that I was, I figured Asia would be an easy place to be a vegetarian – after all, wasn't rice and vegetables a staple part of their diet?

Wrong. Meat, meat, and more meat was all I found. From Hong Kong to Bangkok to Bali – the Asians loved their meat.

But I persevered. I came to believe that eating meat was an indirect act of violence and barbarity. Everything I had read showed meat was not at all necessary for a complete and healthy diet. So when I arrived at The Meditation Shop and read one of their pamphlets promoting vegetarianism, I had to marvel at the synchronicity of it all.

"Valerie," my little voice teased, "here you are enjoying the newness of their teachings and loving their emphasis on purity, and you've arrived on their doorstep only to find out you've been on the same path of purity for quite some time now!"

My little voice was absolutely right. I had given up alcohol and cigarettes and the odd bit of drug experimenting when I first got hypoglycemia eight years ago, and now I had become a vegetarian. I had even taken an East Indian Vegetarian Cooking class five years before, so I guess you could say with all of my other coincidences – I was not at all surprised to find out Raja Yoga originated in India.

The more I thought about why I had chosen a vegetarian lifestyle, I remembered reading a book where the authors of the book called meat eaters, flesh eaters. Then I recalled three of the sayings in the Raja Yoga vegetarian literature. The sayings were kind of gory, but I liked them just the same. They really drove the point home. One of them said, "Animals are my friends and I don't eat my friends." Another one announced, "I like to sit down to my dinner and not wonder what my meal died of!" And my all-time favorite was, "Human beings who eat meat are the living graves of dead animals."

I reached into my day pack and extracted a juicy red apple, bit voraciously into its succulent center and smiled and thought, "Now *that's* some *flesh!*"

TWENTY THREE

Nomadic Goddess
Re-enters
Inner Sanctuary

I walked up the path to the Raja Yoga center, only to see Robert's smiling face waiting there to greet me. He was positively glowing. It was as if his soul really was a brilliant sparkling shining light sitting in the middle of his forehead.

"Welcome home," he said softly.

We went inside, and as we entered the meditation room, I instantly felt enveloped by a lovely, deep sense of rightness and peace. Even though the early morning traffic was being it's noisy, deafening self, I felt as if nothing else existed.

"This feels like a safe little inner sanctuary," I thought, soaking up the tranquillity. "What's really strange, though, is a few months ago I would never even think to use such a word. It must be my new Nomadic Goddess identity taking hold!"

Robert watched me silently taking it all in.

After a few moments, I said quietly, "It's good to be back, my friend. Tulumben and the island sights were quite marvelous, but I was so busy rereading my journal notes and writing down all the questions I wanted to ask you, I couldn't wait to get back to school. You've really stimulated my intellect. As a matter of fact, I've spent the last few days in a daze!"

"Really?" he replied, innocently. "Why is that?"

"Well," I answered, "some of the time I've been filled with wonder – but most of the time I've been inundated with absolutely wild swings of emotion, and feelings of being downright indignant. I mean, this is absolutely crazy stuff you're telling me!"

He looked at my wounded look and furrowed brow and laughed.

"But it's not funny!" I retorted, looking at him accusingly. "My life has been turned upside down – yet all can do is *laugh*?"

He kept on laughing.

Then I laughed. I realized he really had nothing to do with it. He was simply the messenger. I was the one who chose whether to believe it or not. I was the one who decided whether or not to apply it to my life. I was the one who had chosen to take the class, it was I who had chosen to keep coming to classes, and it was I who was now choosing to sign up for even *more* classes!

"What insanity!" I thought. "What next?"

I did not have to wait long for an answer. Robert offered me a cup of tea and launched right in to the next scene of the drama.

"Hey, wait a minute!" I exclaimed. "What do you think you're doing? I've got a gazillion questions to ask you, and here you're going on as if it's all a "Fait Accompli," as you French call it. But this is a pretty shocking story you've delivered. Just what am I supposed to *do* with it?"

"Ah," he said, smiling sympathetically at me. "My apologies. You must think I am being terribly insensitive."

"Not really," I replied. "I just have to get a few things straight, that's all."

"Of course," he said. "But to tell you the truth, I too was upset when I first took the course seven years ago. Then, as I learned more about it, and applied it to my life, I started to see that it all made perfect sense."

"So that's how long you've been in Raja Yoga?" I asked, "seven years?"

"Yes," he replied, "and I can honestly say I have never been happier, because now – whenever something disturbing happens in my life, or in the world, I can just say, "Oh that is the drama. The poor lost souls are simply acting under the influence of their vices. They have forgotten their virtues – they have forgotten they were once complete, elevated, divine beings – and it is all predestined in this amazing, cyclical world drama. We all fall asleep. Then, when it is the right time, we wake up to the truth, and begin to make spiritual effort. I can remind myself to remain completely detached, because if it is all predestined, there is nothing to be concerned about. The World Drama says souls must go from pure to impure to pure again – it is exactly how it is supposed to be."

"Now that's a different way of looking at things," I said, brightening.

"Yes, isn't it?" he replied. "And because it is an *Eternal* World Drama, I can also feel safe in knowing the world never ends; it just goes through some major changes. People today are so afraid of the world blowing up and disappearing; but if they only knew that the world is eternal, and that they *too* are eternal – it would restore hope and faith to humanity."

"That is wonderful news!" I replied, firing up the engine of my mind. "But tell me, Robert now that you've brought up this World Drama stuff again, what is all this about God's introduction and his arrival on planet Earth?"

"Okay – here it goes," he said, settling into a comfortable position. "If God resides in the Soul World, and we humans are here trapped by matter becoming more and more powerless with each passing day, you have to ask how God's knowledge could come to us in the first place!"

"Uh huh. You've got that right," I remarked.

"Well, since we have lost our spiritual power, he cannot exactly reveal his knowledge to us through divine inspiration. That is why *He* has to come to *us*. And to do this, he needs to use a body."

"But I thought you said God never takes a body because he'd lose his power," I piped up – secretly congratulating myself for remembering the course material.

"That is correct," he answered, smiling approvingly, "and that is precisely why he needs to *borrow* a body. He needs something to speak through."

"Oh sure," I said, laughing. "You sure got around that one pretty easily!"

He smiled and winked and said, "Well I never said he couldn't *borrow* a body. You see, Valerie, some 60 years ago, God came into a body of a highly-respected diamond merchant in India. The man's name became Brahma. When God was first speaking, it looked like Brahma was speaking, but he seemed to shine with an otherworldly light and brilliance. Eventually, as people began listening to his teachings, it became clear the source was definitely not human. The power the personality was exerting was so intense and blissful, the guidance offered so high and noble, and the language so poetic, and the ideas so freeing, it was clear it was none other than God Himself. "

"That's some story, Robert," I said, grinning. "Forgive me, but you must admit it sounds pretty far-fetched. There is, after all, tons of people calling themselves God. Gurus, sages, holy men, saints – even Shirley Maclean is portrayed walking up and down Malibu beach calling out, "I AM GOD."

"Yes, that's true," Robert conceded.

"Well," I continued," if he *is* God, why not come in a blinding flash of light and part the heavens and really wow humanity with His presence and power?"

"It is not his style," he said, smiling sweetly.

"Oh," I replied, settling back thoughtfully on my cushion.

"Think of it this way," he said, observing the puzzled look on my face. "God comes in an incognito way – like a " thief in the night", as the Bible says. He is a very subtle energy. That is why, when he first spoke through Brahma, no one knew what to make of him. Brahma's eyes shone out like golden-red lights, and his whole face – in fact, his whole presence – turned a deep golden red, and a voice spoke in Sanskrit and said;

"I am blissful. I am Shiva."

"I am knowledgeful. I am Shiva."

"I am luminous. I am Shiva. "

"Oh my God!" I exclaimed.

I felt my whole body go weak and I began shaking uncontrollably. Robert watched the color drain from my face.

After a minute or so, Robert ventured to ask what was up. He was visibly concerned for my well-being.

I slowly composed myself, and with a slight tremor in my

voice, I replied. "Remember when you first spoke of the Soul World and told me about God being called Shiva," I asked, "and how I said it sounded kind of familiar, but couldn't quite place it?"

"Yes I do," he answered reverently.

"Well, just as you starting talking about this 'I Am Shiva' stuff," I said, "I got a chilled rush of energy up through my scalp because I realized this was the same force which spoke to me through Troy – a psychic reader I met almost three years ago. He too turned a reddish hue, shouted out the name Shiva – then started spouting off something about destruction and fire energies and how it represented the red ray bringing about change and insight and something about cataclytic transformation."

"Well," he said, eyes dancing, "it seems to me you have had your *own* introduction to God."

"Ha ha. *Very* funny!" I exclaimed. "You're quite the storyteller, my friend! I admit for a moment you had me totally captivated me with your bizarre tale – but forgive me if I tell you I'm not convinced God has come – to Brahma *or* to me."

"I can certainly see why!" he exclaimed. "The world had been talking about God coming for centuries. Of course it would be hard to believe that after waiting lifetime after lifetime, he has finally arrived!"

"Yes, well," I replied, "there's only one person in this room who actually *believes* that!"

"As you like," Robert said, smiling.

He turned and inserted a tape into the cassette player, dimmed the lights and said, "How about one more flight before you catch your plane out of Bali?"

I laughed and nodded, "Okay."

"Okay all you little angels," he gently called out. "Get ready for lift off! And remember; all you need is one happy thought, and you can fly – just like in *Peter Pan!*"

I grinned.

He noticed my response and playfully swept his hand across the room and announced, "Calling all souls! It is time to leave for the Soul World. To prepare for lift-off, leave here knowing you have already arrived. It is really that simple. Simply hold the thought in your mind that you are a radiant, shining star-point of light and fly off to the Land of Peace and Timelessness – kind of like the famous Land of Never Never. It is a place where you never feel sorrow and you never feel pain. All you feel is limitless peace. Float freely in that golden-red sea of silence and tranquillity. Take that much-needed holiday from the weight of that costume of yours – your body. Fly home!"

I sat marveling at his theatrics, then let myself be swept away. After a few moments, I felt light and happy and filled with wonder. Then, quite unexpectedly, my plane took a nose dive and my spirits fell. I suddenly realized this would be my last time in my little inner sanctuary.

"It's time for the Nomadic Goddess to continue her soul search," I thought. "But at least now I know where my soul is, so I can finally stop looking for it!"

When the lights came on, we walked slowly towards the door. I could not help feeling a little melancholy; I dearly loved it here on Monkey Forest Road.

I looked at Robert. His big brown eyes shone back at me and he said, "Valerie. Remember who you are. In Raja Yoga, we have a saying: *Om Shanti*. It means, "I am a peaceful soul." So instead of saying good-bye, I'll say, "Om Shanti." It has indeed been a pleasure meeting you, my friend. Maybe we will see each other again – say – in 5,000 years?"

I laughed and winked and said, "Well, we'll just see about that, now won't we, Robert?"

We waved good-bye to each other, and I strode down the road smiling and thinking, "Never in all my life have I met a more unusual treasure of an individual – nor one with a more bizarre story."

"Oh well," I thought. "C'est la vie!"

I walked towards the guest house and my mind went flying off in all four directions – running amok like an out of control monkey. Thoughts of packing and booking a mini-bus and planning a strategy for beating the late-afternoon rush of traffic to arrive at the airport on time, jammed into my mind.

"All this, and I haven't even had breakfast!" I thought. "My little monkey mind is driving me absolutely bananas!"

"Ah, bananas," I thought, calming down. "Now what about those *deeee*licious banana pancakes topped with shredded coconut and fresh pineapple that Made has waiting for me at Nick's?"

I recalled an incident on my way back from Bali's most famous and mystical temple; *Tanah Lot*. It was perched high atop a huge rocky crag, with incredibly high waves crashing in at high tide, making it inaccessible for much of the time. It was pure magic; the mists, the shadows of the rock, the tempestuous, high spray of the waves. On our way back, we stopped in at the Sangeh forest, a favorite monkey-viewing spot for tourists.

My friends and I had just parked our car and were walking through the parking lot, when out of nowhere, a giant-sized furball came flying at me – knocking me off balance. A hairy little monkey had just flung itself mercilessly at my neck. I did not realize what had happened until I saw the hairy beast tear off down the road with my newly-purchased French-made *Bolle* sunglasses. He raced behind a barbed wire fence – effectively sealing himself off from me – then nonchalantly sat gnawing on my glasses – throwing an obnoxiously arrogant look my way – challenging me to retaliate.

"Why you arrogant little beggar you," I thought. "*Now you've got my blood boiling!*"

I madly started shaking the fence – yelling all kinds of obscenities and doing ridiculously embarrassing things like screeching at the top of my lungs, "HEY MISTER. GIVE THOSE GLASSES BACK RIGHT NOW! I PAID $85.00 FOR THOSE LITTLE BABIES IN BANGKOK!"

As an afterthought, I screamed out, "U.S!"

I was obviously hysterical; how else could I account for explaining the intricacies of foreign purchases and the significance of the U.S. currency exchange rate in relation to the falling Canadian dollar – to a Balinese monkey?

"WHY, HE DOESN'T EVEN KNOW I'M CANADIAN!" I yelled.

For a brief second I seriously considered risking bloodying my hands to scale the barbed wire fence. But then a Balinese man came running to my rescue. He adeptly crawled through a tiny, invisible hole in the fence, and offered the monkey a trade; a bag of peanuts for the stolen bootie.

The monkey greedily nabbed the bag and dropped my glasses.

"Little monkey," I muttered, as the man handed me back my precious *Bolles*.

I suddenly began to laugh. I finally realized the cosmic link between man, apes, monkeys, and meditation, and it had nothing whatsoever to do with a guy named Darwin. For me, monkeys demonstrated everything I needed to know about myself; from how I got attached to things, to how my ego made me do stupid things, to how I had to continue to learn to control my monkey mind.

I brought my mind back to the present, and noticed I was walking past my favorite vegetarian restaurant. I started feeling sad again, because leaving Ubud meant I would have to give up Lillie's Restaurant's scrumptious brown rice tempeh curry.

"You're a backpacker, remember?" I reminded myself. "Detach, girl, detach!"

As I contemplated booking a van to take me to the airport at Denpasar to catch my flight to Europe, I smiled to myself and thought, "Life. What a drama it is. All of us little souls riding around in our little costumes down the little highways of life. Well, all I can say is; Holland – here I come!"

TWENTY FOUR

Nomadic Goddess
Meets God

I hopped the train from Schipol airport, and arrived in the little village of Alkmaar – a 45 minute train ride northwest of Amsterdam. My backpacker friend, Gerda, was waiting there to greet me.

Our eyes locked on each other, and we slowly walked towards one another and embraced. It had been four months since we had met in Chiangmai, Thailand – a small city 12 hours-bus ride north of Bangkok. She had been traveling with three of her Dutch friends, and we met each other alongside the pool at a local guest house. She – like I – was a volleyball enthusiast and a tennis player. We got on fabulously.

One day the five of us decided it would be fun to join forces to go on a trek of the northern hill tribe country. By the end of the six-day journey, we had gone through a lot together– slugging through mud and torrential rains, braving dangerously swollen rivers on a treacherous bamboo rafting expedition, and teaching each other how to adjust to the myriad of cultural differences. Through it all, Gerda proved to be one of the most intrepid nomadic goddesses I had ever met. She constantly inspired me to overlook the hardships we encountered,

and had a beautiful gift of always seeing the good in everything. It was great to see her again here in Alkmaar.

After a long, heart-warming hug, she stepped back, smiled
at me, handed me a rented bicycle, loaded my 18-kilo backpack
on to the back of her bike, then – holding it with one hand,
waved me forward with her free hand, and started riding away.

I was flabbergasted. I had never seen anyone perform such
an amazing balancing act outside of Thailand. There, they often navigated the rough roads with all their possessions
strapped to their bicycles.

Her quick departure startled me. I had to race to catch up.

"I forgot how practical you are," I called out, "and how
active!"

We laughed the whole way to her apartment. She constantly
had to remind me to stay on the right side of the road each time
we turned a corner. I was so disoriented by my many months
in the East, I ended up a few times on the left side, heading
precariously in the direction of oncoming traffic.

I looked over at her and hollered, "BUT IT'S LEGAL IN
ASIA!"

She laughed and yelled back in her thick Dutch accent, "But
Valerie – this is Holland! You're going to get yourself killed!"

We arrived at her apartment safe and sound, and I surveyed
my new surroundings. I smiled and thought, "It's just as I expected – simple, efficient, functional and easy to take care of –
just like Gerda!"

One day I was sitting cross-legged on her sofa, trying very
hard to focus on my breath. I squeezed my eyes shut and willed
myself to concentrate, but it just was not working. I started to
think about the volleyball practice the night before with Gerda's
local team. They were a top caliber team, and my body was
still recovering from the shock of what Gerda proudly called,
"Serious, good trrrrraining."

She loved to push herself, and so did I – or rather, I used to;
it did not seem to interest me that much anymore. I sat thinking why, and it began to bother me.

"Three weeks have passed since I left Bali," I thought, "and
something inside of me has definitely changed. All this
meditation and Robert's teachings about seeking spiritual
perfection seems to have calmed my need to push myself to

my physical limits – and yet, I love volleyball. I used to *live* for volleyball."

"What do you suppose is going on?" I asked myself.

"You got what you asked for," my little voice piped up.

"What are you talking about?" I asked.

"Remember your orange socks?" it said. "Didn't they start you on this journey because you wanted to know what more there was to life besides volleyball and the consummate tennis partner? Well – here it is!"

"Did I say that?" I replied.

"You bet your sweet socks, you did!" my voice answered.

"That's right!" I exclaimed. "It was those darned *orange socks!*"

"Uh huh," it replied, looking ever so smug.

"Not only that," I continued, "but when I *am* meditating, I can't keep my mind off of God! Normally my mind wanders off to food, or sports or sightseeing, or looking for someone special to share my life with."

"Isn't that a switch," my little voice teased.

"This is not funny!" I fired back. "Just what am I supposed to do with myself? *I'm not normal anymore!*"

"But that's the whole point!" my little voice remarked.

"Yeah, right," I said, smiling laconically. "The soul is a point, God is a point; but how is that going to help me get on in life?"

"Well, who wants to be normal?" my little voice piped up. "Remember how you liked the saying, "Out there on the fringe, a person's valuable, otherwise, they're just another noise in the zoo?"

"Yes," I replied, "but when my family gets wind of all the changes I've gone through, they'll want to put me in a zoo on display under a sign reading, Rare Species of Screwloose. I mean, how can I return home with all these weird things going on in my mind? I don't even want to work anymore – the whole idea of chasing money just doesn't appeal. And if someone comes by for a visit, I'll probably say, "Would you like a little meditation with your tea?"

My little voice giggled.

"It's not funny!" I retorted.

My little voice fell silent.

I got up from the sofa, got a glass of water, and sat back down again.

"I have to admit Robert said some things that really woke me up," I said. "And it wasn't exactly the wake up call of the Buddha."

Robert's Raja Yoga truths kept creeping in to occupy my mind, and I finally surrendered and said, "Okay, what are your options? You can go ahead and drive yourself crazy with all this mental chatter, or you can take a look at the reason this is happening. Let's try this once again – shall we? Only let's really try to do it Robert's way. Give it your best shot."

I sat up straight, eyes open, and began staring at the white wall in front of me. After a few moments I noticed my mind was all over the map. I shifted my position, got comfortable and started picturing myself as a tiny point of light radiating out from my forehead, and imagined myself bodiless.

Before long, I started to see the wall disappear and I felt light and happy. Then I felt as if there was some sort of a power – kind of like fine waves of energy – emanating out at me from the wall. I could feel a cool sensation in the middle of my forehead.

"This is weird," I thought.

As soon as I thought this, the energy disappeared. I started thinking about being as tiny as an atom, and focused on how much love and peace and power Robert said I had – and I felt myself becoming light and buoyant and sensed the waves of energy coming at me again.

"This is so neat!" I thought, smiling broadly.

The energy disappeared again.

"It's like playing hide and seek," I thought. "It reminds me of my time in the monastery when I was trying to find my breath – only this is 10 times more fun!"

I kept practicing. It seemed every time I relaxed and focused my thoughts on God, or on my original virtues, it was there – a soft, loving, gently pulsating, powerful energy.

"Could this be what God is?" I asked myself.

The energy suddenly started pulsating at a faster speed – slowly increasing in intensity – like someone was turning up the volume. Then, without warning – it increased to an unbelievably high pitch, and I felt swept away in a sea of love and bliss and tranquillity.

"Oh my God!" I thought. "This is incredible!"

The waves of light kept coming at me – until I felt lifted up – miraculously suspended in the invisible arms of a loving being – blissfully absorbing its light, love and power.

When I felt I could take no more, the waves of light lowered me back down, and I could feel the sofa beneath my body again. I sat stunned and thought, "What was *that*?" It took me some time to find my feet. When I *did* find them, I lowered them onto the floor and got up.

All of a sudden I felt incredibly thirsty. I stumbled over to the sink to draw a drink of water. I had to lean up against the cupboard to support my wobbly legs. As I did this, I noticed I was still filled with light; every part of me felt ignited by a strange, cool energy.

"Wow," I thought, scratching my head. "That was *some* trip. What do you suppose happened?"

"Could it be you've just had God's *second* introduction?" my little voice piped up.

"Hey, hold on a minute," I remarked, looking around. "Just what do you think you're talking about?"

"Got any better ideas?" it replied.

"Well, no," I answered, testily. "But give me a minute. I'm sure I'll think of something!"

"I think it's time to get some fresh air," I told myself.

I put on my jacket and stepped out into the crisp December night and felt the air bite at my lungs.

I smiled and started thinking about going home for Christmas – but I could still sense the after-effects of my mysterious encounter.

I decided to set it aside, and pictured how happy my family would be to have me home safe and sound. Until that moment, I did not realize how much I was looking forward to seeing all their shining faces. But I also felt a little sad.

"My return will mark the end of my Nomadic Goddess Quest," I thought, "my Freedom Year! Never *before* have I known *such* freedom! It's been absolutely glorious – no work, no schedules, no telephones ringing, no responsibilities!"

The more I thought about going home, the more nervous and unsure I became.

I could feel my face beginning to frown and a heaviness

started tugging at my heart.

"It's what every traveler goes through just before returning home," I told myself. "Relax – everything's going to turn out just fine."

Then it hit me.

I was not going home to stay.

TWENTY FIVE

Shiva The Firelord Makes A Return Engagement

I walked into the arrivals area of the Calgary airport and found myself swept into the strong, warm arms of my sister, Laura.

"How I've missed you!" I cried, burying my face in her long blonde hair.

"Likewise, sis!" she exclaimed. "It's about time you honored us with your presence. We've missed our little Nomadic Goddess!"

When we arrived at my house, Lisa was there to give me a big, "Welcome home, you little Nomadic Goddess, you," hug.

I smiled and laughed so much my smile muscles hurt.

A few other friends dropped by later on to welcome me home. We stayed up late into the night exchanging stories of our year apart. After they left, I went upstairs and slept in my very own bed for the first time in 350 days. What a feeling it was, laying there revelling in the softness of my goose-down duvet – my cat Athena stretched out luxuriously at my feet, purring contentedly.

I sat up and leaned forward and whispered, "The Nomadic Goddess has returned."

She shook her ear and scratched it with her back paw.

"My breath must have tickled you," I said, giggling and stroking her shiny black fur.

She looked at me sideways, as if to say, "*Who* are you *anyway?*"

I laughed and laid back and closed my eyes and tried to drift off to sleep.

That turned out to be wishful thinking. All I could think of was that I would be leaving again. I lay awake most of the night feeling incredibly unsettled and tense.

The next morning I was completely out of it; groggy, sleepy-eyed, and totally disoriented.

"Welcome home," I mumbled, scratching my head and rubbing my neck.

I got up and looked in the bathroom mirror. I looked awful. I looked like I had been run over by a cement mixer – then tossed into the mixing bucket for good measure.

"Tell me," I said to my reflection. "Who does your hair? Why – it's positively divine!"

My hair resembled a bird's nest.

I stood in the shower for a long while, soaking up the hot water, letting its steaming spray pelt my tired, aching body, trying to see if I could work out some of the kinks which had mysteriously crept into my neck.

I slowly stepped out of the shower, put on my housecoat, and walked over to the wardrobe cabinet and pulled open the bottom drawer. Staring up at me was the cassette tape of Troy's Life Reading session from three years before.

I got out my Walkman and laid down on the bed and inserted the tape.

Troy's voice came to me loud and clear. It was as if no time had passed. I lay completely mesmerized. I was surprised at how much I now understood what he was talking about.

"Boy," I thought. "What *happened* to me out there?"

As I listened, I knew beyond a shadow of a doubt I had to go back to Bali. Troy was speaking of brahmins, of fire initiations and yogis, and about how in the past I had been an Indian yogi helping to bring souls through their initiation by fire and show them the gateway to Heaven."

"I wonder if that's the fire of yoga Robert talked about – the fire of remembrance," I thought.

I listened some more, and when Troy burst out with the name Shiva, I laughed.

"Oh God," I said. "Here we go again!"

"It represents a consciousness of change," Troy said. "It is transformative, cataclytic...it is power, it is directorship."

I turned up the volume. "There is an energy here of a sword carrier – in terms of gods and goddesses," he said, "which are looked upon as guides and principles of guidance for others who are capable of that level of intelligence. You are of what is called the higher angelic energy fields. You are a portion of that energy that brings transformation through the fire principle, so the Shiva consciousness is that sound of fire which represents what would be termed as destruction!"

"Oh God," I said silently. I looked down at my body. It was shaking uncontrollably.

I unplugged my Walkman, got up, and went outside.

I decided to walk towards the river.

As I wandered through my once-familiar neighborhood and over the bridge towards the downtown core, I felt like a lost soul. Everything had changed. They had torn down a row of my favorite older houses and put up new stylish buildings. I felt like a tourist in my own city. It was a strange feeling.

As I gazed at the wall of office buildings outlined against the clear blue sky, I thought, "You know, Valerie – you can always *work*, but can you always *play*? You've got enough money to go back to Asia – why not do it? Besides – you know you won't rest until you know if Robert's story is true."

I wandered down to the YMCA for a swim, but my mind ended up swimming more than my body.

The next day I phoned my travel agent and asked her to look into the cost of a flight to Asia. She was surprised to hear I was going back so soon. I told her I had to.

She laughed. She too was a world traveler. She said she would send over the tickets just as soon as they were ready.

I boarded a plane three weeks later, waved goodbye to Laura, and flew off to Vancouver. I was off on another adventure – but this time I knew exactly where I was headed. I even knew which bus I would catch when I got to Bangkok. I was going to take the Buddhist course again, then return to Bali to learn more about Raja Yoga. Only then could I make a rational, informed choice as to which path was right for me. I knew I was only half-cooked. What's more, I had to know the truth.

"And Bangkok will never ever get the best of me again," I said, resolutely, smiling to myself. "Once is enough."

I was happy to put my mind on the journey again, and started humming Willy Nelson's song, *On the Road Again*. I began thinking about my life as a traveler – a nomad.

"Didn't Robert say all souls were travelers?" I asked myself. "And if that's true, I guess that makes us all nomads. We wander from costume to costume and lifetime to lifetime, playing our roles in different cultures and different lands."

"So what's the most consummate point for being a Nomadic Goddess?" I asked myself. "The most perfect, most eloquent point of all time?"

"Point number adinfinitum of being a Nomadic Goddess," I said, sitting back smugly in my seat. "All souls are points of light. All souls are nomads. All souls are gods and goddesses who have lost their way. All souls are nomadic gods and goddesses!"

"So what's the point?" I gamefully asked myself.

"Why, you're a point," I sung out, "I'm a point, God's a point....everyone's a point, point...Old MacDonald had a farm, ei ei OOOOOOMMMMMMMMMMM!"

"Point number adinfinitum and a half," I thought, "Remember point number one: Never lose your sense of humor. Keep it light!"

TWENTY SIX

Nomadic Goddess Gets Hit Between The Eyes

Five days into the course at the monastery, I came to realize just how nuturing and beautiful the silence could be. I loved the peace and quiet. I also found I was much more successful at calming my mind. The course was so much simpler the second time around – probably because I was now familiar with the retreat environment as well as with their Vipassana method of meditation. But what surprised me the most, was how I felt right at home – bedding down on my rock-hard cement bed and saying goodnight to my ever-present roommates, the giant spiders. I even started playing a game of dare and double dare with the scorpions – challenging them to come stalking me. "You just wait, you guys," I teased. "I've got my confidence up, so don't you go messing with me, y'hear?"

It seemed somewhere along the way, between leaving the monastery and taking the Raja Yoga course, I had lost my fear of being harmed. I really wasn't sure why, but I felt a quiet, sure strength.

I stayed on at Wat Suan Mokh for two weeks after the 10-day course ended. I felt no compulsion to leave. I loved the lifestyle – rising in the early morning, getting in a full day of studying, walking, meditating, and enjoying Mrs. Bethoun's cooking. Then one day I felt it was time to go. I toured around the southern islands of Thailand, snorkeling and taking lots of quiet walks along the beaches – meditating five, sometimes six times a day. In between, I would feast at the quaint little thatched-roof, bamboo restaurants – experimenting with the local extraordinary, but simple, Thai culinary delights. I ate like a king.

I would sit contentedly at my bamboo table on the beach, feet toasting in the sun-warmed sand, watching the huge waves roll in, feeling myself growing wistful as the sun dipped below the horizon. The restaurant owner's family was working away in the small, simple kitchen – hovering over red-hot coals, preparing the evening's menu items – the light of the flickering kerosene lamps dancing on their faces.

One morning I woke up feeling uncharacteristically antsy – like I was putting something off. I knew it was time to seek out Robert.

I headed back to Bangkok to hunt down a discount flight ticket to Bali. It was now August, and I knew it would be busy in Bali. The Australian tourists would be flooding in. It was wintertime in their homeland, and Bali was their equivalent of Canada's Hawaiian vacation. Bali was also a favourite holiday destination for many other tourists from around the world. I winced at the thought of running into so many tourists, but then I thought, "What does it matter? This is your *future* we're talking about. You *have* to go back so you can get some clarity about this Shiva – God stuff. So – git along little yogi!"

As I got out my back pack, the Gene Autry classic, *Back in the Saddle Again* jumped into my mind, and I found myself humming a few verses as I packed. I also thought about how fortunate my time at the monastery had been. Even though the Buddhist concepts intrigued me, and complemented what I had learned in the Raja Yoga course, I was now pretty much sure that Buddhism, and the closed-eye, following-the-breath meditation really wasn't for me – much as I wanted them to be. I asked myself why, and I realized the Raja Yoga stuff about God really bothered me. I had never been looking for God – I was just looking for The Answer. But this God business both surprised me and frightened me – and I wanted to know why.

When I reached Ubud, I headed straight for Nick's Pension. I adored the little red brick bungalows overlooking the terraced rice paddies – my home away from home. As I crossed the small bamboo bridge to take me to the pathway leading to the guesthouse, Made emerged from the kitchen. When he saw me, he broke into a huge grin and called out, "Valerie!" in his adorable Balinese accent, and started waving wildly. He yelled something in Balinese, and I saw Nick and his wife poke their head out from inside the office. They called out a big, "Welcome back!" I waved and smiled. It was a great homecoming. They were like family to me.

The next morning I walked down the sun-soaked street of Monkey Forest Road and noticed myself picking up the pace as I approached The Meditation Shop. I smiled to myself. I had missed Robert.

He did not seem at all surprised to see me walking up the pathway.

I laughed and called out, "Yes, I'm back! I've decided to study with you awhile, my friend!"

"Oh?" he asked, smiling broadly. "Why is that?"

"Because I've had more proof of this God stuff since I last saw you," I replied.

"Marvellous!" he exclaimed. "That's what usually brings people back."

"Oh?" I said, raising my eyebrow. "This has happened before?"

"Oh yes, numerous times," he replied.

My knees suddenly felt weak.

He patted a spot on the step next to him and said, "Here, sit down."

I gratefully lowered myself onto the step.

"Sheesh!" I exclaimed, turning and looking at him incredulously. "This journey of discovery is getting weirder by the moment!"

"It has only just begun!" he said – eyes gleaming.

I turned my face to the noon-day sun to bask in its warmth. I wanted to gather my thoughts. There was just too much happening – too fast. I could feel him looking on in amusement.

After a few moments I turned back to him and began relating what had happened to me. We talked for a long while and

I told him about my pulsating wall experience in Holland, and about the details of Troy's tape back in Canada. He listened intently, then suggested I read a few of the Raja Yoga books outlining Brahma's life experiences. He also recommended a book on scientific findings to back up their idea of the cycle of time. Then he went inside, gathered up what he called My Homework, and sent me on my way.

After a couple of weeks of twice-daily visits, I decided it was time to take a holiday. The knowledge was fascinating, but a bit overwhelming. I looked into booking myself a ferry ride to the nearby island of Lombok, and asked around about making arrangements for a trek up Mount Rinjani – a spectacular five-day hike to the top of a magnificent dormant volcano in the north of the island. Then I telephoned Gerda, and she agreed to fly over and meet me. We had talked about going on another adventure together, and it turned out to be an ideal time for her to take time off from her teaching job.

The day before we were to climb, we went looking around the small village of Banglor in search of warm sleeping bags. Many of the more experienced hikers told us it was freezing on the mountain at night. They strongly recommended we shop around carefully for some of the better quality bags. After a day-long search, we ended up empty-handed. All we had to show for our efforts was a promise from the park warden that he would save us two of his rental bags if they were turned in early. He warned us it didn't look too hopeful. Our only other choice was a couple of cheap, damp, polyester-style bags from a local homestay.

We decided something was better than nothing, and deposited 50,000 Rupiah – about $25.00 Canadian – on the two polyester bags. Walking up the dirt road through the centre of the village – our sleeping bags tucked up under our arms – we debated whether or not there would be enough sun for the bags to dry on time. Up ahead, the park warden suddenly appeared. He was frantically waving his arms in the air, signaling for us to join him.

We ran towards him. Once we were within earshot, he proudly announced a miracle had happened. Two hikers had just returned a full two days early, and two top-quality bags were now available. We thanked him profusely, then ran back down the road towards the homestay. Since only ten minutes had passed, we were certain there would be no problem getting a full refund on the other two bags.

We arrived and explained to the homestay owner what had happened. He looked at us blankly, as if we were talking gibberish – then announced he didn't understand English. Gerda and I looked at each other – dumbfounded. He had conversed with us in perfect English only minutes before.

"He can't be serious!" I exclaimed.

"I think he is, Valerie, " Gerda replied. "Look at his face."

He turned and started walking away, and I yelled, "HEY! WAIT A MINUTE. THIS ISN'T FAIR!"

He ignored me and kept on walking. A few feet away, his wife came out from a small building. He stopped to talk to her, then pointed in our direction.

I turned to Gerda and said, "What do you think we should do?"

She shrugged her shoulders.

"He can't possibly think we're going to take this lying down!" I exclaimed. "Who does he think he is?"

The owner suddenly started walking back towards us and stopped in front of me and said, "My wife says, 'No.' She says you must pay for the full five days – just as we agreed."

I looked at him – stunned. I could not believe what I was hearing.

I walked over to a nearby table and sat down. I had to think.

"Better check in with your intuition on this one, Valerie," I thought to myself. "This is, after all, another culture. You don't want to make any mistakes jumping the gun."

As I sat contemplating what to do, my little voice piped up and said, "Remember in Bangkok when you refused to pay for the food because it tasted rotten, and the owner started yelling at the top of her lungs for the police? Remember how she reached up and grabbed you by the t-shirt and just about ripped your shirt from your body and demanded payment?"

"Yeah," I replied, smiling. "I decided right then and there to surrender. I remembered the saying, "Do you want to have health, happiness and peace of mind, or do you want to be right?"

"Well?" my little voice replied. "What makes this case any different?"

I smiled and looked the owner in the eye and said, "Okay. We'll pay for one day out of the five, but I feel it's only fair you refund the rest."

He started pacing and yelling something in Indonesian. A crowd of male neighbors gathered around to see what was going on. He went over and started talking to them. "Oh, oh, Valerie," I thought. "You forgot Lombok was predominantly Muslim! No wonder he's upset. Not only are you a woman challenging the unquestionable authority of a man, but you are also a western woman – so you're a disrespectful foreigner challenging their culture, too."

I sat back, closed my eyes, and focused on my inner light – just like Robert had taught me. I figured it could not hurt. I had already made a pretty big mess of things. It was time to call in a second opinion.

"Okay God," I said. "I give up. I've tried all my own ways – now it's your turn."

A thought popped into my head.

"Ask him to look into your eyes," it said.

"What?" I exclaimed. "You've got to be kidding! Are you nuts? Why – he's so hyped, I'd be lucky to get him to stop pacing – let alone get him to come close enough to look me in the eye!"

The owner suddenly stopped pacing, left his circle of supporters, and came and stood next to where I was sitting.

I was stunned.

"What is going on?" I asked myself, feeling my heart beginning to race.

I recalled Robert telling me how everyone was inherently good and pure, and that they only acted badly because they had forgotten their original nature.

I sat up straighter, gathered my courage, looked him straight in the eye and said, "Would you do me a favor? Would you sit down here and look me in the eye?"

He looked at me a little oddly, but then sat down.

"Okay," I said, "you believe in Allah, right?"

He nodded.

"Well," I replied, "do you think Allah would see what you are doing as right and honest?"

"Oh yes!" he exclaimed, sitting up straighter – his body

swelling with pride and conviction. "Allah would most certainly agree!"

"Uh huh," I thought, smirking to myself. "This is definitely not going to be an easy victory."

"Okay," I said, bracing myself for another round. "I believe you are truly a good, honest man – and I believe Allah knows this too. If Allah were to choose, what would he do?"

As I said this, our eyes suddenly locked, and I felt an incredible surge of energy come in through the top of my head, and out through my eyes. Everything went blank.

A split-second later, I came to. The man got up, turned his back on me, and crumpled. It was as if his entire body had suddenly deflated. He slowly began walking in the direction of the the building where he had been talking to this wife, and disappeared inside.

I looked across the table. Gerda stared back at me – speechless.

My head suddenly felt light and airy – like someone had taken a vacuum and sucked out all of its contents. I had the distinct feeling something was sparkling – like I was radiating some sort of powerful energy. It didn't particularly feel like it was mine. Rather, it felt more like it was there for me to use.

I looked back towards the house, trying hard to focus on what had just happened. I could not really comprehend it. It was as if my mind had suddenly taken a vacation.

As I struggled to compose myself, the man came out of the building holding something in his hand. As he came closer, I could make out a number of 10,000 rupiah notes.

"Oh well," I thought, "at least he's giving us back some of our money."

He came to a stop directly in front of me and extended his hand.

In his hand lay not four, but five notes.

I could not believe my eyes.

"What's this?" I said, looking up at him. "You're giving us back all of our money?"

He looked at me sombrely and replied, "I don't know who is right. Allah will decide. Take this and go."

He gathered up the sleeping bags, turned on his heel, and walked back in the direction of the little building.

I looked at Gerda. We both broke into a huge grin. She raised her eyebrows and gave me a, "Who would have ever guessed?" look, and shrugged her shoulders.

I stood up to leave. My knees suddenly buckled underneath me and I fell back down into the chair.

"Whoa!" I exclaimed, catching myself. "That must have been some energy!"

Gerda quickly came around to help me. She lifted me by my arm, and I held on to the table with my free hand, then tentatively removed it. Leaning against her, we walked together towards the main road.

Suddenly it hit me. "This is how Jesus made fishers of men!" I exclaimed, feeling another surge of energy.

Gerda looked at me – puzzled.

"What a brilliant revelation!" I raved on, completely ignoring her confused expression. "I've always wondered about the stories in the Bible – you know – the ones about how God worked through Jesus to gather his disciples? Don't you see? This is how he made them believe! He created miracles through them – just like what happened back there!" I exclaimed, wildly waving my hand in the general direction of the homestay.

"Valerrrrie," she said, rolling her r's. But then she stopped in mid-sentence, and began to laugh. "Maybe it's my English," she said, grinning, "but what exactly are you talking about?"

"Oh!" I exclaimed. "I must sound like a raving lunatic to you!" I looked self-consciously down at the ground, and began remembering how I had always disliked what I called 'Jesus Freaks' – yet here I was, sounding just like one.

"God," I thought, "What have I done?"

"Well," she said, smiling sweetly back at me – completely oblivious to my reaction. "You certainly aren't making much sense, Valerrrrie – that's for sure!"

We walked on in silence, while I gathered my thoughts.

"Poor thing," I thought. "Of course she doesn't understand. How could she? She has no idea what happened to me in this morning's meditation. Plus – how could she possibly know I've always had a secret longing to have lived when Christ walked the earth; to have been part of that incredible, momentous time – a time when the greatest spiritual teacher of all time arrived on earth to tell us that within us lay the greatest power and the greatest love and the greatest purity. A love and power that had the ability to transform our lives – if only we could learn how to access it."

"Hm," I thought, feeling a deep, pervasive quiet come over me. I felt a heightened sense of awareness. I looked around and the ground seemed a richer shade of reddish-brown, and the trees seemed to sway to my every breath. I sensed the same presence was with me as when I confronted the man, and it was now resting comfortably deep inside of me.

"Didn't Robert say that God himself was now teaching us?" I thought, "and that it was up to us to access our own power through having yoga – that is, linking our thoughts to him? That's incredible! God! Imagine that!"

We rounded the corner and started heading up the main road of the village. I looked back towards the homestay and was surprised to see the man still standing where we had left him. He was staring up at me with a strange blank expression on his face. He appeared to be in a daze; as if he was desperately trying to comprehend what had just happened to him.

"I wonder if he thinks we used some kind of Black Magic on him?" I said.

Gerda followed my gaze and smiled back. "I don't really know what happened back there, Valerrrrrie," she said. "What I do know, is it's really amazing how we got our money back."

We wandered further up the road, collected our sleeping bags from the park warden, then headed back in the direction of our guesthouse.

When we arrived, Gerda announced she was going out for a run. I sat down on the bed to meditate. I started by focusing on the wall in front of me and smiled and said to the wall, "God – you sure do have a sense of humour! Just this morning I asked you to give me a sign whether Raja Yoga was the path I should follow, and here you go and do this!"

I sat and smiled and reflected on Gerda and our afternoon together. After a few minutes, I felt myself beginning to relax, and as I did, silent waves of energy began slowly flowing towards me. At first they were barely perceptible, but the more I directed my mind to concentrate, the more I could feel their sweetness and their delicateness – and their unmistakeable, absolutely compelling power. I could feel myself ; to beam from ear to ear – as if something was filling :h an exquisite, almost childlike form of delight. Then – feelings of peace and wonder began to flow in – followed by a sense of awe. But not the kind of '*Oh wow!*' awe, but one more like, 'How very simple and real this feels' kind of awe.

"If this is what God feels like," I said wistfully to myself, "He sure is one lucky fellow. To be so wonderfully sweet and positive and pure – and not just sometimes, but I suspect He must be this way all the time. Imagine....no fear, no doubt, no anxiety, no questions.......just being.... forever being – calm, cool, and easy. What a marvellous existence He has."

The door suddenly opened and in walked Gerda. The energy abruptly vanished – as if the gross action of a door opening had snapped it into oblivion – like it had been dangling from some invisible elastic band. The physical action was so totally incongruent with its presence – I felt the energy had to disappear, leaving me sitting on the bed looking up at her with a silly grin pasted on my face. Gerda looked at me – smiled sweetly – then casually walked over to her back pack and started rummaging around inside.

"I guess by now she must be getting used to my unusual activities," I thought, trying hard to fight down my ego. It was doing its best to make me feel stupid. I remembered Robert telling me the ego was a form of vice. He called it being body-conscious. He said it robbed us of our true self-respect – that of being a pure, powerful, peaceful soul, and that we should try to replace those feelings of embarrassment with a those of a virtue – like humility. I smiled as I remembered him saying the best way to learn humility was to be thoroughly humiliated.

"Well," I thought, "I'd say I'm well on my way to becoming *very* humble – and I've got a feeling this is only the beginning!"

At first, I could not bring myself to move from the bed. I was frozen to the spot. What's more, I didn't really want to move. I liked the sensation of feeling complete and loving – as if no negative force or thought could ever touch me – as if they were now somehow grossly unacceptable. I realized I had experienced just seconds of God's pure positivity, yet in those brief moments, I knew beyond a shadow of a doubt it was not only my true nature, but everyone else's true nature.

"Robert was right," I mused. "We really *were* once like this. What's more, I think we can be that again! Why else would I have felt it just now, unless it wasn't something already inside of me? Besides – I like these new feelings of limitlessness and joy and self-confidence."

We journeyed back to Bali the next day. When we arrived, I said goodbye to Gerda and went off to find Robert. He was just finishing up with a couple of students. When he was done he came over and asked me how I was doing. I told him about the incident in Lombok and he said, "Oh, that was *drishti*."

"What, pray tell, is *drishti*?" I replied, flabbergasted.

"It is something we do here in Raja Yoga. It means to look at another soul with spiritual vision – to see only the good in each soul – rather than focusing on their defects. It's a very powerful way of seeing the light and purity in each other."

"You can say that again!" I exclaimed. "The guy just gave up right there on the spot!"

He laughed and replied, "How could he not? He recognized his true self. He may not consciously have been aware of it, but his soul knew."

"So he had no choice but to follow it, you mean?" I asked.

"Precisely," Robert replied, smiling brightly.

"Wow!" I exclaimed. "I've never experienced anything quite like it. I can see why you do this stuff. The results are nothing short of miraculous!"

"Well," Robert replied, smiling. "Not always. What you experienced, is actually quite rare."

"Really?" I replied, sitting up straighter. "How so?"

"Normally," he said, watching my amused expression, "people practice Raja Yoga for some time before they can transmit that kind of power."

"I guess God wanted to make sure I got the point!" I said, trying hard to suppress a grin.

"Well," Robert said, "don't take this too lightly, Valerie. Did you also notice how He did not waste any time getting back to you with an answer to your morning meditation request, back there on Lombok?"

"Yeah," I replied. "That really was something, wasn't it?

"Well," he went on, "I believe that is because he knew you were ready!"

"Ready for what?" I asked, bemused.

"Ready to go the next step," he replied, smiling slightly.

"Just what does *that* mean?" I said, feeling myself beginning to squirm.

Noticing my reaction, his face visibly softened and he gently replied, "It is nothing to be alarmed about, Valerie. God – or Shiva – comes to all of us in different ways. It simply means you asked for an answer, and He gave it to you. Now it is your turn."

"My turn?" I said. "My turn for *what*?"

"To make a commitment, of course!" he replied.

"I'm not interested," I replied curtly.

"You have misunderstood me," Robert said. "What I mean, is, you were waffling between Buddhism and Raja Yoga, and wondering which one to choose. Well – now you know."

"Yeah," I replied. "I *have* heard commitment is freedom, but I never understood what it meant. But I think I do now. And you're right – I *have* wasted a lot of energy bouncing around between the two. It's really quite exhausting."

He nodded.

I suddenly began to laugh as a saying popped into my mind.

"I remember reading a saying that appeals to the athlete in me," I said. "It went something like this: "When God hits the ball into your court, it's up to you to hit it back with a comittment."

Robert laughed.

I looked at him, and smiled even more brightly.

"So, Robert," I remarked, grinning. "I guess the answer is pretty obvious. How would you suggest I proceed from here?"

"Well," he said. "I would recommend you study a little longer here, then think about heading home; since you got what you came for."

"No, no, no," I replied, suddenly feeling alarmed. "You don't understand. That's the *last* place I want to go. Don't you *see*? I'm weird enough here in Bali. But at least I've got *you* here with me. You're even *weirder* than I am, so I feel right at home!"

"I'll take that as a compliment," Robert replied, smiling with amusement.

"Back home, I'll stand out like a sore thumb," I continued. "Nobody will understand me. But then, how can they? I've changed so much *I* don't even understand myself!"

"I felt the same way," Robert said, consolingly. "But eventually I kind of grew into it."

"But there's no one back there for me to relate to!" I exclaimed.

"Oh, yes there is!" Robert remarked, a mischievous smile playing at the corners of his mouth.

"What are you talking about?" I replied. "The last time when I asked you if there were any Raja Yoga centres in Calgary you said, "No."

"Well," he said, reaching for a handful of papers. "That is true. There were not any – then. But while you were on Lombok, I received an updated listing from our western headquarters in London, and there has been one more person added to our small, but growing list in Canada – and it just happens to be in Calgary!"

"You've got to be kidding!" I exclaimed. "That's positively remarkable!"

"Well," he replied, "you wanted an answer, and I cannot think of a more definitive one than this!"

"God!" I exclaimed.

"Precisely," Robert replied, winking back at me.

I read the address and burst out laughing. The person lived just a few blocks away from me.

TWENTY SEVEN

Orange Sock Talk

I arrived home, talked with my sister for an hour or so, then went straight to the telephone and dialed the number Robert had given me.

A man answered and I identified myself and told him I had been studying Raja Yoga in Bali, and that I needed a little guidance now that I had returned home. He said he was very happy to hear from me, and asked if I could come by the house the next day.

We agreed on a time, and I hung up.

"He has a strange accent," I thought, as I walked into the living room.

The next day I walked up the cliff behind my house, and felt the warmth of the sun on my face, and began marveling at just how close this gentleman really lived.

As I approached what I guessed to be the correct address, I let out a peal of laughter. Directly in front of me stood the most adorable little pure white house in the entire neighborhood.

"Why, of course it would be white!" I thought, recalling the first time I spotted The Meditation Shop. "These Raja Yogis love white. Robert told me it stands for purity and positivity, so I guess it suits them perfectly."

I walked up the steps and rang the doorbell. A few moments passed, and I entertained myself looking around the yard. I turned back and found myself face to face with the largest, deepest, brownest eyes, and the most extraordinarily long dark eyelashes I had ever seen.

"Hello," the young man said, in a gentle, melodious voice. "You must be Valerie! Welcome. Please – come in."

He opened the door, and motioned for me to step inside. He extended his hand and introduced himself as Eric. I stared at his curly dark hair and strong, handsome face, and realized I was looking into the eyes of a slightly taller, slightly thinner version of Robert.

"This is uncanny," I thought. "I've come half-way around the world, and look what I've found – a Raja Robert Clone!"

He noticed my strange reaction, but didn't say anything. He simply invited me to leave my shoes in the entranceway, and guided me inside.

The house smelled of incense and room deodorizers – a sweet, pleasant scent. I could make out fresh vacuum cleaner tracks across the living room carpet and looked around and thought, "It looks *so* clean – just like the house on Monkey Forest Road."

"I have just put the tea kettle on," he said, smiling and watching my eyes scan the room. "Please make yourself at home and I will be right back."

I was grateful for the reprieve. I needed some time to absorb everything. Wandering around the room, I noticed how empty the room was, except for a stereo cabinet and a few plants and cushions. He returned moments later with a tray of teacups and a teapot and we sat down on the floor. He apologized for the lack of chairs and explained how they used the room for meditation.

"So," he ventured, "you took the meditation course in Bali? Aren't *you* the lucky one. What an exotic place to study!"

"Yes," I replied. "I found it fascinating, but I also found it a little unsettling. That's why I've come looking for you. I'm really glad you're here, Eric. I was petrified to come home. After my Spirit Quest I'm speaking a whole different language, and you're the only one who can understand me in the whole of Calgary!"

He laughed.

"I'm not kidding!" I exclaimed.

"I know you're not," he replied, gently. "It happens to all of us."

"I bet!" I replied. "But you know what kept me going to the classes? My teacher, Robert. He was a little bizarre, but I think that's why I stuck around – he was so incredibly entertaining. Do you know him?"

"I don't think so," he replied. "Where is he from?"

"France," I said.

"Really?" he replied, his face breaking into a wide grin. "That's where I am from – from Brittany, actually."

"Of course," I said, smirking. "Why am I not surprised? That explains why your accent is so similar to Robert's, and why you two even look kind of alike!"

"Oh?" he said, smiling. "Fancy that. I guess we really *were* meant to meet."

"There's not a doubt in my mind," I replied. "Ever since I started this course, I have experienced one coincidence after another."

He poured the tea and we talked for an hour or so, and I shared my list of coincidences. He didn't seem at all surprised – especially about my story of Troy and Shiva. After we were done, he put on a guided commentary and we relaxed into a lovely, soothing meditation.

I bid him a warm farewell, and began walking home. I felt a little lighter, knowing I now had someone I could confide in. He was sweet, kind, and very gentle – and a terrific host. I had a strong sense of having known him before.

I laughed and thought, "Maybe I met him 5,000 years ago!"

"Listen to yourself!" I exclaimed, laughing even harder. "Now you're even talking like them!"

I stopped and stood on the ridge looking down at the wall of city lights lining the valley below, and reminisced about the lush, picturesque, terraced rice fields I had left behind in Bali. Suddenly, I felt a wave of melancholy wash over my heart.

I sighed deeply.

"Well," my little voice piped up, "you're home to stay, now

aren't you little Nomadic Goddess? But who would have guessed you would come home a yogi?"

"Yeah," I replied, smiling slightly. "Over three years ago, I put on a pair of orange socks and just look what happened. I'm a Yuppie Goes Yogi! I'm getting up at 4:00 in the morning to meditate – which used to be the time I got in – and I'm insisting on eating only the purest vegetarian food, and every chance I get, I'm looking for solitude! How am I ever going to get my head back into life and business in Calgary?"

"It is no wonder you're feeling a little disoriented," my little voice said, consolingly.

"Yeah, what happened to me out there?" I remarked, rubbing my forehead.

"You'll see," my little voice said.

"I don't like the sound of that," I said, feeling more than a little disturbed. "You seem to know everything even before it happens, so I can only assume it's going to be something big!"

"You'll see," it repeated.

"Typical," I thought.

I arrived home, had a bite to eat, lit some candles, and sat down for my evening meditation – but I had a devil of a time concentrating. My mind was racing with worries about money and a new career, and how to relate with my old friends and how to be a yogi in the West – to name just a few. I felt like my mind was a locomotive speeding wildly along at 200 kilometers an hour, and I – the panicked conductor – was pulling helplessly on a skinny little frayed emergency cord called Soul-Consciousness – trying unsuccessfully to stop the train.

Suddenly – out of the blue – it came to me to try replacing my troubled thoughts with thoughts of being a carefree child – to allow the Supreme Soul to play the role of my father – to allow him to provide for all of my needs.

"I don't know if I can do that," I thought to myself. "I'm still having trouble seeing God as my father. A companion and a protector – yes; but a father, no."

I considered the idea a little longer, and decided to give it a whirl.

"What have I got to lose?" I asked myself.

"Why – your worries, of course!" my little voice answered, tumbling onto the stage of my mind, executing three perfect cartwheels in quick succession.

"You're such a child!" I teased.

"So are you, my friend," it cried out. "Try it! You might like it!"

I did, and I instantly felt like I didn't have a care in the world. Robert had called it being a Carefree Emperor. All of my troubles evaporated, and the area between my eyebrows began to sparkle. I could sense myself becoming bodiless. Then – suddenly – I felt a warm, ever-so-gentle hand on my knee. The warmth intensified, then emanated upward and outward – becoming two loving arms that embraced me from behind. I felt totally enveloped in a gentle, comforting, glowing hug. It was as if God was saying, "It is going to be okay. It will happen. I am here now."

I burst into tears. I had no idea how much I had been holding back. I wanted so much to be the powerful Nomadic Goddess who had conquered the world – alone; fearless, self-assured, and most of all – independent. I realized I had been carrying the weight of the world on my shoulders – and I didn't even know it.

"It is only natural," my little voice piped up. "That's where you've been – *around* the world. You simply decided to bring the whole thing back with you – on your shoulders! You're such an athlete, you've taken up weight-lifting. But don't forget what you learned out there. Remember the stuff about God."

I smiled. Then I began to cry some more – only this time it was out of immense relief. I now knew – beyond a shadow of a doubt – that I wasn't alone. God had made sure of it by giving me His signal.

I realized I had happily allowed God to come along with me while I was traveling; as my invisible companion – someone to help me out in case I got myself into a tight squeeze. But now, as soon as I had set foot back in Canada, I had tossed him out. I guess I figured I was on my home turf; I didn't need him anymore.

I smiled and thought, "Thank God he knows better!"

Climbing into my warm, welcoming bed, I nestled myself securely under its pillowy-soft duvet. I thought about God and how he had taught me my most valuable lesson. Suddenly, as if to confirm that he had heard me, I could feel the area between my eyebrows begin to glow again. I smiled and drifted off into a deep, peaceful sleep – with dreams of hopscotch and double-dutch skipping floating through my consciousness. I felt myself in my Baba's warm, apron-covered lap – basking in the glowing afternoon rays of the sun as they flooded the verandah. We were sitting quietly enjoying each other's company – looking out over the garden; the faint sweet scent of caraganas wafting by our nostrils. And as I gratefully drank in their fragrance, I felt as if every part of my hungry soul was rejoicing.

I woke up the next day feeling a little more optimistic and confident. I looked out at the sunshine streaming down, and thought, "Isn't it interesting that I happen to live in a neighborhood called Sunnyside, and that Robert said something about God being the Sun of Knowledge shining down on humanity. I like that – and I'll take it as a good omen that there are sunny days ahead!"

I decided to go for a stroll through the crunchy granola district of the neighborhood and came upon a schedule for a weekly metaphysics breakfast. I looked over the list of speakers and recognized a few names. I decided I would attend a session – just to see what was going on in town.

I called up Susan, the woman in charge – who also happened to be my spiritual counselor a few years before. She had helped me work through my issues with my dad. It was fun to listen to her cry of surprise when she heard my voice. After relating some of my adventures, she asked if I would consider doing a talk at one of her breakfast meetings.

I froze.

"You mean – public speaking?" I replied, nervously. "Like getting up in front of a group of people and *talking*?"

I paced around the house for what seemed like an hour, then called her back and said I would do it.

It was my little voice that convinced me.

"You had the courage to quit a successful business and take a two year sabbatical," it said. "You can certainly tell a little story to 40 or so people! It's the perfect Personal Best stretch. I mean, what self-respecting graduate would miss such a chance?"

"Are you by chance implying I would be a coward if I didn't do it?"

My little voice smiled.

264

I looked over at the corner closet of my bedroom. Peeking out from behind the glass door, was one very bright – one very fluorescent – orange sock.

"I hate that," I said, stomping around the bedroom. "You always know how to get me!"

"Guess what the title of your talk is going to be?" my little voice teased.

"Yeah, yeah," I said, walking towards the sock.

I dug around inside the closet and found the second one. It wasn't hard to find; everything else in the closet was beige, black, or blue.

"Corporate Yuppie colors," I said, smirking to myself.

I picked up both socks and began to laugh.

They hadn't changed a bit – even though I was taught orange actually *stood* for change. They were *still* bright, they were *still* demanding, and they *still* annoyed me.

I held them up in front of me and said, "Okay. I surrender. How does, 'Orange Socks Lead the Way on a 2 1/2 year Walkabout – The Journey Within and Without' sound to you?"

The orange socks smiled up at me.

"You're losing it, Valerie," I said, staring incredulously at the socks.

"You've been out there way too long, little Nomadic Goddess," my little voice piped up.

"Tell me about it," I said, scratching my head.

I went to my computer and started typing out cue cards.

Three weeks later, I arrived at the breakfast meeting sweating profusely.

"It must be 105 degrees in here!" I exclaimed. "This is the stupidest idea I've had in a long time! I can't believe I actually fell for my little voice's ploy. Cowardice – ha!"

"Actually," my little voice piped up, "it was what you call 'those darned orange socks' – the ones you have in your bag. They're the ones to blame!"

"Yeah, right," I retorted, bending down to check if they were still in my day pack.

I pulled them out and began to chuckle.

They smiled up at me and sang out in unison, "Why don't you put us on, Valerie?"

"Not so fast!" I replied. "You guys will just have to wait

your turn! Now cool it!"

I looked over at Susan, and she signaled to me it was time to begin.

I grabbed my bag and walked up to the podium, and busied myself spreading out my notes. Then – I looked up.

"Oh God!" I thought, surveying the crowd.

"Precisely," a voice said.

"What?" I said.

"Precisely," the voice repeated. "Don't forget you are the instrument, Valerie. All you have to do is just stand up here. I will do the rest."

"What are you talking about?" I said, looking around.

"If you think you *alone* are doing this," it said, "you will just be scared and nervous. Let me help you."

"Okay," I said. "You're on."

"This is a riot!" I thought. "Who would have ever guessed *God Himself* would come to the rescue?"

I began to speak. The words tumbled out all askew.

"You're speaking gobbedly goop," I said. I could hear an alarm beginning to ring in my head.

"You're making a fool of yourself," my little doubting voice piped up, "just like in your Grade Four Whooping Crane speech."

The color began to rise in my cheeks and I could feel myself beginning to hyperventilate.

I quickly caught hold of myself, took a deep breath, and willed myself to begin again. I did not look at a soul.

I decided to let the voice do the talking.

Much to my surprise, the words began flowing out effortlessly.

"Wow!" I thought. "This is a cinch! Why didn't I do this right from the start?"

I kept on going, and as I did, I began to feel myself glowing. I was surprised how easy it felt – how natural it all seemed. All I had to do was imagine myself standing up in front of a few friends and telling stories.

"Didn't you read somewhere," my little voice piped up, "that what distinguishes man from beast, is the compelling art of story-telling – and that by sharing our stories, we help each other along the road of life?"

"Yeah," I replied. "It's really not such a big deal, now is it?"

As I went along, my ego kept trying to jump in to do the talking. Each time it did, I stumbled over my words.

"Get out of my way," I said, under my breath. "Can't you see I'm *busy* here?"

I took a deep breath, gathered my senses, and sent my ego packing.

When I was done, and the applause had died down, I looked down at my feet. Staring up at me were my orange socks.

"How did *you* get there?" I asked, laughing.

They beamed back at me.

I looked around the room. Everyone was smiling and laughing. I could hear some of them talking about going out and buying orange socks.

My sister came running up to me and tackled me and wrapped me in a big bear hug.

"Hey, hey!" I exclaimed. "You're a weight-lifter! You'd better watch it! You're going to crush my bones!"

Suddenly a group of people came rushing at me, and started queuing up to talk to me. I was overwhelmed. I had been so detached for the whole event, I felt as if I had been one of the spectators. It took me a moment to realize they actually wanted to talk to *me*.

"You were the speaker, remember?" my little voice said, giggling. "This is who you *are*, Valerie. Remember what Troy said? He said you'd be talking in front of multitudes. This is just the beginning, my friend, so you'd better get used to it!"

I smiled. I was speechless.

The woman in front of the queu started talking to me. I tried to listen, but I was having trouble concentrating. I was still thinking about Troy.

"Didn't he also say you would be writing?" my little voice continued.

"Funny," I replied. "I had that thought when I was in the monastery in Thailand; I thought how valuable it would be to share my discoveries – to help others experience peace of mind."

I rubbed my chin, then tried again to give my attention to the woman in front of me. After a few moments, I managed to concentrate on what she was saying.

After virtually everyone had left, another woman whom I

had noticed earlier, came up and introduced herself as Patricia. She asked if I was doing anything afterwards. I said I did not have any plans.

No sooner had I said this, than my bicycle and I were loaded up in the back of her Subaru station wagon and whisked away to her house – a cute little white house with a red door – which – funnily enough – was located a few blocks from where I lived.

"Not again," I said, laughing. "A white house close to where I live, and a red – for Shiva – door. What next?"

"You'll see," my little voice said.

"Uh oh," I said.

She brought out her tea kettle, fired up her propane stove, placed the kettle on the burner, then calmly sat down and started reading from a large hand-bound manuscript. The chapter she chose was the story of how Ulysses came home to his birthplace, only to find everything had changed.

"I thought this would appeal to you," she said. "I'm a writer. This is a book I wrote. It interweaves astrology with the essence of mythology. When I heard your story, my voice told me to bring you here."

"What?" I said. "*You* have a little voice too?"

"Why, of course!" she exclaimed. "Doesn't everybody?"

"I don't know," I said. "I only discovered mine just before going on my Walkabout."

"Mine's been talking to me since I was a child," she said, smiling brightly. "Most of the time it got me into a lot of trouble. I knew it was my truth, and I knew I had to follow it, but it really made me very different from everyone else – and that was tough."

We talked for over two hours. I told her about how I wanted to write a book of my travels, but how I lacked the confidence to do it. My Grade Five teacher had told me I had no sense of continuity, I was hopeless in grammar, and assured me I would never become a writer – and I believed her. Yet I had made a living as a corporate writer for eight years.

Patricia looked at me with great interest and said she could relate. She too had suffered from a lack of confidence.

"I've written three books and I'm working on my fourth," she said, laughing. "I finally decided I must be a writer!"

We drank down our last cup of tea, and as I was rising to go, she put her hand on my shoulder and asked me to stay sitting. She quickly ran up upstairs. A few minutes later, she returned, holding something in her hand. She came and stood directly in front of me, smiled – looked me directly in the eye – and softly said, "Close your eyes and put out your hand – I have something for you."

I smiled and did as she said. She placed a warm, metal object in my hand. After a few moments, she told me to open my eyes. As I did, I saw a beautiful yellow-stoned silver ring gleaming up at me.

"What is this?" I asked.

"It is what I call my Writer's Ring," she replied.

"I can't accept this!" I cried, pulling back. "It's too valuable!"

"You're right," she said, eyes sparkling. "It is! When I first began writing, and I didn't have the confidence in myself, I put on this ring and sat myself down at my computer, and said to myself, "I'm a writer, I'm a writer." I didn't believe it at first. As a matter of fact, I didn't believe it for the longest time. Some days it was all I could do to just put it on my finger and stare at the computer. Eventually, I began to write – and I've never stopped. The words just pour out onto the pages. That was five years ago."

"That's incredible!" I exclaimed.

"Be careful!" she said, eyes twinkling. "This ring will make all your dreams come true!"

A few moments passed. I could feel a dead calm beginning to surround us. The kitchen suddenly looked brighter – as if flooded by a soft, glowing, golden light. It was as if all time stood still. Suddenly – it hit me. Nothing would ever be the same again. I knew I was going to write the book. There wasn't the slightest trace of doubt in my mind.

I rose to leave, and she quietly fell into step behind me. When we reached her car, she helped me lift out my bicycle. I climbed on and was about to wave goodbye, but noticed she was standing motionless with an incredibly intense expression on her face. It was obvious she had something to say. I quickly got down from my bicycle and waited for her to speak. She said nothing.

"Yes?" I said, smiling gamefully.

"Could I have a hug?" she said, shyly.

"Why – of course!" I exclaimed. "You bet!"

I set down my bicycle, scooped her up into my arms and whispered, "Thank you, Patricia – for everything." Then I quickly jumped on my bicycle, and turned to wave good-bye.

"You're a writer!" she called out, as I rode down the lane. "Writers are here to tell the stories for those who cannot speak for themselves! Never forget this! You're a writer, Valerie! Always remember who you are!"

"Funny," I thought. "That's what Robert kept saying – and so did that Meditation Shop poster about God. Remember..."

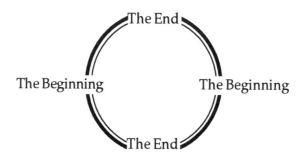

Epilogue

I not only wrote the book – it is resting in your hands – but I also ended up helping to run the Calgary Raja Yoga center after Eric left the city to take up a post as a CBC television producer for Canada's French-Canadian channel. Then – shortly afterwards – I started a new business in the investments field. Talk about a stretch. I had never sold anything in my life. But I figured if I had traveled the world alone for two years, I could certainly sell a few investments. Even so, the thought was pretty scary. I had also become quite disinterested in, and even turned off, material pursuits through my *Yuppie Goes Yogi* freedom days. I didn't really know if I could re-enter the corporate world again. But I knew I was as 'cooked' as I would ever be. It was time to take up a new challenge.

At first I struggled like any beginner would – phoning up people and asking them how much money they had, and would they give it to me, please. The whole thing seemed ridiculous. And as if that was not bad enough, having been out of the downtown scene for over three years, things like weekends seemed even more ridiculous. How could one possibly refuel from a whole week in just two days?

After two months of fighting back feelings of being invaded by the once-familiar culture, I found myself becoming more and more disheartened. I constantly had to remind myself of what I had learned in Buddhist Summer Camp – about the Law of Impermanence, and that everything that was happening would pass. I also had to tell myself to stay positive – no matter what. Slowly, things began to gel. I began to earn some excellent money, and I really started enjoying showing people how to invest in good, secure investments. They often phoned me to thank me for my guidance.

As time went on, I realized my world travels had given me a new sense of identity. I now knew my true nature was that of being a peaceful soul, and my challenge was to remain so, no matter what the circumstances. I had to remind myself that I was a soul *in* a body playing out the part of an investment consultant, and that everyone else was a soul *in a body* playing out *their* roles – according to their specialities and characters. It was, in fact, their *duty* to play out their roles. Wasn't it, after all, a pre-recorded world drama? And what would a drama be without actors?

I often hike up the steep ridge behind my house and sit high above the city looking down at the wall of office towers teeming with life. I marvel at the synchronicity and signs along the path of life that have guided me to my truth, and I realize it is really quite the drama; scene after fascinating scene laid out in front of me.

I read somewhere that if you follow your truth, and you have the courage to take the first step – and even if you are not wearing orange socks – it is as if the *Divine Hand of Providence* moves at the same time, and delivers gifts unimagined by the soul. But if you are not thoroughly convinced, perhaps you should try buying a pair of fluorescent orange socks. They changed my life – and they can change yours. But remember – if you DON'T want to change your life, DON'T BUY* orange socks!

*CAUTION: BUYER BE AWARE

Nomadic Goddess
Comes Full Circle

Once upon an eternity, there was a little Nomadic Goddess who had broken her wings. She knew she had lost something of great value, but didn't know where to look for it; she only knew she had to find it. She left the shores of Canada, and flew off into the big unknown world to discover the answer. After searching many foreign lands – she arrived at the Paradise called Bali. It was there she found what she was looking for. It was a brilliant, glowing, ever so tiny, magical diamond.

At first she didn't see it because it had been covered up by lifetimes of disuse. But she was determined to find her treasure, so she dug and dug and when she uncovered it, it was *so* beautiful and *so* enchanting, its power radiated upwards and outwards and filled her with a love and a light and a peace like she had never known. She was happier than she could ever remember in her entire life. In her heart, she knew she had finally come home.

The little Nomadic Goddess spent day after day in her idyllic paradise learning as much as she could about the essence of her beautiful diamond, but soon it came time for her to return to the land of her birth. She didn't want to go, but she knew she had to.

When she landed on its quiet, familiar shores, she was still clutching her new-found treasure close to her breast. She vowed to never let go of it again. That diamond meant more to her than all the gold and jewels in the whole wide world, because there – shining back at her – was her soul.◊

The Game

Picture God saying to you, "See only me, just watch and listen to me and I will carry you on my shoulders to your destination".

And sitting on His shoulders, what a different view we get of the world! We can watch it at a slight distance and yet see so much of it. We can remain free of it and yet have more effect on it. And above all, we can feel ourselves to be children.

That is important. For if we think in an adult way about walking this path, we may make it complicated. But if we think of ourselves as children, then what is clearly the most challenging task we have ever been given in our whole existence, becomes just a wonderful game. And if you play a game with God, He always makes you win!

BRAHMA KUMARIS*
Raja Yoga Centres in North America

CANADA

Main Centre
Brahma Kumaris
897 College Street
Toronto, Ontario
M6H 1A1
(416) 537-3034

1245 Chemin Ste-Foy,
local 140
Quebec City, Quebec
G1S 4P2
(418) 682-0203

767 Avenue Querbes
Outre Montreal
Montreal, Quebec
H2V 3W8
(514) 272-0671

Unit 3-90 Roslyn Road
Winnipeg, Manitoba
R3L 0G6
(204) 284-8935

112-1822 10th Ave. S.W.
Calgary, Alberta
T3C 0J8
(403) 209-2988

205, 10132 - 105 Street
Edmonton, Alberta
T5J 1C9
(403) 425-1050

3467 Monmouth
Avenue
Vancouver, B.C.
V5R 5R8
(604) 436-4795

UNITED STATES

Main Centre
Global Harmony
House
46 S Middle Neck Road
Great Neck,
New York 11021
(516) 773 0971

Brahma Kumaris Office
at UN
Room 4054
866 United Nations
Plaza
New York
New York 10017
(212) 688-1335

Brahma Kumaris
Mind's Eye Museum
2207 E Busch
Boulevard
Tampa, FL 33612
(813) 935-0736/4836

1821 Beacon Street
Brookline
Boston, MA 02146
(617) 734-1464

8009 Hollywood Boul-
evard
Los Angeles, CA 90046
(213) 876-5545

410 Baker Street
San Francisco, CA
94117
(415) 563-4459

International
Headquarters
Brahma Kumaris
World Spiritual
University
Post Box No. 2
Mount Abu
Rajastahn, India
307501
91-2974-3348/49/51

Internet address *http://www.rajayoga.com/*

* All courses offered free of charge

Order Form

Here's The Book You've Been Waiting For...

For a friend, a family member, a partner, an associate, a co-worker, a teacher, an ex-partner...why, the possibilities are limitless! To obtain your copy, please mail this completed form, along with a cheque or money order to:

Eternal Giving Inc.
P.O. Box 61108
Kensington Postal Outlet
Calgary, Alberta T2N 4S6
CANADA

Name —————————————————————————

Street Address ————————————————————

City/Province ————————————————————

Postal Code ——————————————

Enclosed is my cheque or money order for:

$18.75 X   books   = $ ——————

$ 4.50 X   books(shipping/handling) = $ ——————

SUBTOTAL = $ ——————

7% GST = $ ——————

PST (if applicable) = $ ——————

TOTAL = $ ——————

Please allow 4-6 weeks for delivery. Orders must be prepaid; no C.O.D.'s Please write to ask about quantity discounts or public speaking engagements.

The *Orange Socks* are looking forward to joining their new owner!